FICTION
IN SEVERAL LANGUAGES

THE DÆDALUS LIBRARY

Published by Houghton Mifflin Company and
The American Academy of Arts and Sciences

A New Europe?, edited by Stephen R. Graubard
The Professions in America, edited by Kenneth S. Lynn
The Woman in America, edited by Robert Jay Lifton
Science and Culture, edited by Gerald Holton
Utopias and Utopian Thought, edited by Frank E. Manuel
The Contemporary University: U.S.A., edited by Robert S. Morison
The Negro American, edited by Talcott Parsons and Kenneth B. Clark
Creativity and Learning, edited by Jerome Kagan
Fiction in Several Languages, edited by Henri Peyre

FICTION

IN SEVERAL LANGUAGES

EDITED AND WITH AN
INTRODUCTION BY
HENRI PEYRE

HOUGHTON MIFFLIN COMPANY   BOSTON   1968

First Printing   R

Copyright © 1968 by the American Academy
of Arts and Sciences

Library of Congress Catalog Card Number: 68-15214

The Introduction by Henri Peyre, "The Modern Novel in
the Low Countries" by Seymour L. Flaxman, and "The
Hungarian Novel in the Last Fifty Years" by Valérie
Korek are here published for the first time. The
other essays in the book appeared originally, some
of them in slightly different form, in the Fall 1966
issues of Dædalus, the Journal of the American Academy
of Arts and Sciences.

Printed in the United States of America

CONTENTS

CONTENTS

HENRI PEYRE

Introduction

LIFE HAS often been defined by skeptics as a process, pleasant or unpleasant, of shedding one's fond illusions, and by optimists as a process of building up new illusions joyfully. International affairs in the middle of the twentieth century have certainly shattered some of our hopes about "one world." Technological progress, easily transmissible from the Western countries to those elsewhere whose development has lagged, decolonization, the building up of a democratic façade in lands which could not well afford it, the partial raising of the Iron Curtain in Europe and the greatly expanded facilities for exchange of persons between East and West, Northern and Southern hemispheres, have not brought about a parallel increase in mutual goodwill and an end to recriminations. "We must love one another, or die," declared peremptorily the poet W. H. Auden. The advice, which had already been proffered two thousand years ago, has not been conspicuously heeded. While we are still endeavoring to live up to it, many of us believe that we might, at the very least, try to understand each other better. Speedy communications, exchange of students, missionaries of the Peace Corps, scientific aid and two-way trade may help. Sincere interest in other countries on the part of the very rich and powerful ones, untainted by any patronizing condescension and free from any complacent conviction of the West's superiority, may well be the best road to such an improved understanding.

Music has been called a universal language, although it is doubtful that it can be enjoyed uniformly in very different cultural settings and fully express the aspirations and the anxieties of a people. André Malraux has made an eloquent case for the pictorial and plastic arts as more universal than music and more likely to help us recapture, or mold anew, a notion of man's unity in place and time.

Poetry, if it could be translated skillfully enough, would perhaps best reveal the traditions, the popular feelings, the sensibility, the heroic urges of peoples whom we imagine to be less sophisticated than ourselves. Very few cultures can boast of a national theater; the drama, presupposing a certain level of urbanization, a sense of ritual, linked in its origins with myths and beliefs, dominated in the West by a very few traditional currents (Greek, Spanish, English, French, much later Scandinavian and American) has not afforded us much insight into what may be called "the soul" of Poland, Hungary, Rumania, Portugal, Egypt, or Israel.

It may well be that the latest born of all the literary forms, the most flexible and loose, fiction, is also the one through which we might come closer to the spirit of a number of countries which, in America and Western Europe, we have seldom attempted to understand. For a long time, the English remained insular and little concerned with the literary achievement of the peoples (even when they were Indian, Burmese, Nigerian, Canadian) among whom their political and commercial influence had spread. The impact of Gogol, Tolstoi, and Dostoevski abroad, that of Chekhov and Gorki never owed anything to efforts by the Czarist regime to display a liberal or an evangelical face of Russia outside her frontiers. The French were so accustomed to having other nations, in Eastern and Central Europe, in the Near East and South America, look up to them for cultural refinement or for vanguard movements (the *philosophes*, the rebels of Realism and Impressionism, the Symbolists) that they considered themselves as givers, but seldom as receivers. Still, Paris remained the metropolis where writers from Brazil and Peru, Lebanon, Rumania, and Greece were proud to win recognition and to be translated. Not a few novelists from those countries, indeed, wrote their books in the French language.

A very significant innovation of our time, especially since World War II, is the vivid interest which we take in the so-called "exotic languages." Military, diplomatic, and economic motives primarily, entailing more disinterested cultural ones, have impelled foundations, universities, and government agencies to undertake the systematic study and teaching of languages from several continents which, in happier or more complacent isolationist days, this country at any rate had placidly ignored. We have likewise, though more slowly, become aware of the power of imaginative literature to reveal nations which, in spite of travelers, journalists, and diplomats, had remained mysterious to us. All the hundreds of volumes written by visitors and inquirers about the South American continent have not succeeded in arousing a passionate interest in Venezuela, Chile, Uruguay, and Ecuador. James Reston hinted once that the American people would do anything for South America except read about it. It may be that only novelists who would do for those cultures what Russian novelists achieved for the steppes and the spring thaw of their country, for the Cossacks and the "Dead Souls" of the Ukraine, might succeed in building up for their countries the same inalienable capital of goodwill which has survived Czarist inefficiency, Bolshevik ruthlessness, purges, and threats. Stendhal and Balzac similarly won for France devotees abroad, among intellectuals (Tolstoi, Nietzsche, George Moore, Theodore Dreiser) but also among schoolboys, office clerks, women dreaming of an elsewhere, movie audiences; the erratic policies of the French and their occasional arrogance never lost friends thus made.

The epic once played the role which, in many lands, has now been assumed by the novel; cultures, like that of France, where fiction seems rather to have been the successor to tragedy, because the epic tradition had been less rich there and a certain trend to rational organization and to feverish condensation was deeply marked in the national character, are the exception. Yet even in France, with the recent fashion for the *roman fleuve,* with Marcel Proust, Céline, Michel Butor, a yearning for a sprawling, poetical, and multifarious form of fiction closer to the epic has been conspicuous. Georg Lukács, the dean of European philosophical critics, is fond of asserting that while tragedy expresses solitude and the negation of life, and the epic conveys the sense of a correspondence between the soul and the universe, between the world within and the world without, fiction is today the dialectical form of the epic: It revolves, according to him, around solitude in the midst of the community, presence in absence. No abstract theory can be put forward to embrace, or to chain, the eight or ten literatures represented in the present volume. Reducing them all to a few common denominators would be tantamount to mutilating them. The very purpose of this series of essays is to maintain the claims of diversity. The most earnest request of the countries now emerging from a prolonged literary silence (modern Greece, Israel, Arab lands, Brazil, the Philippines) is that the Western and wealthy powers, while assisting them technically, financially, culturally, respect what

Goethe termed the one most precious possession of earth's children: their personality.

Those essays appeared originally in *Dædalus,* in the issue of the fall of 1966, under the title *Fiction in Several Languages.* They were concisely and pertinently presented to the reader by Stephen Graubard, the editor of the Journal of the American Academy of Arts and Sciences, a true Dædalus himself, skillful deviser and explorer of many labyrinthine ways, the tamer of several minotaurs whom he has convinced to write in a civilized fashion for a cultured audience on a number of abstruse topics. The original essays in that 1966 issue purposely left out any consideration of fiction in English, French, Spanish, German, Russian, and any discussion of theories of the novel; on the latter subject, an earlier number of *Dædalus,* prepared by a novelist and critic, Albert J. Guérard, had appeared three years ago, in the spring of 1963. The countries whose recent fiction was treated here in a separate essay constituted only a small portion of those which might have been included, the choice depending upon the availability of authors familiar with the American public to which their articles were addressed. Several other such collections might and, we hope, will be made, perhaps encouraged by the publication of this one in book form: Mexico, Venezuela, Chile, India, Iran, China, Turkey, and several of the new nations of Africa as well as Finland and Iceland should someday be thus presented to the English-speaking world through their modern fiction. That is one of the essential long-range tasks which UNESCO should make possible and in which American cultural attachés in those countries might well assist. An insight into the most mysterious of all elements in a nation could thereby be gained: their attachment to the past, and to their language, the tensions resulting from the rapid introduction of foreign ideas and of modern techniques, social disruption in the home and through the schools, the ideals subconsciously cherished by the people, the heroes after whom they try to model themselves, the eagerness with which they wish to hurry the advent of a future that is both feared and devoutly desired. Whether we are justified or not in doing so, we inevitably seek in a novel, by the nationals of a country about which we know little else, information on their national character. Even more than for Mark Twain and William Faulkner, Dickens, Flaubert, or Pérez Galdós, a novelist from Poland or Syria or Bolivia or French Canada will be viewed abroad as a representative of his country.

One of the chapters which follow treats the present trends of the novel in the one country of the Western hemisphere in which the language is derived from Portuguese: Brazil. The author, Emir Rodriguez Monegal, was born in Melo, Uruguay, in 1921. He is the editor-in-chief of *Mundo Nuevo*, a magazine on Latin-American affairs published in Paris. He is the author of several volumes of fiction and of criticism which appeared in Montevideo and in Buenos Aires between 1950 and 1966. He shows how the Brazilian novel, starting from a strong regionalist perspective, has tried to transcend the limitations of such an approach and to broach universal themes. Realism has lately become a secondary concern of Brazilian novelists; they have, like several of their European contemporaries, been more preoccupied with form and language. Their recent novels strive to be less documentary and more artistic.

N. V. M. Gonzalez, born in the Philippines, in Romblon, occupies a chair of comparative literature at the university of his country. He is very familiar with the literatures of Britain and of the United States, the author of several fictional works himself: *A Season of Grace* (1956), *The Bamboo Dancers* (1959), *Look, Stranger, on this Island Now* (1963), all published in Manila. He was in 1960 the winner of the Republic Cultural Heritage Award and in 1961 of the Rizal Pro-Patria Award. He is keenly aware of the difficulties presented to the writers of his country by the multiplicity of languages and by the hesitation of some authors between one of those languages and English. It seems clear, however, that the authentic novels of the Philippines are, and must be, written in the native languages. Tagalog, recently recognized as the language of the archipelago, is spoken by nearly half of the population. Another difficulty standing in the way of native fiction is the existence of a lively daily press, which deals with subjects of burning immediacy and with which, as in Western countries, the novel must compete in intensity and sense of urgency. It will take a powerful imaginative talent either to elicit the lasting and the universal from the ephemeral or to lend to an invented world the vividness and the sense of personal involvement in the reader, which the mass media more easily capture. The Philippino short story, relying more upon dramatic values and less upon slow collaboration with time, appears to have thus far drawn more talents than the novel itself.

Japanese fiction has been treated by an American expert, Howard Hibbett, born in 1920 in Akron, Ohio. He holds a chair of Japanese literature at Harvard University. He lived and studied in Japan for several years at the universities of Kyoto and Tokyo. He translated

The Key, by Tanizaki Junichirō in 1961, *Seven Japanese Tales* in 1963 and *Diary of a Mad Old Man* in 1965. He published a critical study, *The Floating World in Japanese Fiction,* in New York in 1959. The chapter on the Israeli novel is by Robert Alter, an American scholar born in 1935 in New York City who teaches at Columbia University. He is the author of *Rogue's Progress: Studies in the Picaresque Novel* (Cambridge, 1964) and of many articles in *Book Week, Midstream,* and *Commentary.* His most recent undertaking is a book on Fielding. He lucidly explains the very special dilemmas confronting the novelist in a new country, Israel, whose literary language, Hebrew, the language of piety and of the Old Testament, has become the current vehicle of expression. The perils were great: artificiality, archaism, remoteness from the common reader, esoteric symbolism. New techniques had to be devised to convert "the obstrusive literariness [of Hebrew] into an artistic resource." Other difficulties lay in the sharp cleavage between the younger generations, attuned to the modern world, aware of the need for action and constant vigilance amid a hostile environment, and their older compatriots, for whom a national home had long been a mystical dream and in whom distrust of the modern Western world might well have run deep. The one very great Israeli novelist, Shmuel Yosef Agnon, now near eighty, happens to belong to the older generation, that of Kafka and even of Thomas Mann, with whom he can sustain comparison. The younger novelists have attempted a more realistic portrayal of life around them, but also a type of fiction marked by the metaphysical issues of our time, which have come to the fore in Existentialism.

It is harder to generalize about the Arabic novel, since the language is spoken by millions from Java and Pakistan through the Middle and the Near East, through Egypt and North Africa. For a long time, it seemed that the requirements of structure and of searching self-analysis which have been stressed in fiction since Flaubert, Henry James, and Joyce would not easily be met by the writers of Egypt, Syria, or Tunisia, who had never been prone to strictness of composition or rigidity in planning. Further obstacles lay in the duality of languages: one spoken by the people, the other, more literary and highly respected, being the written one with an august tradition behind it. It would take several essays to cover the several literatures written in the varied lands where Arabic is spoken, not to mention the fiction in French by Syrians, Lebanese, Tunisians, Berbers in Algeria, North African Jews. The social issues and the conflict of ethical values vary from country to country. The events of 1956, in the second war with Israel (then assisted by two European powers), and even more those of 1967 may unleash an intellectual revolution in Egypt, Syria, and Algeria similar to the Russian and Chinese revolutions of our century or to the profound changes in the moods of Spain which followed the Spanish defeat of 1898 and the advent of the prodigiously gifted "1898 generation" in Spain. Many new issues are emerging in Arabic lands which the novel of the future will have to face: condition of women, tension between the village and the city, conflict between the hallowed traditions and the need for a new technology. The promises of fiction in Arabic and its present rich confusion, more auspicious than detached artistic refinement would be, are ably brought out in the essay by George N. Sfeir. Mr. Sfeir, born in 1922 in Lebanon, is the author of numerous articles in Arabic and English on literature, but also on Arab banking and law. He is Assistant Manager and Counsel for the Intra Bank S.A. in New York City.

Modern Greek literature has won recognition and admiration in Western Europe and America through its remarkable poetic renaissance. Palamas, Kavafis, Sikelianos, Seferis, and others have been favored by able translators. The Spaniards alone, since 1930, have displayed an equal variety and combined to a similar degree musical evocativeness and density of imaginative thought in their verse. Nikos Kazantzakis, in verse and prose, has also reached world fame. Yet Greek writers, like those of Arabic and Israeli cultures, had to wrestle with many odds: the overwhelming memory of an ancient and universally respected literature which might well have discouraged new creation, a powerful fascination with the local scene and in consequence some provincialism, the long rivalry between a learned and literary language and the current or "demotic" language (the latter, for many years held under suspicion by fastidious scholars and traditionalists, finally won acceptance). Since 1930 or so, the novel has become the main literary form of the modern Greeks. Among the seven or eight prominent practitioners of the genre, Angelos Terzakis is the one whom the author of the chapter on Greek fiction, Costas M. Proussis, has selected as most representative. Terzakis, born in Nauplion in 1907, has had plays acted by student groups in America; his experience as playwright and director has served his fiction, which shows dramatic tension, sense for atmosphere, and a rare gift for dialogue. Flaubert and Dostoevski are the two authors whose impact on him he generously acknowledges. He stands as a witness to the decline of old values and the social and political turmoil through which a confused, anxious, younger Greek generation is now going. The essay, centering on Terzakis, is a penetrating critical analysis. Its author was born in Cyprus in 1911. He teaches classics at the Holy Cross Greek Orthodox Theological School in Brookline, Massachusetts. He has published, in Athens and in Cyprus, several volumes on Cyprus letters, on Greek writers, on criticism and aesthetics and a *Grammar of Modern Greek* as well as one of the Latin language.

With the fictions of Poland and Hungary, the reader finds himself closer to native grounds, or at least to Western European traditions. Yet those two literatures are very seldom studied in America or in Atlantic Europe and far too few of their works are translated. Nevertheless, in science as well as in the study of politics, in the fine arts and in literature and literary criticism, those two countries have sent to the United States probably the most gifted groups of cultured *émigrés,* matched only by the greatest boon done to America by the cruelty of the Nazis: the integration of German and Austrian Jews into American society and culture. The martyrdom of the Poles under the German conquest and the Russian distrust and ruthlessness in 1939–1945, their courage and new prospects since then, the blend of tragic anguish and of humorous resignation with which their present regime is received have offered great themes to fiction. Some of the most moving and graphic portrayals of the horrors of war have been written, one in French, the other one in English, by writers of Polish origin: *Éducation européenne* (1945) by Romain Gary, at present a French diplomat and author of eminence, and *The Painted Bird* (Boston, 1965) by Jerzy Kosinski, now a scholar and man of letters in New York. The essay on recent Polish fiction, preceded by a lively letter by the author to the editor which describes the predicament of one who tries to give an account of a literature in a state of flux, torn between poetry and prose, between the past and the future, is by Czeslaw Milosz. Born in Lithuania in 1911, Mr. Milosz is Professor of Slavic Languages and Literatures at the University of California at Berkeley. He is a poet himself in his native Polish language and a translator of poetry from English and French into Polish. He published a novel in French, *La Prise du Pouvoir,* in Paris in 1953 and another one,

Tal der Issa, in Cologne in 1961. The sufferings of Poland and the monstrosity of the crimes of genocide have been so enormous as, in the trite cliché, to beggar description and to intimidate Polish novelists. Only with a perspective of more years and the ability to recollect emotions, if not in tranquillity, at least with some poetic irony, may the writers of Poland do justice to the nightmarish events through which their country has lived.

Poland had recovered its national personality at the end of World War I and learned then to live perilously between two hostile neighbors, but also with a new lease of hope. Hungary suffered more, both territorially and in humiliation, from the treaties of 1919–1920 than any other European land. Whole segments of her soil passed under the control of other nationalities; the turmoil of a revolution afflicted her; her capital had to undergo, in 1945, one of the longest and most destructive sieges; the events of 1956 were a new ordeal and the future is far from assured. The Hungarian language is one of the most difficult, hence one of the least studied, in Europe and America. Musicians, painters, even poets from Hungary have reached recognition outside their frontiers more readily than novelists. Nevertheless the originality, jealously and victoriously preserved, of Hungarian culture throughout the half century when Hungary was associated with Austria is one of the amazing cases of survival of the will, and of the soul. The energies of the Hungarians will be among the strong pillars on which a new Eastern-Central Europe will someday have to be erected. For political and social reasons as well as for its aesthetic value and fresh creativeness, Hungarian fiction deserves to be better known in this country. The achievement of Hungarian novelists, the dilemma they face due to the conflict between the Communist demands for socialist realism and the preservation of the freest of all pursuits, that of literary creation, are expertly discussed in the fine essay by Valérie Korek. Trained in philosophy at the University of Budapest and the author of a thesis in the philosophy of history, versed in three or four Western literatures, a writer of tasteful elegance and of intellectual vigor, Valérie Korek, the only woman writer represented in this volume, published a novel in Hungarian at Brussels in 1960, whose title in English would be *Visit to Buda.* She is engaged in a study of the Hungarian novelist Zoltán Ambrus.

Seymour L. Flaxman, for some years professor at New York University, then at the State University of New York at Stony Brook, and more recently at the Graduate Section of the New York City

Colleges, has long been a missionary for one of the least studied among the literatures in Western Europe: that of Holland. Portuguese letters, those of Scandinavia and of Iceland have won a place in our academic institutions more readily than the writings of the Dutch and the Flemish. Proficient students of foreign languages themselves, generously and remarkably pliable readers of other literatures, the citizens of the Low Countries have been, since the seventeenth century, shy either at producing fiction in their own languages (several of the best-known Belgian poets, dramatists, and novelists who wrote in French were of Flemish stock) or in making their novels accessible to other countries through translation and criticism. Seymour Flaxman shows convincingly that the literature of Holland is in no way provincial today. It started with a revolt of young writers late in the nineteenth century and the strong impact of Naturalism. Criticism of society then became a feature in a country which is wrongly taken to be complacently conservative. The sufferings endured during the German occupation in 1940–1944 and the subsequent loss of the Indies with which Dutch life, economy, and imagination had been more closely bound up than those of Britain with India or of France with Africa have profoundly disturbed the Dutch psyche. Recent literature reflects those traumatisms: conflicts between father and son, the individual and society, religious morality, and the sexual liberation are portrayed by the most gifted of today's novelists, the prolific and influential Simon Vestdijk, born in 1898. Marnix Gijsen, whose real name is Jan-Albert Goris and who spent the World War II years in New York, is also a satirical and biting social critic. He is of Belgian nationality and keenly aware of the modern influences on today's European fiction: psychoanalysis, Proust, Mann, Hesse, the *antiroman*. The impact of modern English, Irish, and American novelists somehow appears to have been weaker in the two countries of Europe, Belgium and Holland, which are, in other fields, the closest to Anglo-American moods and views.

Deducing elaborate generalizations from necessarily sketchy essays on vastly different modern novels would betray the originality of those literatures. A few remarks, however, may point to the value of that fiction in itself and for its own sake, and to the broadening of our "Western" ideas on the novel which may accrue to America and Europe from a closer attention to literatures too long neglected.

Too many of us, in the United States, Britain, France, or Italy, have been guilty of a pharisaic provincialism of our own, complacently convinced that our humanistic culture was bound to be absorbed and imitated by other countries of Asia and Africa as they rose to our own exalted level of development. If those young or rejuvenated countries have something to learn from our examples and from our failures, we too may well envy their fresh audacity and the earnestness which makes them stress the subtleties of technique less, and the contents of fiction more

The obvious reasons for which the novel is more likely than poetry, the drama, or the essay to become the art which will mirror the deepest concerns of new or rejuvenated nations have to do with the form of the novel, on the one hand, and with the facilities for dramatically portraying social and psychological issues, on the other.

Many a fastidious mind in the West, in France particularly (Paul Valéry being the most prestigious among them), has taken issue with the art of fiction for allowing too much arbitrariness and for being subjected to no rules whatever. Any novelist is free to dispose of his imaginary characters as he likes, to challenge verisimilitude or disregard logic in his plot, to juggle with time and make it reversible ad libitum. The very notion of perfection, which implies that certain unwritten rules or conventions are satisfied, that there are no flaws in the development of the action or in the evolution of the characters, is alien to the art of fiction. The greatest of Russian, English, and American novels are also the least free from faults. That same absence of rules and independence from theorizers, pedants, or critics, no longer enjoyed by the novel in America and in France where theorizing has since proliferated and tends to stifle creation, may well be a boon to fiction in cultures where (as in Japan, Israel, Greece) it is hardly half a century old.

At the same time, the obstacles raised by the long-standing opposition between a literary language and a popular one appear to have been lifted, or surmounted, almost everywhere. The pedantic stress upon too literary a language, florid as it was with many humanists or overly poetical and stilted because it harked back to the epic or to lyricism, had long impeded the development of a powerful novel in Italy. Racy dialects would not easily yield to one literary tongue, even one glowing with the authority of Dante. In countries like Greece and the Arabic lands, it was far harder for the language of the common man to gain enough prestige to tempt fiction writers. The literary style cultivated by the scholars and writers enjoyed the advantages of tradition, polish, and refinement, but it suffered from artificiality. Why and how exactly does a language severed from the masses fail, even when wielded by great talents, to acquire the vitality, the imaginative suggestiveness needed for great literature? We do not appear to have the satisfactory answer. Petrarch, Du Bellay, Jean Second, John Milton wrote remarkably good poetry in Latin, from the fourteenth to the seventeenth century. Prose writers in that same era were easily, at their best, the equals of Livy and Cicero. Somehow an element was missing which was not missing in Spaniards like Seneca and Martial, in a Gallo-Roman poet like Ausonius or an Egyptian one like Claudian in the fourth century A.D.

The peril presented by too rich a literary legacy was especially great for Israel, which adopted and chose to recreate the Hebrew language, thereby conjuring up memories of the prophets and of the rich imagery of the Biblical narratives. Even in Britain, the hallowed model provided by the universally admired Authorized Version of the Bible (1611) has not always served writers of English prose. Some moderns like Somerset Maugham have contended that far too long it hampered English prose, depriving it of simplicity and of familiar terseness, as indeed is the case with the prose of Jeremy Taylor, of Sir Thomas Browne, Macaulay, Newman, and others. On the whole, nevertheless, Israeli authors, like the best of the Greeks since 1930, have shunned what might have been the direst result of the language duality. At the same time, in many countries where the spread of education once lagged, in South America, North Africa, Asia, the spread of literacy has suddenly swollen the reading public, and presumably the purchasing public, for works of fiction. The isolation of the novelist has come to an end.

Realism, once the main force in European fiction, began to lose ground when poets, painters, sophisticated storytellers set to preferring dreams, symbols, fantastic excursions into the unreal, plunges into the subconscious, to the depiction of a reality deemed to be gross and inert. The disintegration of our conventional notion of reality and the disintegration of our notion of a coherent ego occurred in the first decades of the twentieth century. The last volume of the Proustian saga, the playful irony of Giraudoux and Cocteau, in England the seductive skirmishes of Virginia Woolf against the pedestrian novel of manners of Galsworthy and Arnold Bennett, the disaffection from H. G. Wells' social propaganda succeeded in luring storytellers to more elusive pursuits than that of reality. A return to *Chosisme* and to an affectation of scientific objectivity in photographing and measuring objects, keeping shy of all anthropomorphism, has been staged in some of the French new, or anti-, novels since 1955, but it is as yet too calculated and too sophisticated a movement to hold much appeal for the countries which hope, through their fiction, to acquire a fuller awareness of themselves.

Socialist realism as dogmatically ordered by Soviet cultural propaganda has thus far yielded pitiful results in Russia, mediocre ones in Hungary or Poland. It has proved even more of a failure in the pictorial arts. Clearly, it is preposterous to expect masterpieces ever to arise under duress or under command from an authoritarian ruler. Those attempts at portraying national events or national figures, at rendering the excitement of peasants' riots or the plight of prisoners in extermination camps need not, however, be doomed to eternal failure. After all, dedications of their plays by Corneille or Molière to sovereigns and noblemen, portraits of Italian cardinals, of Richelieu and Mazarin in France, historical and monumental paintings of Bonaparte at Arcole or at Jaffa, of his coronation in Paris, and tapestries of Le Brun at Versailles are respected, often revered, today. Much of the art of the past was official and intended to serve propaganda. Much of the literature was didactic, from Hesiod, Lucretius, and the *Georgics* to the religious drama of Spain, to the French *philosophes* and even including the nineteenth-century novel of Balzac, of Dickens, and of Dostoevski. Our century is more sophisticated, but it has revived the notion of commitment on the part of the artist, and it is not so certain as some of our critics proclaim that art and propaganda (understood as the fervent propagation of one's convictions) are never to be reconciled. But such a reconciliation has not occurred under any dictation from above and probably never will.

For the present, the value of fiction as dramatizing or focusing the social problems of countries like Japan, Brazil, the Philippines, Egypt, and even Holland or Scandinavia lies in the sharp relief with which some tensions are set. The fiction of these countries reveals, better than any journalists' inquiries, at what depth of sensibility changes are being effected, and with what traumatisms, nostalgic regrets, or hopes. The sources of conflicts are many: the individual in revolt against the once unquestioned authority of the family; the remoteness of the youth from the older generations (grandfathers and grandmothers fond of their dialect, slow to adapt to the new technology, trying to live thirty years back and unable to adapt to the changes wrought in Asia and Eastern Europe by World War II). Another source of conflict is the liberation of women, which caused especially acute dilemmas in Islamic countries, and the sexual liberation of married and unmarried women elsewhere, which is powerfully helped by literature. The boldness of Japanese novels like *The Key,* discussed by Howard Hibbett, the breaking away in Poland of the puritanical standards imposed during the Stalinist era described by Czeslaw Milosz, the discarding of the restraints which both Catholics and Calvinists in Holland had once meekly accepted—all point to one value, jealously cherished by literature in those countries as political life often attempts to stifle it: a search for a more drastic sincerity in the writer, a protest against cant and hypocrisy. Themes of disintegration and decay, lurking behind the conformity of small-town life, are treated by Dutch, Hungarian, and Greek novelists with the same glee as they once were in the fiction of Balzac, Flaubert, and Mauriac, in the dramas of Ibsen and Pirandello. In still one other respect does the novel in these new or renovated countries recall the big issues once agitated in the fiction of the last hundred years in the West: it reveals a potential conflict, which is likely to become especially grave in Israel and in Islamic countries, between the traditional religious faith which has long made their cultures and even their politics theocratic and the agnosticism more and more openly professed by the younger generations. The recent humiliation suffered by Arab nations in their 1967 war with Israel may lead either to a revival of Moslem fanaticism or to a conviction that only through the adoption of Communist ideology and technology can they hope to match the industrial modernization of Israel and of the West.

Volumes and articles have been published in several languages on politics and the novel; the best-known one in English is Irving Howe's (1957). They have, as a rule, confined their attention to the fiction of the two countries, France and Russia, in which literature and politics, or philosophy and politics, have never been very far apart. They have tended to be severe with the books which enjoy an enormous sentimental and historical importance, like *Uncle Tom's Cabin,* but do not rise to the level of artistic literature. Debates on the social role of literature may well rage in highly sophisticated countries. Controversies on the Sartrean theory of the commitment of the writer may comfortably be carried on in societies where dissent and heresy represent an old tradition. Feelings may run otherwise in countries which are still in the process of forging their national unity and of asserting their literary personality. There the smooth artistry of the 1966 Nobel prize winner, the Israeli Agnon, or the epic loftiness of Kazantzakis may appear to readers of the West less fruitful and less significant than novels which would reflect the tragic dilemmas of Israel, Greece, and other countries in process of metamorphosis might well be some day.

The cultivation of aloofness from the circumambient world and of purity in art is also sometimes a confession of defeat. Writers abdicate from the rendering of the momentous crises lived by their readers. Even when they do so out of a desire not to tarnish their Olympian serenity in the confusion of pressing and strident quarrels, they may, unbeknownst to themselves, be acting as the playthings of tyrannical regimes of the Left or of the Right, thus reassured by keeping writers neutral and uninfluential. Stendhal has been, as a political novelist, claimed with equal plausibility by liberals (Irving Howe) and reactionaries (Maurice Bardèche). Balzac was in the last century extolled by those (like Paul Bourget) who hailed in him the monarchist and the Catholic and by revolutionaries for whom the Legitimist and conservative Balzac was also the author who satirized the nobles most fiercely and admired those whom he opposed politically. Karl Marx's delirious praise of Balzac is well known and Friedrich Engels lavished admiration on *The Human Comedy*, "that complete history of French society from which, even in economic details, I have learned more than from all the professional historians, economists and statisticians of the period put together."

Balzac himself somewhere defines a fictional character as "anyone on the street who goes to the limits of himself." The peoples of Poland, Hungary, Israel, Greece, Japan, not very long ago, those of Cuba, Colombia, Egypt, India someday, have lived or may have to live limit situations. Few outstanding novels on the war, the bombings, the concentration and extermination camps, the civil war feuds, the Israeli *émigrés* of 1946–1947 prevented from seeking a refuge in the Palestinian land, the Arabs betrayed by the inefficiency of their leaders have as yet been written. The most tragic events of the years 1965–1967, the plight of the harassed and bombed Vietnamese of the two warring sections of Indo-China and, indeed, that of the American soldiers fighting there thousands of miles away from their homes have not yet, in spite of much reporting, impressed the imagination of the non-Asiatic world as that momentous struggle should have. Only powerful fictional volumes (some, by Frenchmen and by Indo-Chinese, had appeared in French between 1945 and 1955 which evinced authentic talents) might do justice to the suffering endured and to the heroism displayed in that new Trojan war. Like the war of Troy, and the destruction of "holy Ilion," as Homer calls the city, it may well leave complexes of guilt in the subconscious of the conflicting nations, such as long haunted the epic narrative and the tragic theater of the Greeks. Napoleonic battles only found a literary presentation commensurate with their magnitude twenty and thirty years after they had taken place. It seems to be a law of artistic creation that it occurs with a lag of a quarter of a century after the events, of which authors may treat, have occurred. Those who are most powerfully affected by events such as the Spanish Civil War, the battle of Stalingrad, the Normandy landings, the martyrdom inflicted by the Nazis are likely to be, not those who fought those battles or survived torture, but those who were then impressionable teen-agers and are only now, twenty-five years after, fully probing the intensity of that vicarious experience.

The implicit ideals of the novel as practiced, since 1950 or 1955, in the nations of Western Europe may thus not prove valid or worthy of being pursued by the novelists of the cultures represented in this volume or of India, Indo-China, Senegal, Kenya, Bolivia. *"Toute maîtrise jette le froid,"* Mallarmé pronounced. "Any virtuoso mastery sends a cold shiver down our spines." The highly sophisticated and self-conscious novel of several groups in France (notably the group "Tel Quel"), represented by Claude Ollier, J. P. Faye, Robert Pinget, Philippe Sollers and by their most talented elders, Nathalie Sarraute and Alain Robbe-Grillet, can hardly be pregnant with useful examples (except perhaps in Japan) for the novelists of Asia, Africa, or Eastern Europe. The French have waged a fight against both narrative and character. The reaction against too well structured a plot, too consistent characters, and the psychology of introspective Solipsists like those of Proust and Gide may have been a healthy innovation in the hothouse atmosphere of aesthetic debate of Paris. Elsewhere, it may not sound naïve to continue maintaining with the dean of English writers on the novel, E. M. Forster, that the prime requirement of that form of literature is that it be "sogged with humanity." A half-forgotten critic, E. S. Dallas, brought to life again by Cecil Day Lewis, had already asserted, a century ago, in *The Gay Science* (London, 1866), while George Meredith was attempting to make English fiction hyper-intellectual: "After all, the question upon which depends our whole interest in art, is, what are its relations to life." That primary question, that *unum necessarium*, has been conspicuously missing from a certain vanguard literature in France since Existentialism ceased to be the dominant current. That may account for the fact that the French novelists mentioned as influential in Poland, Greece, Arabic lands, Brazil in the present volume are Malraux, Sartre, Camus, whose fictional output was practically complete by 1950.

Mention of the English novels—those of Jane Austen (never truly enjoyed outside Britain), Dickens, Thackeray, or the twentieth-century giants like Henry James, Joseph Conrad, James Joyce, and D. H. Lawrence—is conspicuously scarce. The more recent English novel (from E. M. Forster to Angus Wilson, John Wain, Lawrence Durrell, Muriel Spark, Iris Murdoch) may be too subtly ironic, too self-conscious in its mastery of style, perhaps also too thin in content, to exercise a potent attraction on the men of other lands, endeavoring with Arnoldian "high seriousness" to understand life better and perhaps see it steadily through their literature. The criticism of fiction itself, which has, since Henry James, been practiced with more sharpness and high technique in England and America than anywhere else, is of scant value for literatures which have to create fictional works instinct with life and its tensions, rather than to speculate on how others have achieved it. One of the ablest English critics of fiction today, Graham Hough, in *The Dream and the Task* (New York, 1964), remarked courageously, if severely: "There appears to be something about the study of English literature as a separate subject that leads inevitably to a boring provincialism." Lionel Trilling, in this country, more discreetly, regretted that English literature by itself had become too remote from philosophy and politics, from the tragic portrayal of "the human condition," so that it could not provide the sole basis for a literary education. Dostoevski, Mann, Kafka, Proust, Camus, Beckett, the American dramatists and novelists had to be introduced into college syllabi of English courses so as to enrich the usable context which students and readers must today have at their disposal.

The Russian novel of the twentieth century has lacked the universality of appeal and the poetical charm which had won for it so many admirers in an earlier era. It has ceased to count as an element of an active Russian influence in other countries and is practically never mentioned in the essays here collected. It may appear stranger that the impact of American fiction, which was great in France, Spain, Italy, Germany between 1930 and 1945, should not have been similarly powerful on the novelists of Brazil, Greece, Poland, Israel, and Japan. Sinclair Lewis and Ernest Hemingway have been read everywhere. William Faulkner's name is mentioned with awe, but one may have doubts on how widely he is actually read. The violence, the pessimism, the destructive spirit of revolt of the American novel should, it seems, have offered challenging models to the practitioners of fiction in young literatures. The fact that, as Malraux once remarked, American literature is the first to have been in majority composed by writers who were not professional intellectuals is another reason which should have surrounded it with a halo for nations which see in the writing of fiction a form of strenuous action and not the pastime of mandarins. But the impact, if any, of the American novelists who have come to the fore since World War II, when American supremacy was unchallenged, has nowhere matched that of the earlier American authors of the years of the Depression. John Horne Burns, Paul Bowles, Norman Mailer, Irwin Shaw, Saul Bellow, Bernard Malamud, Ralph Ellison, James Baldwin, John Updike, even William Styron, who has been warmly received abroad, have not impressed the fiction of other lands as their predecessors had done. Is it due to a latent fear of American influence at all levels? To a conviction that the problems of other nations, even of European ones, are not similar to those of the "people of plenty"? Perhaps also the coming to the fore of the two groups of American writers of the most marked originality, the Jews and the Negroes, has, in the eyes of the rest of the world, detracted from the universality of American fiction. Certainly many signs point to an influence of the East and of Europe on the Americans who have resided there, at least as all-permeating as the much talked about, and often superficial, Americanization of India, Japan, Iran, Turkey, or South America. It is, in any case, refreshing to discover that diversity has not disappeared from the literatures in three continents in this age of easy communications and of exchange of persons and of ideas, if not always of harmonious meeting of minds.

For Americans and Western Europeans, the initiation to the fiction of other lands is a healthy reminder of the provincialism of our own prejudices or conventional views on the art of fiction. The novel of Arabic lands, of the so-called "popular democracies" of Eastern Europe, or Asiatic, African, and South American countries

belies all our generalizations about that literary form being necessarily linked with "individualism and liberal culture" (V. S. Pritchett's
phrase as quoted here by N. V. M. Gonzalez) and the triumph of
the bourgeoisie. The vitality of that novel in ten or twenty countries
now emerging from a long slumber or from political ordeals likewise
contradicts the disillusioned prophecies of many of us that the novel
is now a dying art and has to make way for mass media. That
novel, self-confident, vigorous, not overconcerned with the subtleties
of technique, fulfills the two functions of fiction which have been
defined by an American critic (R. B. Blackmur) as an addition to
"the stock of available reality" and by an English novelist as poetry
in a broad sense: "the expression of life in relation to eternity that
was once the poet's exclusive province" (Olivia Manning).

HENRI PEYRE

New Haven, Connecticut
August, 1967

FICTION
IN SEVERAL LANGUAGES

E. R. MONEGAL

The Contemporary Brazilian Novel

Toward a National Diction

THE VIENNESE writer who called Brazil "The Land of the Future" was offering more than a slogan for Brazilian chauvinism or a pretext for the obvious retort that Brazil will always be the Land of the Future. In Brazil, the *amanhá* is as deeply ingrained in the national character as the *mañana* is in the rest of Latin America. Stefan Zweig's remark implies, nevertheless, a simple but elusive truth: Brazil as a coherent unity does not yet exist. Politically, it has existed since the Grito de Ipiranga (1822) severed the country from Portuguese rule—but not from Portuguese rulers. (D. Pedro, who proclaimed independence, was the son and heir of the King of Portugal.) As a free country, Brazil has existed for nearly a century and a half, but as a national and cultural unity it is still a Land of the Future. Thus, to assume that there is such a thing as a Brazilian novel is to assume too much. There are Brazilian novels, but there is no such thing as *the* Brazilian novel.

Because of the wide differences between the Amazon jungle and the North-East desert, the arid plateau of Minas Gerais and the soft, luxuriant coastline around Rio de Janeiro, the humid forest of Sta. Catarina and the temperate open spaces of Rio Grande do Sul, Brazil encompasses a wide variety of cultures. The microcosms that form the macrocosm of Brazil are richly reflected in the novels of the country. The Brazilian novelists of today, like the nineteenth-century novelists of North America, cannot avoid being regional in their writing. For this reason also, the all-embracing Brazilian novel, like that other mythical prototype, the "American novel," does not exist.

Literary critics in Brazil have pointed out the obvious contrasts between fiction written in the North-East—the tragic land of desert and famine, of epic and bloody revolt—and the fiction of the South —the *gaúcho* country of rich grass, cattle, and temperate climate

1

similar to the North-American West. They have also discussed the differences between the introspective novelists of Minas Gerais and the more brilliant and extroverted novelists of the large Atlantic ports. But it is as misleading to view Brazilian writing only in terms of a literary map of the country as it is to speak only of the school of southern novelists or of the New York "international" group in writing about the novel in the United States today. Although there is some merit in the approach, it is founded on an erroneous assumption. It implies that the Brazilian novel is conditioned solely by the milieu, that novelists are writing exclusively realistic novels, that the novel, in short, is a documentary form. Twenty or thirty years ago such views were unchallenged in Brazilian literary criticism, as they were in all Latin-American criticism. The impact of Nature over Man in the vast subcontinent, the rediscovery of political commitment by the French school of existentialist writers, and the theories of socialist realism that permeated the Soviet Union were all discussed and widely accepted throughout Latin America. Not only in Brazil, but also in Mexico and Argentina, in Ecuador and Cuba, writers were engaged in mapping out their native lands, describing rivers and mountains, denouncing the local oligarchies or the all-pervading (although not always visible) "American imperialism." In that period, novels were written to show the plight of the Andean Indians or the shocking misery in the spreading slums of Caracas. Very few of these Latin-American novelists were, in fact, concerned with reality. They seldom wrote about men but only about Man. Although their aim was documentary realism, the books they produced were highly stylized exercises in abstract description, pamphlets thinly disguised as novels, or pious tracts.

In Brazil the regionalist movement of the late twenties grew up as a reaction against the extreme academism of Brazilian literature, which was still culturally dependent on Europe. The movement itself had begun somewhat earlier, and, paradoxically enough, its origin lay with a group of writers who felt the need to sever all ties with Portuguese diction and rhetoric. To achieve that, they turned to France and Italy. The Semana de Arte Moderna (Modern Art Week) held in São Paulo in July 1922 had a tremendous impact on the cultural life of the whole country and marked the beginning of a wave of renewal that had important consequences. The group was baptized the "Movimento Modernista"; it should not be confused with Spanish-American *Modernismo*, created some forty years earlier by Rubén Darío and other Latin-American poets under the influence of symbolist poetry and pre-Raphaelite painting.

Although clearly inspired by Italian *Futurismo* and other European "isms," the Semana de Arte Moderna was oriented toward a creative discovery of Brazil. Contact with and imitation of Marinetti and Dada and the surrealists led the Brazilian writers (rather unexpectedly) to a search for Brazilian essences. Mario de Andrade (1893/1945), a poet and critic of a very personal turn of mind, was one of the leaders of the movement. He was among the first to see the dangers of regionalism and to urge the rediscovery of Brazil. His only novel, *Macunaíma* (1928), is a deliberate attempt to produce a poetic narrative based on the whole of Brazilian folklore and to explore the possibilities of a Brazilian language that is as different from the Portuguese as the American idiom is from the British. As a novel, *Macunaíma* is a beautiful failure. Too incoherent, obscure, and episodic, too loosely woven, it has many of the defects of an experimental work like *Ulysses* and few of its virtues. As a milestone, however, *Macunaíma* is a success. It pointed out, at the very beginning of the modernist movement, two extremely important truths: documentary realism is a dead end; language is the first and most critical problem faced by the novelist. Through Macunaíma, the lazy antihero of his novel (*Qué preguiça*—"How tired I feel"— is his slogan, and a national one of a sort), Mario de Andrade showed that the novel could be a mythopoetic creation and need not be a mere recording of reality. By focusing more on language than on plot or characters, de Andrade was dealing with first things first. Unfortunately, *Macunaíma* never managed to be more than a wonderfully lucid and poetic experiment.

In many respects, this attempt in the late twenties ought to be compared with that of Jorge Luis Borges during the same period in Buenos Aires. Borge's short stories, deliberately presented as *Ficciones* (Fictions), emphasized, as *Macunaíma* did, the mythopoetic qualities of narrative imagination and the urge to break with a dead tradition in order to create a truly new Latin-American language. Although Borges was extremely successful in his experiments and became the leader of a small group of writers supported by *Sur* magazine, the main line of Argentine fiction continued until very recently to follow a more realistic and documentary trend. Mario de Andrade was equally successful in changing the literary outlook of Brazil; he indicated the right path, but he apparently got no further. In 1926 a new movement had already grown up as a polemical reaction to the São Paulo modernists. A renewed emphasis on regionalism marked the North-East group that challenged the Paulistas.

Regionalism as a Dead End

The starting point of the countermovement was the Primeiro Congresso de Regionalistas do Nordeste (First Congress of North-East Regionalists) that met in Recife in 1926. If São Paulo represents the dynamic, modern Brazil of the nineteen-sixties, the North-East in the twenties represented the Brazil that was left behind by the new industrialism. It was the region of the obsolete economy of the sugar-cane industry, the decaying feudal world of slaveholders' heirs, and the marginal society of poor *retirantes*, internal emigrants who periodically ran away from the arid hinterland. In many respects, the land combined the harsh realities and nightmarish visions familiar to the readers of Sherwood Anderson, William Faulkner, or John Steinbeck.

Inspired by men like the sociologist Gilberto Freyre (b. 1900), the Congress of North-East Regionalists saw the beginning of an important literary movement—it put the North-East on the map of Brazilian fiction. It did this with a vitality and splendor that tended to conceal the fact that the novel of the North-East is not *the* Brazilian novel. One of the classics of Brazilian sociology, Euclides da Cunha's *Os Sertoes* (*Rebellion in the Backlands*), written in 1902, had already explored the vast epic possibilities of that corner of Brazil; in *Casa Grande e Senzala* (*Masters and Slaves*), Freyre, in 1933, added to Da Cunha's poetic insight his own l e and meticulous vision of a decadent feudal past.

Starting with writers like José Américo de Almeida (whose *A Bagaceira,* 1928, was a pioneering work) and Raquel de Queiroz (who, before she was twenty, wrote *O Quinze,* a classical, spare document on the *retirantes,* published in 1930), the novelists of the North-East, including Graciliano Ramos, José Lins do Rêgo, and Jorge Amado, soon became known throughout Brazil. Of these novelists, only Jorge Amado has achieved international fame. A follower of the Communist leader Luiz Carlos Prestes (whose biography he wrote), Amado was widely translated in the socialist countries. He has also achieved success in the United States; one of his books, *Gabriela, Cravo e Canela* (*Gabriela, Clove and Cinnamon*), 1958, was the first Latin-American novel to become a best seller in the States. The American edition, published in 1962, was reviewed on the front page of *The New York Times Book Review*. Recently, *Hopscotch* (*Rayuela*), a finer and infinitely more creative book by the Argentine Julio Cortázar, also received a front-page review in *The New York Times*.

Despite his international success, however, Amado is not so highly regarded by critics in Brazil as are Lins do Rêgo and Graciliano Ramos. The reasons are obvious. Amado, a born story-teller and a writer of great charm, was until recently one of the sincere followers of the sterile theories of socialist realism. His first books (particularly those in the *Cacau* cycle) are mere tracts, occasionally relieved by graphic and near-pornographic descriptions of life in the North-East plantations and big-city slums. *Jubiabá*, which appeared in 1935, is an extravagant novel, a kind of Grand-Guignolesque suite of horrors, presented as a piece of documentary realism on the social situation in or around Bahía in the thirties. Since 1956, when the Soviet leaders officially declared a thaw in the restrictions placed on literature, Amado has felt free to write novels in a purely narrative vein. *Gabriela* is perhaps his best: the characters are alive, the local color brilliant, and Gabriela charming. But its shortcomings as a novel are obvious. It never moves beneath the surface; the language, although adequate, is rarely creative. Amado, like O'Hara in the United States, or Maugham in England, is a master of the obvious, the typical, and the superfluous.

More interesting is the case of Lins do Rêgo (1901/1957). He also started with a cycle of novels on the sugar-cane culture, but his approach is totally different from Amado's. Lins do Rêgo wrote not with a Marxist blueprint in hand, but out of his experiences as a boy born and educated in the sugar mills. He was the son of the owners; what he wrote in rich, chaotic, and undisciplined prose was his own remembrance of things past. Like *Don Segundo Sombra* (1926), a masterpiece by the Argentine Ricardo Güiraldes, his books are full of nostalgic memory. Lins do Rêgo had a less poetic and more comprehensive vision of his world than did Güiraldes. He wrote with bravura and feeling, and with a deep personal concern for the harsh reality of the North-East. His blueprint was the work of his master, Gilberto Freyre, to whose charming theories and observations he contributed his own experience, enriched by literary contact (in Alagoas, during his formative years) with people like Raquel de Queiroz and Graciliano Ramos.

Later, the success of his novels and his long residence in Rio de Janeiro attenuated the warmth and immediacy of his reporting. While in Rio de Janeiro he completed three of his more ambitious novels: *Pedra Bonita* (1938), *Fogo Morto* (1943), and *Cangaceiros* (1953). Writing now from a purely narrative point of view and not simply from his memories of the sugar-cane world, Lins do Rêgo showed his limitations as a novelist. Only the first novel is a really solid piece of work. This fictional account of a mystical rebellion in the deserts of the North-East, kindled by a fanatic who pretends to be a new Christ (and perhaps believes it), is presented through the eyes of a very young boy, Antonio Bento, a descendant of the fanatic. The story pursues two layers of time—one present, one remote—that merge at the end of the novel. The point of view is both distant and immediate.

Lins do Rêgo did not possess the creative powers to achieve his ambition; his last two really important pieces of fiction clearly demonstrate this. While *Fogo Morto* is occasionally relieved by the vigor of certain of the characters, such as the captain, Vittorino Carneiro da Cunha, *Cangaceiros* relies too heavily on the basic appeal of its subject: the colorful bandits of the North-East desert. In balance, Lins do Rêgo's limitations as a novelist do not obliterate his achievements. In many respects he was moving in the right direction. He had discovered that documentary novels must depend on the imaginative transcription of language as it is in fact spoken. From São Paulo, Mario de Andrade had fought hard to free Brazilian Portuguese from the diction and grammar of the old metropolis. (In Spanish America, the main fight was fortunately concluded by the middle of the nineteenth century.) Although Lins do Rêgo opposed many of the European influences that pervaded the São Paulo movement, he shared de Andrade's concern about spoken Brazilian. While de Andrade's aim was really to replace an old-fashioned rhetoric with a new one, Lins do Rêgo sometimes created the impression that he wanted only to eliminate all rhetoric. In his novels, which are characterized by great freedom of speech, he attempted to transcribe the "real" language of his characters. What he lacked was the discipline to keep the spoken language continually creative. Because of his effort to be faithful to the actual words and sounds used by people, he occasionally became literal, monotonous, and ungrammatical to the point of distraction. The result often justified the charges of certain of his critics that he wrote badly.

Up to a point, Amado and Lins do Rêgo did not really care about good writing and relied, sometimes too heavily, on their storyteller's intuition. Among the North-East novelists, the writer who did care about good writing was the novelist most Brazilian critics hail as the best of that period: Graciliano Ramos (1892/1953). Ramos was as marginal in his job as a civil servant on the fringes of the North-East as the North-East itself was marginal to the new Brazil. An introvert, shy to the point of total silence, Ramos was reticent to publish his first book. He was forty-one when *Caetés* appeared in 1933. Ramos learned to read when he was nine; his formal education was sketchy. During his early years, he was influenced by Gorki and by some of the masters of his native language, including the Portuguese novelist Eça de Queiroz and the Brazilians Euclides da Cunha and Raul Pompéia.

Some critics have proclaimed Ramos' *Vidas sêcas* (1937) a masterpiece of the regional novel. The judgment is debatable, but, even if it is not a masterpiece, it is an impressive book and the best of his works—though some people prefer his autobiographical *Infancia* (1945). *Vidas sêcas*, which describes the plight of a family in the *Sertão* of the North-East, is written in a spare and economical style. Each of its chapters is autonomous (in fact, they were originally published as separate short stories), and the whole structure of the novel reveals a great concern with form and style. Although Graciliano Ramos avoids psychological analysis in this book (he indulged in it in a previous novel, *Angustia*, 1936), he manages to reveal, more by implication than by direct statement, the inner life of his destitute characters through their relationship with the milieu and with animals. The sun, a dog, and a shadow are as legitimate characters in this tale as the human beings are.

Ramos was a silent man, and *Vidas sêcas* is a silent book—the kind that needs frequent reading to reveal itself. With the perspective of nearly three decades, it is easy to discover that it fails precisely because of what appeared to be its virtues at the time of its publication in the thirties. In a period when the vital books of Amado and the loosely constructed novels of Lins do Rêgo were best sellers, *Vidas sêcas* was a lesson in austerity, in depth of observation, and in antiheroic attitudes toward a stark and cruel reality. Since the late thirties, new literary forces have transformed Graciliano Ramos into a respected but not deeply influential master. Lins do Rêgo once called him "Mestre Graciliano." The title was well deserved, but during the last ten years Brazilian novelists have discovered another master: João Guimaraes Rosa. Paradoxically, his first book was published the same year as *Vidas sêcas*, but, instead of ending a creative trend, *Sagarana* was opening a new one.

Mestre Guimaraes

The problem of regionalism as it was discussed in the twenties and thirties in Latin America is a false one. It was presented as primarily geographical rather than literary. From a strictly literary point of view, all novels are regional because they belong to a certain linguistic area. For example, the first novel of modern times, *Don Quixote*, is about an imaginary knight in a forgotten region of the Spanish empire; *Madame Bovary* is about a lady daydreamer who has read too many romantic novels in her sordid French province; and *The Brothers Karamazov* is about a bunch of drunkards, inflamed by mystical thoughts, in a small Russian village. But it is not only the so-called realistic novels that are strictly localized by language and *Weltanschauung*. The fantastic novels are also regional. Swift's *Gulliver's Travels* is as nationally rooted in eighteenth-century neoclassical prose as Voltaire's *Candide*, but their views of the world reveal different national characters. Kafka's *The Trial* and *The Castle* overwhelm the reader with the most concrete Central-European minutiae and with an Old Testament notion of guilt. When Borges writes about Scandinavian or Chinese or Irish heroes, he is always writing about an enormous library, filled with British books, in a cosmopolitan suburb of the world: Buenos Aires. It does not actually matter very much what the writer's geographical situation is. What really matters is the nature of his approach to reality. From this point of view, some books are more regional than others because they tend to present only the typical aspects of a given place and milieu, only the local color— never moving beneath the surface of what they are describing. It is the difference in depth, and not the difference in subject matter, that makes Amado more regional than Ramos.

João Guimaraes Rosa (b. 1908) managed to be universal in his outlook without being unconcerned with his own native territory. So far, he has published one book of very short short-stories, two books of *nouvelles*, and one novel—not very much by the standards of some of his colleagues. Today, he is acclaimed as the greatest Brazilian writer and one of the best in Latin America. Originally published in 1956, his only novel, *Grande Sertâo: Veredas* (*The Devil to Pay in the Backlands*), is written in the form of a monologue. Riobaldo, the protagonist, was once a bandit or *jagunço*, as they are called in the *Sertâo*; he is now an honorable rancher, growing old. The monologue—which proceeds almost without pause, though the narrator stops occasionally to answer some unrecorded questions put to him by an unknown listener—describes Riobaldo's life of love and adventure. The unknown listener is a more ambiguous character than the interlocutors used, for example, by Conrad in his novels. Yet it is for the listener's benefit that the protagonist tells his story. Every monologue needs a haunted listener (as the Ancient Mariner well knew) because his presence justifies the confessional attitude and implies at the same time that there is some deep secret that will be revealed. Riobaldo, of course, has a secret.

Riobaldo's monologue creates a world. It is the world of the Minas Gerais backlands, a high and deserted country that borders on the northeastern *Sertâo*, a smaller desert which had already been explored by Brazilian novelists and sociologists. Guimaraes Rosa once told me with visible pride that, compared to the Minas Gerais, the *Sertâo* is but a fringe of desert, not far from the coast and the sea. The title of his novel, literally translated, indicates this extra dimension of land, *Big Desert: Little Rivers*. Compared to the enormousness of Minas Gerais, his long book is the record of only a small excursion.

The world that Riobaldo evokes is a violent one of treason and burning rivalries, of misery and exploitation, of a territory run by bandits, politicians, and a ruthless army. The story is set in the late nineteenth century, but the problems Guimaraes Rose describes are still very much alive, as today's headlines prove. The novelist is not really concerned with the documentary aspects of the world about which he is writing. Like some of his more brilliant counterparts in the Spanish-American fiction of today (such as Alejo Carpentier of Cuba and Julio Cortázar of Argentina), Guimaraes Rosa does not overlook the misery or exploitation around him— but he knows that reality goes deeper than that. His experiences as a country doctor and later as an army doctor made him familiar not only with the men of the region but also with their inexhaustible language. Through the artistic re-creation of this spoken language, he manages to convey the whole reality of this brutal and tragic land. His childhood was spent listening to old men telling tall

9

stories about the fierce and bloody bandits of the *Sertâo,* the grotesque errant knights of a dubious crusade. In his youth, he traveled extensively through the strange, hard, haunting landscape of the Gerais, spent a great deal of time exploring very small towns or pacing down roads that led to nowhere, and became intimately acquainted with the squalor and misery of his very wealthy country. His life was a quest for a creative language.

Through a technique and sensibility that were molded by the experimental writing of the twenties and thirties (his debts to Joyce, Proust, Mann, Faulkner, and Sartre are obvious), Guimaraes Rosa, in *Grande Sertâo: Veredas,* plays with time and space, telescopes events and persons. He uses the most shameless conventions of melodrama and never slips into the stale conventions of documentary realism. Indeed, he even makes fun of these conventions, sustaining (like Cervantes) a subtle note of parody from the beginning to the end of his tale. One of the best-kept secrets of Riobaldo's monologue, for example, is the name of his real father. When it is discovered, the whole book assumes the form of a quest for identity, one of the basic literary themes since the Greeks. The most sensational secret, however, is the real nature of Diadorim, the protagonist's closest friend and constant companion, a young man of unusual beauty and purity to whom Riobaldo feels sexually attracted, though he fights against this. Playing on the ambiguity of this relationship, Guimaraes Rosa transmutes a melodramatic cliché into a deep insight concerning the nature of desire. Thomas Mann would have liked this book, and Italo Calvino could have recognized in it some of the motives and ironies of his *Cavaliere inesistente* (1959).

As the best Brazilian critics have already pointed out, *Grande Sertâo: Veredas* is in many respects similar to the medieval *Novela de Cavalaria,* the epic fiction of the errant knights that Cervantes parodied in *Don Quixote.* Like those prototypes, Riobaldo is inspired by honor, by unearthly love, by pure friendship, by a noble cause; and he fights against treason, carnal temptations, the obscure power of darkness. The vast, sprawling intricacies of accidental meetings and unexplained separations, brusque discoveries of a hidden past, and tragic anagnorisis that constitute the plot are projected, as Professor Cavalcanti Proença has pointed out, in different layers of meaning: the individual, the collective, the mythical. The whole novel is divided into episodes that are carefully interwoven into the fabric of Riobaldo's monologue, as the

medieval rhetoricists advised; even the technique derives from this
type of novel, so popular in the late Middle Ages. In Spanish
America, one of the most promising young novelists, the Peruvian
Mario Vargas Llosa, reflects the same model in his most recent
novel, *La Casa Verde* (1966). That Vargas Llosa wrote this splendid book without any direct knowledge of Guimaraes Rosa's masterpiece (Brazil is less connected with the rest of Latin America than
with Europe or the United States) shows that there are some deep
undercurrents that link the epic style of the *Novela de Cavalaria*
and the narrative style of some Latin-American writers today. The
feudal world of the Peruvian jungle or the Minas Gerais *Sertão*
somehow matches the feudal world of the late Middle Ages.

But the real theme of *Grande Sertão: Veredas* is diabolical
possession. Riobaldo is convinced that he has entered into a pact
with the devil, that it was the devil who first drove him to a life
of perversity and crime. But his is not the classical devil of cloven
hoof and ironic mien. Guimaraes Rosa's devil is everywhere: a voice
in the desert, a whisper in the conscience, a sudden glance that is
full of temptation, the irresistible depravity of a powerful bandit.
By the devil's side, in this morality tale, stands the figure of an
angel, the beautiful and ambiguous Diadorim. But this is a modern
morality tale, and therefore not a simple one, so Guimaraes Rosa's
angel and his devil are not always clearly distinguishable. Torn
between good and evil, often unable to decide which is which,
Riobaldo vacillates, beset by doubt and anguish.

At the center of this epic tale—full of battles, murders, and
sudden death—is the story of a soul divided between love and
hatred, friendship and enmity, superstition and faith. It is nothing
less than a mythopoetic creation, a literary microcosm of the com-
ponent elements of Guimaraes Rosa's own huge, chaotic, angel-and-
devil-ridden Brazilian motherland.

If *Grande Sertão: Veredas* is an allegory, it is an allegory that
is saved from pure abstraction by the concrete poetry of diction
and character. Hesitantly at first, then more and more easily as
the long tale gathers momentum, it manages to take on the pure
narrative charm of a Western. As the sheer force of the narrative
takes over, a whole world is re-created through language. Guimaraes
Rosa's relation to the world of the *jagunços* is indirect and distant.
Unlike Euclides da Cunha's masterpiece, which was based on his
own experiences during a campaign that ended the bloody rebellion
of one of the most famous Northeastern *jagunços*, this novel was

11

written from tales told by survivors, tales rewritten by Guimaraes Rosa's imagination. For the novelist, this distance in time and in direct experience was more advantageous than the closeness of Da Cunha's sociological reporting. By his very detachment, Guimaraes Rosa was able to get nearer to the core of things. What happened to him while he was writing about the *jagunços'* world is similar to what happened to Sarmiento when he wrote Facundo's biography and described the *pampa* in 1845. The Argentine author had never been in the *pampa,* although he had lived not far from it. What he knew about it came from hearsay and the accounts of English travelers, who were the first to attempt to write about its vastness and desolation. In effect, Sarmiento re-created in Spanish what was actually a foreign vision, but, despite this, he "nationalized" the *pampa* through his style. The same double point of view operates in *Grande Sertão: Veredas.* Guimaraes Rosa has used his own experience of the *Sertão* and documents gathered by people like Da Cunha to evoke, in the language of an imaginary *jagunço,* the world of the Brazilian backlands in the late nineteenth century.

Every phrase of this novel is written as if it were a line in a poem. The invisible but omnipresent structure of verbal sound is as important as the story itself. The distribution of accents in each phrase and the general movement of each paragraph sometimes reveal more about the real mood of the protagonist than any given situation or episode. This is the main reason why, at the beginning of the long monologue, Guimaraes Rosa makes his protagonist so reluctant to tell the full story of his life; why Riobaldo is so reticent and ambiguous about Diadorim and about his pact with the devil; why he begins to confess in earnest only when the flow of memory, the incessant stream of evocation, possesses him completely. The narrative then mounts and accelerates. The last quarter of the novel is completely free of asides, of mental reservations, of the relentless activities of the inner censor. When the confession comes to a climax, the novel ends. The catharsis is complete.

It is this peculiarity of style that accounts for the difficulties Guimaraes Rosa's novel presents to translators and even to readers of Portuguese. In fact, the American translation (done with tremendous care by James L. Taylor and Harriett de Onís) reads much more easily than the original, for to a certain extent the translators were forced to simplify and explicate the text. According to the author, only the recent Italian translation of *Corpo de*

Baile, a volume of *nouvelles,* and the German version of *Grande Sertâo: Veredas* achieve the almost impossible task of being both faithful to the original and readable. Translating Guimaraes Rosa is like translating Joyce: his, too, is a purely verbal world.

O Novo Romance

The deep regionalism of Guimaraes Rosa's fictional world is not the only answer to the regionalist challenge of the thirties. While Ramos, do Rêgo, and Amado were developing the North-East movement, writers in other parts of Brazil were exploring new possibilities. In the plateau of Minas Gerais, Cyro dos Anjos (b. 1900) and Lucio Cardoso (b. 1913) were creating a more introspective type of fiction; in the vast spaces of the South, Erico Verissimo (b. 1905, in Rio Grande do Sul) was achieving fame through novels written in a more international idiom. None of these writers, however, succeeded, as Guimaraes Rosa had, in crossing the very subtle line that separates the regional from the universal. Even Rosa was not always successful. While European critics praised him, the North Americans reacted with indifference. Misled by critics who did not understand or perhaps even read his novel, the American public let *Grande Sertâo: Veredas* pass almost unnoticed in 1963. It is a pity because Rosa's work deserves a wider audience.

During the last ten years or so, a new group of Brazilian writers has been experimenting with a form that has been baptized *O Novo Romance Brasileiro.* The term *novo romance* acknowledges the influence of the *nouveau roman* and, to a degree, underlines the deep cultural ties that still exist between Brazil and France. (This is less true of the new group of Spanish-American novelists, who are strongly attracted to the Anglo-Saxon world as well.) But if some of the *novo romance* is only an adaptation of the *nouveau roman,* the best of it is really a new movement. Among the prominent novelists now writing in Brazil, Clarice Lispector is one of the most widely respected. She is not alone in the field: Maria Alice Barroso, Adonias Filho, Mario Palmeiro, and Nélida Piñón are also recognized as important or promising new novelists. But Clarice Lispector is the acknowledged master of the experimental fiction of the sixties.

She has already produced five novels: *Perto do Coração Selvagem* (1944), *O Lustre* (1946), *A cidade sitiada* (1949), *A Maça*

13

no escuro (1961), and *A Paixão segundo G. H.* (1964). She has also published three volumes of short stories. Her first three novels passed almost unnoticed at the time they were published. Success came with her last two novels, which are undoubtedly her best. But success, even of a very limited and specialized kind, is something that cannot affect Lispector's attitude toward her fiction. She writes to fulfill a very tyrannical vocation and because she cannot stop. What she writes has very little to do with what is fashionable at the time. Up to a point, her attitude is similar to that of Graciliano Ramos: They are both reticent and very personal in their approach, although their works have very little else in common.

Her last two novels reveal a turn of mind and an imagination deeply involved with a quest for reality, a determination to force appearances, and a burning desire to grasp the core of things. To a degree, she can be compared to Virginia Woolf (as some of her critics have suggested) because of her rather obsessive philosophical attitude and obviously feminist bias. But it would be wrong to believe that Clarice Lispector is simply turning back the clock of fiction. In a sense, her novels are poetic novels, but they seek to go further than Virginia Woolf's experimental novels of the twenties and thirties. While the author of *To the Lighthouse* was influenced by writers like Frazer, Bergson, and Joyce, Lispector is influenced by the contemporary school of social and psychoanalytical anthropologists. In a very subtle way, her whole enterprise is linked with the one prematurely attempted by Mario de Andrade. As one of her critics pointed out recently, her novels are mythopoetic creations in which morose, and even exasperating, explorations of a given reality are reflected in very primitive types of consciousness. It has also been noted by the same critic that her two most recent novels retrace from the so-called primitive mind man's discovery of philosophical consciousness. According to José Américo Motta Pessanha, the mythical consciousness of man that Lispector explored in episodes of her previous novels and in her short stories is fully organized into a mythology in *A Maça no escuro*. The plight of this novel's main character becomes a symbol of the hero's return to the origins, to the roots, to the native land. In *A Paixão segundo G. H.*, the problem of the origins of everything is presented in a more philosophical vein. Phenomenology and existentialism help Lispector to search beneath the surface of man's consciousness. Her task becomes increasingly more difficult and hard to follow. Quite

14

recently, one of her most successful short stories, "O Ovo e a Galinha" ("The Egg and the Hen"), presents subliminal, almost quartet-like variations on an age-old question.

But even if one fears that Lispector's philosophical assumptions are sometimes a bit too lofty (it is easy to predict that they will be considered so by the generally pragmatic North-American reviewers when the forthcoming translation of *A Maça no escuro* is published in the United States), her skill in creating a totally fictitious world, her hypnotic power to extract from words, simple words, all their incantatory virtues, and the single-mindedness of her tragic vision tend to act on the reader as a charm. In *A Maça no escuro* (*Apple in the Dark*), the inner struggle of a man who believes he murdered his wife is the pretext for an unmitigated exploration of man's grasp of reality (both external and internal), of his power to cope with concrete objects, of his insertion into a foreign and always hostile environment—the world. At the beginning of the novel the man becomes lost in a desert, and in this emptiness even words are hard to find. In *A Paixâo segundo G. H.*, the main character, a woman, talks endlessly. She is trying to understand, trying very hard and obsessively to understand reality. Her effort to grasp the naked reality of the present moment and to recover her own soul reveals her *passion*, a word Lispector uses deliberately in a double sense, the Greek (to suffer) and the Christian. Paradoxically, the use of religious language in this novel indicates her profane turn of mind. As one Brazilian critic has remarked, the religious language serves to mask her vision. It is an oblique way of de-sacralizing the real world just as the effort to rediscover a primitive mode of consciousness in her previous novel revealed the intention of destroying the assumptions of rational psychology. Both novels are at the beginning of a new and private mythology.

Part of Lispector's works is lost to the common reader. What he generally finds is a brilliant and hard surface, a very morose tale, mysterious characters that suffer from some obscure disease of the mind. Captured by her prose, the reader discovers, in her novels, that everyday reality becomes hallucinatory. At the same time, hallucinations are presented as commonplace. Because of her mythological turn of mind, she is more a sorceress than a writer. Her novels show the incredible power of words to act on the reader's imagination and sensitivity. On the whole, she has proved, going by a different route, what Guimaraes Rosa has also demonstrated: the importance of language in the novel.

All her work reveals an almost maniacal determination to use the right word, to exhaust the possibilities of each word, to build up a solid structure of words. Her last two novels are written like poems. They demand of their reader a concentration similar to that required by the best contemporary poetry. Once I asked Guimaraes Rosa what he thought of Clarice Lispector's work. He told me very candidly that every time he read one of her novels he learned many new words and rediscovered new uses for the ones he already knew. But, at the same time, he admitted that he was not very receptive to her incantatory style. He felt it was alien to him. His reaction is not unique and explains Lispector's limitations as a novelist. Critics often talk about some form of art that needs an acquired taste. Lispector's novels belong to this category, I think, while Guimaraes Rosa's have a more universal appeal.

The Latin-American Context

What Rosa and Lispector represent in the Brazilian novel of the last decade is the new trend in Latin-American fiction. Nineteenth-century realism tended to obscure a novelist's obligation to present more than individual characters, social or national descriptions, ideas or beliefs. This realism overshadowed the fact that a novelist's fight is mainly with language. Flaubert, Henry James, and Conrad had already shown the way to a new type of fiction, widely conscious of its dependence on language, structure, and style. The experimental novel of the twenties and thirties in Europe and the United States made this commonplace. But in Latin America it took the writers some time to discover and accept it. Only in the last decade has it become obvious in Latin-American fiction. The works of pioneers like Borges and the Guatemalan Miguel Angel Asturias, of people like Alejo Carpentier of Cuba, Onetti of Uruguay, Juan Rulfo of Mexico, Ernesto Sábato and Julio Cortázar of Argentina made the Spanish-American novelist widely aware that documentary (or socialist) realism is finished; that regionalism as a mere expression of local color is dead; that the novelist's real and only commitment is to his personal vision and craft. The emergent new writers such as Carlos Fuentes in Mexico, Gabriel García Márquez in Colombia, Mario Vargas Llosa in Peru, José Domoso in Chile, and Carlos Martínez Moreno in Uruguay followed this creative and deeply literary line, like their counterparts of the new Brazilian novel.

For the new novelists of Latin America, the center of gravity has shifted radically—from a landscape created by God to a landscape created by men and inhabited by men. The *pampas* and the *cordillera* have yielded to the great city. For the older novelists the city was no more than a remote presence, arbitrary and mysterious; for these new writers, the city is the axis, the place to which the protagonist of their novels is ineluctably drawn. The somewhat depersonalized vision of the novelists of the beginning of the century has reacquired flesh and blood. Suddenly, powerful, complex fictional beings are emerging from the anonymous masses of the great cities. This dramatic change corresponds sociologically with the growth of the conurbations, but also reflects the spreading influence of psychoanalysis. This change has not spared the novelists who adhere, by and large, to rural themes. Even if, on the surface, they still record the traditional struggle of man against nature, the characters they are now presenting are no longer abstractions or ciphers that justify some political or sociological approach. They are complex and ambiguous human beings. A forerunner of this new vision, the River Plate storyteller Horacio Quiroga discovered early in this century that the natives of Misiones and the outcasts of the European world who were stranded there could be as sophisticated as people living in big cities. The Brazilian novelists no longer write epics of pure and exploited *campesinos* and *gaúchos* and *indios,* with their two-dimensional characterization, their "documentary" mechanical structure. The cities and their chaotic inhabitants monopolize the attention of the younger novelists. Today, in Latin America's great sprawling cities—Rio de Janeiro, Buenos Aires, Mexico City, Lima—each of the young writers aspires to be a Balzac, a Joyce, a Dos Passos, a Sartre.

Yet these. new novelists do more than imitate European and American models. Though linked to these models by a continuous, living tradition, and by a study of their technique and vision, the new novelists have an acute social and political awareness. They combine this awareness with a remarkable subtlety and a personal engagement that is marked by sensitivity to other, transcendental dimensions. Through these men, Latin America shows its face to the world and communicates its hopes and despairs. A new man is emerging from the chaos and revolutions, and the Latin-American novelists are the mentors of this new man. Because of their efforts, the Latin-American novel is beginning to take wing and rise above its present linguistic limits. The novels are being translated, discovered, and discussed in Europe and the United States; the number of international prizes they win and their foreign editions are beginning to multiply. Latin-American writers are now having some impact on milieux that had been, until quite recently, rather unreceptive to their works. Perhaps not since the introduction of the Russian novelists into nineteenth-century France, or the modern Americans into postwar Europe, have similar potentialities existed, both for Latin-American writers and for their readers overseas.

In the present situation of the Western novel, dominated by the arid writers of the *nouveau roman* or by the secluded, personal fiction of the best American, British, or Italian novelists, the all-embracing and over-confident attitude of the new Latin-American novelists is worth considering. An enterprise of such vastness and courage—the portrayal of a whole new society and the representation of a contradictory, still unclassified type of man—is seldom attempted with such vigor in our days. It is easy to believe that the Latin-American novelists have a vision to communicate and to share: the common vision of a continent that is torn by revolution and inflation, but also emboldened by anger and mounting expectations, by its awareness that it speaks for a truly emerging world.

To this continental task, the Brazilian novelists of this century have already made a great contribution. In the works of the best novelists a very clear line of development can be traced—the line of anti-documentary and extra-realistic fiction. Mario de Andrade's *Macunaíma* first revealed this development, but more as a possibility than as an achievement. It was visible occasionally in some of the novels of Lins do Rêgo and Graciliano Ramos, but it achieved concrete form in Guimaraes Rosa's vast fictional world. It is bravely if obscurely present in Clarice Lispector's hard, uncompromising books. It is the line of writers who believe in the re-creation of a whole reality through language: the old line of literature.

A NOTE ON TRANSLATIONS

Alfred A. Knopf published Jorge Amado's *Gabriela, Clove and Cinnamon* in 1962; Guimaraes Rosa's *The Devil to Pay in the Backlands* in 1963; Guimaraes Rosa's first book, *Sagarana* (a cycle of nine related but independent tales set in Minas Gerais), and José Lins do Rêgo's *Plantation Boy* (the first three volumes of his sugarcane cycle) in 1966. It is also planning to publish this year a second novel by Jorge Amado and Clarice Lispector's *Apple in the Dark*.

18

N. V. M. GONZALEZ

The Filipino and the Novel

To THE Filipino the world of the imagination has a singular appeal, for the work-a-day world is particularly depressing. The per-capita national income last year was slightly less than a hundred dollars. A recent survey revealed that only 4.7 per cent of over five million households enjoy an income of $1,250 a year and nearly 80 per cent must make do on $500 a year.[1] The Filipino imagination must confront or gloss over life lived at this level; it is here that the novelist finds the "vast but finite quarry"[2] which, with luck, becomes his fulfillment.

In areas where the twentieth century has become a reality, radio, television, and the movies have cashed in on an audience that seeks escape from the harsh conditions of life in the Philippines. Tagalog, which recently became officially known as Pilipino, is spoken by 44 per cent of the population, and English by 39.5 per cent; the literacy rate is 72 per cent.[3] Upon this wide base, fortunes have been built by entrepreneurs, even in the field of publishing. But this has not worked to the best interest of the novel as an art form. As Ortega y Gasset has said, "There exist a definite number of possible themes for the novel. The workmen of the primal hour had no trouble finding new blocks—new characters, new themes. But presentday workers face the fact that only narrow and concealed veins are left them."[4] In the Filipino novelist's milieu, the large and obvious veins have not, as yet, been worked out. His themes are writ large in the daily press, which enjoys an unusually vigorous and jealously guarded freedom and exhibits an amplitude of moral indignation with which fiction cannot seem to compete. It is perhaps for this reason that few serious novels are being written in the Philippines today.

The insistence upon a new Rizal, a new *Noli me tangere*, is understandable in the light of corruption in high places, ideological evasions, assorted venalities, and the like. A man of abundant gifts, Jose Rizal (1861/1896) was only twenty-six when he wrote *Noli me tangere*, a book which, with its companion volume, *El filibusterismo*, written four years later, unleashed upon the author the full wrath of the Establishment. Rizal died a martyr's death and today occupies a revered niche in the Philippine pantheon. His two books are required reading for college students, and their popularization has assumed the proportions of a minor industry. In regard to their status as novels, however, qualifications have been expressed. Of *Noli*, particularly, the following is typical: "The book is a novel only in the sense that the technique employed by the author is that of fiction. It is a mistake to suppose that because it is written in novel form it is, therefore, fiction."[5]

The much-sought relevance of history to fiction has become a special feature of the milieu in which the Filipino novelist works. It is expressed in the call for the Great Filipino Novel, a depiction, possibly, of private lives that would encompass Philippine experience within living memory. Rizal's aim, while immediate and practical in terms of the conditions about which he wrote, set the canon for the form. Flaubert's *Madame Bovary* (1857) and Turgenev's *Fathers and Sons* (1861) might have shown Rizal and his contemporaries what the novelist's idea of order could create; but this was not in their sights. Rizal's target emerged from a personal conviction that reforms were due in the country. His fiction was meant to veil his purpose, though thinly. The novel must lead to an epiphany of self-knowledge and the will to reform. Writing to a friend, Rizal attested to his confidence in history: "The facts I narrate are all true and actually happened; I can prove them."[6] His milieu today could well ask the Filipino novelist for similar assurances and could count indeed on getting them.

A problem that immediately presented itself to the serious writers after Rizal was not quite that of the novel itself; rather, it was the question of language. Charles E. Derbyshire's English translation of Rizal's *Noli me tangere* suggested the possibilities for fiction in English—the language instituted as the medium of instruction in the growing school system under the American regime; but the pleasures of reading about the Philippine scene in this new text did not assuage the nationalist's yearnings. He was aware that Tagalog, while not widely spoken in the country at that time, could best express the sentiments of the Filipino writer.

The first decade of the American regime witnessed a new fervor for writing in Tagalog. Sold at Manila church patios, side by side with votive candles and *novenas*, were metrical romances, popular love stories, and *Florante at Laura*, the masterpiece of an early heyday, by Francisco Baltazar (1788/1862), better known as Balagtas. The theater was active and not adverse to presenting anti-American plays, even at the risk of being closed down. Some eighteen years had passed since the writing of *Noli*, and Tagalog intellectuals in Manila were following a newspaper serial entitled *Banaag at Sikat* (Glow and Sunrise). A long discursive narrative, it offered readers progressive ideas barely disguised by a contrivance of romantic events.

Its author, Lope K. Santos (1879/1963), was not a newcomer to the field of romantic fiction in Tagalog. As a printer's son, he had worked on galley proofs and written several love stories for the trade. To Mariano C. Javier, he was to describe years later how he turned schoolteacher and newspaperman. Javier set down the story as a preface to a critical reading and a complete English translation of *Banaag at Sikat*, the first attempted in fifty years.[7] To his firsthand experience in the labor movement, Lope K. Santos added the knowledge he had gained from reading some four hundred books by such authors as Vicente Blazco Ibañez, Ruben Dario, Karl Marx, Victor Hugo, and Leo Tolstoi. Although Javier may be correct in saying that *Banaag at Sikat* is essentially a long definition of socialism, this novel remains the most ambitious single effort of its day in Tagalog prose. The work did not find readers too readily, and Santos' printers relentlessly hounded the author.[8]

The book did win a measure of recognition for its author, for it appeared when labor unions were beginning to be organized in secret and when it was nearly seditious to speak about mounting a strike. Quick to see the qualities of the author, Manuel L. Quezon, then the acknowledged Filipino leader in the government, projected Lope K. Santos into public life. He became a provincial governor and was later appointed senator by the American Governor General, Francis Burton Harrison. Quezon some years later was to launch a strong program for Tagalog as the national language, and Lope K. Santos crowned his literary career by presenting his friend with a comprehensive grammar of the language.

Lope K. Santos and his *Banaag at Sikat* illustrate the tension between talent and milieu. It was not quite the book that the author's friend and critic, Macario Adriatico, would have liked to see.

21

In introducing the book to its public, Adriatico could not help suggesting: "Indeed the author might do well to model his work after those by the great masters—Zola, for instance; he must observe and study life well before attempting a portrayal of it."[9] The remark did not discourage the author: Time would prove him right, as he was to emphasize later in his "Afterword." His interest had not been on character but on ideas. Adriatico's comment indicated that the milieu asked of its writers, on the one hand, those impossible romantic narratives intended for sheer entertainment, several of which Lope K. Santos provided himself, and, on the other hand, serious fiction in the cast and direction of *Noli*, a costuming of actuality in order to project a measure of social reform.

A definition of the novelist's role was evolving. Jorge C. Bocobo, in 1925, gave the following description of the proper subject for the Filipino novel:

There is a bounteous store of material that awaits the magic touch of the dreamer of dreams and the teller of tales. Our rugged, simple home virtues, than which there is no richer heritage from our forebears, could breathe the genial spirit of beauty into any song or story. Nature in her tropic moods—her radiant lavishness, her throbbing radiance, her infinite calm, her wrathful upheavals, and terrible agitations: these generously lend themselves to poetic fantasy. The iron fortitude of our heroes, who with their blood have "tinged the dawn" of freedom, the unfaltering struggles of our people for their God-given right to live their own life—these must claim the inspired pen of him who has the gift to utter them in lofty accents and vibrant strain.[10]

The rhetoric was typical of the period. In any case, more English was being spoken and written in the country than ever before. The intellectuals as a class had acquired an enthusiasm for the language; the essay had become a favorite form, and samples of the "vibrant strain" were turning up in verse by undergraduates at the University of the Philippines. As early as 1912, it was apparent that there was a need for criticism that would indicate whether "the Filipino public is susceptible to the imaginings of a native Tennyson . . . whether the ideals and aspirations of the race could be expressed in English and yet remain distinctively native."[11] Bocobo, however, was hardly that critic; his interests were elsewhere.

"The great Filipino novel," he wrote, "or the great Filipino drama, or the great Filipino poem, will not be in English; it will be in one of the Filipino languages." To underline his view, he cited Dante, Cervantes, and Chaucer, whose masterpieces were written at a time when "Latin was the language of high culture in Europe."[12] This issue has remained unresolved even though the Filipino creative imagination has preoccupied itself with the fictional forms, particularly the sketch and the short story.

In 1928, the twenty-five best short stories from an annual crop of six hundred were gathered into a small volume under the imprint of the English-language weekly *Philippines Free Press*. "The aim, apart from self-interest," the sponsors wrote, "was to develop a school of Filipino writers or authors, partly as filling a want in the local literary field and partly with a view to the possible development of some literary genius who might make a name for himself in the United States."[13] This last note, because it posed the status of best seller as a factor of success, has probably caused great harm to the Filipino imagination. In any case, by 1933, Jose Garcia Villa, the editor of the *Free Press* anthology, had collected his short stories under the title *Footnote to Youth*—a collection that drew from Edward J. O'Brien a more than approving smile. O'Brien marked Villa as "among the half-dozen short story writers in America who count"; he further observed that Villa's individual viewpoint in "the interpretation of American life, as well as the energy which these stories reveal, suggest that he might well give us a new reading of the American scene in novels of contemporary life."[14] This expectation —insofar as it concerned the writing of novels in general and not necessarily novels about the American scene—was shared by the younger generation of writers; Villa might indeed come up with *the* Filipino novel in English.

He devoted his main attention from then on, however, to poetry. But he also heightened the consciousness of form and substance in the Philippine short story by evaluating the annual crop in the manner of Edward J. O'Brien, who himself followed the literary work in America and Britain. The direction was indeed timely. With the institution of the Commonwealth Literary Awards in 1940, the milieu was ready to accept the reality of a new literature—a literature written in English.

The justification for appropriating tax-money for literature derived from a provision in the Philippine Constitution which committed the state to a role as patron of the arts and letters. It required, however, some promotion on the part of the newly organized Philippine Writers' League. The League encouraged social consciousness in the growing literature in reaction to the creeping dilettantism in poetry, the essay, and the short story. The League's leadership came, ironically, from the University of the Philippines

Writers' Club, that is to say, from the same group of young writers who, in 1927, had introduced themselves "to the general public as the faithful followers of Shakespeare," and who in twelve years were to disown their motto ("Art shall not be a means to an end; but an end in itself") in favor of something more pertinent, more immediate. The League's best spokesman, Salvador P. Lopez, wrote: "The writer, therefore, who works upon the belief that man is a mere fancier of beautiful words and golden phrases, has missed the essential element in man. He works in a vacuum and, therefore, works in vain. . . ."[15] This sense of urgency was heightened by the fact that Nazism had, by then, overrun Europe; in a few more years Japanese imperialists were to mount their invasion of the Philippines. "Go through the history of literature, and you will find that the greatest writers are ever those whose feet were planted on the earth regardless of how high up in the clouds their heads might have been," Lopez wrote in 1940.[16] This reminder is reflected in the novels in English that even then were being written.

Juan C. Laya's *His Native Soil* received the Commonwealth Award for the Novel in 1940. Using a Filipino who had returned from America as its central character, *His Native Soil* considers the problem of social change. In a second novel, *This Barangay* (1950), Laya examines a similar theme, the return to traditional community living.

A concept of character, flat and in the round, was becoming a feature of fictional writing; this was developed further in the novels that followed. It is particularly evident in Stevan Javellana's *Without Seeing the Dawn* (1947), Edilberto K. Tiempo's *Watch in the Night* (1953), Nick Joaquin's *The Woman Who Had Two Navels* (1961), and, more recently, Bienvenido N. Santos's *Villa Magdalena* (1966) and *The Volcano* (1966). A reading of these works discloses a tremendous creative vitality trying to come to grips with actuality. The question Manuel E. Arguilla put to Hemingway in 1940, How much of fact should there be in one's writing? was indeed pertinent to Filipino fictional development.

Arguilla, author of the short-story collection *How My Brother Leon Brought Home a Wife* (1940), had raised the point at a private party where the American novelist, in Manila on a brief visit, was a guest. The record of this incident is largely in paraphrase, but it is nevertheless credible.[17] Hemingway reportedly replied that "one had to know the subject thoroughly and from there invent, because if [one] wrote cold facts, they would not be at all interesting, as nothing ever happens to us anyway." This advice hardly comforted the Filipino writer who was well aware that he was in the vortex of public events. In due course he was to cope with Bataan, the Japanese Occupation, Independence in 1946— material, in short, that would be sufficient to atrophy the imagination.

Neither was William Faulkner, in 1955, of much help when he told his audience: "Just to report facts, to report injustice, sometimes is not enough. That doesn't move people. The writer's got to add the gift of his talent; he has to take the truth and set it on fire so that people will remember it."[18] Actuality, not unlike the cosmos of Tolstoi's *War and Peace*, has seemed to be always on fire. Worse, the novelist, if he could tend his fire at all, could not count on a large audience.

The reason is not hard to find, in fact, for the Filipino writer lives in a country where there is no "middle class." What passes for it is the educated sector of the national community which has middle-class aspirations, but not the corresponding economic freedom to attain them. The novel as a saturation of "individualism and liberal culture," as V. S. Pritchett puts it,[19] cannot but become for the Filipino primarily a tract for the evolution of that middle class. Faulkner suggested to his Philippine audience in 1955 that the best way to get a "certain portrait in the legends, the customs of the people that are valuable" is to work these into the body of a national literature and, later, into that of universal literature.[20] Reviewing a collection of Philippine short stories, Donald Keene wrote, by way of a progress report on Philippine literature: "It [the collection] is an admirable testimony to the emergence of another important branch of English literature."[21] But this was not the kind of success that really mattered. In view of the Filipino's aspirations to middle-class status in terms of individualism and liberalism (which are central to the portrait that Faulkner mentioned), the Filipino novel seems to have been evolving as a tool to clear the ground for social action rather than as an art form trying to find its proper setting.

Still, the Filipino shares with writers the world over "a glut of new means, new manners, and new styles" which V. S. Pritchett identifies as the heart of the troubles of the modern novelist.[22] According to Pritchett the novelist's views on his art and on the practices of his antecedents and contemporaries are indeed "hardly more than steam rising from a simmering pot. Or, more precisely, clues to his own conflicts." One of these conflicts concerns his moving away from or remaining in the direction set by *Noli*. Writers, so far, have concentrated on the Filipino, unique in his time and place. The intended subject is Man, as he has always been and however Filipino he might be.

A contemporary example is Nick Joaquin's *The Woman Who Had Two Navels*, a work which Professor Leonard Casper has described as embodying a style and theme "perfectly adapted to one another's needs, in this novel proving Joaquin is Faulkner/ Dostoevsky."[23] In it Casper discovers the dimensions of a moral memory to be "not just the coexistence of the divinely oriented Spanish past and the pragmatic American-influenced present but the intersection of time and eternity as well"; in those "navels" are the dualities "of the diabolic and the angelic in man."[24] For all this, however, national self-consciousness has blurred much of the reading of Joaquin and of those of his colleagues who have attained a similar level of performance. This audience has preferred to read Joaquin as an illumination upon a past and upon an uneasy present, combining a sweet nostalgia with an understandable anxiety.

There have been interesting refinements in the short story, which, since the twenties, has offered private enjoyment to the individual reader in the solitude of his critical awareness and fellow feeling. If nowhere else, it is from the ranks of short-story writers that the rich metaphorical resources of Philippine culture are finding their discoverers and users. These writers reflect a wide acceptance, perhaps largely unconscious, of "the very richness of our social experience, the diversity of our cultural traditions," and this has raised a serious "problem of synthesis."[25]

But it is quite possible, even today, to offer such a synthesis in terms of the short story in English while keeping alive the hope that a critical investigation of the short story in Tagalog, Cebuano, Hiligaynon, and Iloko, to mention the principal language areas where the form has been very much in use since the thirties, can present a similar achievement. There is still another way of looking at the matter of synthesis: by examining a selection from works by such writers as Sinai C. Hamada, Manuel E. Arguilla, Bienvenido N. Santos, Francisco Arcellana, Gilda Cordero Fernando, and Gregorio C. Brillantes. This listing covers thirty years of the short story in the Philippines, but it can, to a perceptive reader, appear to include material by only one hand. These works express a sensibility which, during the Commonwealth period, World War II, and thereafter, has developed a maturity of style, technique, and themes.

The conflict between country and city, youth as the "fair hope of the Fatherland," the idea of the Lost Eden, and the intricate interaction of illusion and reality, of form and substance, of intention and outcome have successfully engaged the imagination of four generations of Filipino short-story writers. Only now is their success being noticed, thanks to critics like Leonard Casper and Donald Keene, and to a very few magazine editors in America. The truly new in Casper's critical anthology, *New Writing from the Philippines* (Syracuse University Press, 1966), is the composite image that the reader inevitably must form of an emerging literature that is essentially a response of Philippine society and of the creative imagination to the circumstances of history and cultural exchange.

The brevity of the short story, its modest appeal for attention, the relative ease of publication, and the wide variety of truly small subjects possible of illumination are ready assets that the Filipino writer has used to advantage. He has been further aided in his progress by the criticism on the short story that began to gather after World War II. The attention that the Filipino writer gave to Robert Penn Warren and Cleanth Brooks, to Allen Tate and Caroline Gordon, and to Robert W. Stallman, V. S. Pritchett, and Mark Schorer was an investment in the fifties that today is handsomely paying off. Among the writers in the native languages, those in Cebuano have been especially responsive to the insights derived from these critics, while those writing in Tagalog, hampered by the demands of an extremely large but peculiarly undiscriminating audience, have been less so.

In contrast to the Filipino short story, with its diversity of voices and sophistication in performance, the Filipino novel has tended somewhat toward simplification, perhaps because of the novelist's inability to cope with the Rizal tradition. Its scope and its obvious social relevance have made an intensity of illusion, to use a Jamesian distinction, difficult to attain. That such intensity must come from a fine mind, as James prescribes, still needs unequivocal demonstration. It may well be that for some time the short story will provide a testing ground; but one cannot overlook the fact that the novelist's imagination is, in its reach and intentions, quite different from that of the short-story writer's. To arrive at this insight through trial and error is too time consuming; yet for most writers this will have to be a necessary phase. It is from those who have come to terms with the demands of these two forms of fiction that impressive performances will come. Their emergence on the literary scene, incidentally, may well coincide with the hurried efforts to introduce industrialization and to raise the per-capita national income. The increased tempo of economic development may minimize the appeal of the short story and generate more ardor for the novel, as has happened in England, for example. In all likelihood, however, it will take many years before this stage of growth can be reached.

It must be pointed out that the *ex abundantia* which Ortega y Gasset speaks of as a feature of the density from which a novel comes into being[26] is perhaps another aspect of self-consciousness. This density presents a real challenge. It requires strategies that must defeat, for instance, the current convention in Tagalog publishing which, as a simple matter of editorial policy, discourages the rendered scene. It must, at the same time, rise above the picturesque and charming, which, especially in the case of the Filipino novel seeking an attentive and respectful audience abroad, are allegedly endearing qualities that are proudly announced on the dust jacket.

Indeed, such strategies will be discovered as the Filipino novelist perseveres; to certain of today's critics their occasional presence should be no surprise. The Filipino novelist's role, in any case, will not be unlike that suggested in a Tagalog riddle about a rich man's house which is full of treasures and which a burglar explores, keeping for himself whatever object strikes his fancy, and yet—so the riddle insists—leaving every work of value, every gem and heirloom, in its original place.

The riddle describes how a thoughtful reader might, like this burglar, go through the Filipino novel with profit. It offers the Filipino novelist a purpose and defines his scope and method.

REFERENCES

1. *Manila Chronicle*, June 5, 1966, Business Sec., p. 7.

2. Jose Ortega y Gasset, *The Dehumanization of Art* (New York, 1956), p. 54.

3. *Manila Chronicle*, *op. cit.*

4. Ortega y Gasset, *op. cit.*

5. Teodoro A. Agoncillo and Oscar M. Alfonso, *A Short History of the Filipino People* (Quezon City, 1960), p. 169.

6. *Ibid.*

7. Mariano C. Javier, *A Study of the Life and Works of Lope K. Santos, with Special Reference to* Banaag at Sikat (unpublished Master's Thesis; University of the Philippines, 1960).

8. Lope K. Santos, *"Huling-Kabit"* ("Afterword"), *Banaag at Sikat* (2d ed.; Manila, 1959), pp. d-e.

9. Macario Adriatico, *"Paunawa"* ("Foreword"), Santos, *op. cit.,* p. vii.

10. Jorge C. Bocobo, "Cultural Independence of the Philippines," *Philippines Herald,* Dec. 2, 1924, ed. Leopoldo Y. Yabes, *Filipino Essays in English* (Quezon City, 1954), p. 34.

11. Fernando M. Maramag, "A Call for Critics," *The College Folio,* Oct. 1912, Yabes, *op. cit.,* p. 8.

12. Jorge C. Bocobo, *loc. cit.*

13. "Publisher's Note," ed. Jose Garcia Villa, *Philippine Short Stories/Best 25 of 1928* (Manila, n. d.), p. 3.

14. Edward J. O'Brien, "Introduction," Jose Garcia Villa, *Footnote to Youth* (New York, 1933), p. 5.

15. Salvador P. Lopez, *Literature and Society* (Manila, 1940), p. 105.

16. *Ibid.,* p. 165.

17. Elmer A. Ordoñez, "Literature of the Commonwealth," *Philippine Social Sciences and Humanities Review,* Vol. 28, No. 4 (Dec. 1963), p. 400.

18. William Faulkner, *On Truth and Freedom* (Manila, n.d.), p. 3.

19. V. S. Pritchett, "The Future of Fiction," ed. John Lehmann, *Penguin New Writing 32* (London, 1947), p. 104.

20. Faulkner, *op. cit.,* p. 11.

21. Donald Keene, "Native Voice in Foreign Tongue," *Saturday Review of Literature* (Oct. 6, 1962), p. 44.

22. Pritchett, *op. cit.,* p. 106.

23. Leonard Casper, *The Wounded Diamond* (Manila, 1964), p. 134.

24. *Ibid.,* pp. 132-133.

25. Horacio de la Costa, S. J., "The Responsibility of the Writer in Contemporary Philippine Society," *Literature and Society* (Manila, 1964), p. 111.

26. Ortega y Gasset, *op. cit.,* p. 90.

HOWARD HIBBETT

Tradition and Trauma in the Contemporary Japanese Novel

VIEWED FROM abroad, the really "novel" characteristics of modern Japanese fiction seem to derive from the venerable literary tradition linking an age of Peace and Tranquillity, that of the Heian court a millennium ago, with the age of anxiety of the present reign. But it is a long way indeed from the serene world of Prince Genji, whose accomplishments included incense-judging and performing Chinese dances, to the traffic-choked Tokyo of a novel dominated by the *noirōze* ("neurosis," now a household word) of its antihero. It is no wonder that younger writers in Japan sometimes assert that any meaningful link with the past has been broken. Most Japanese novelists, especially in the early stages of their careers, have rebelled against their native literary tradition. Writers and public alike are familiar with a vast range of Western thought and literature, extending from Greek mythology to American Zen; the Tokyo avant-garde in all the arts is seldom outdistanced by New York or Paris. Yet the comparatively few novels that have been translated from the Japanese retain a special flavor unaccountable except for the lingering, pervasive influence of the traditional culture.

The literary themes and techniques imported so eagerly since the Meiji Restoration of 1868 were often successfully grafted onto the ancient stock, and soon seemed indistinguishable from it. Often the attempt was made to transplant whole genres or ideologies, as if they could be expected to survive without modification. Innumerable hybrid and variant forms began to flourish in the Meiji era, to be labeled romanticism, realism, naturalism, neo-idealism, or whatever, with a fine enthusiasm for each new exotic bloom. But there was always a more or less traumatic process of change, as

30

intellectuals discovered and defined their *Angst,* as writers adopted alien conventions of fiction, and as a newly revitalized literature began to influence as well as to reflect one of the most rapidly developing societies of modern times. Despite the extraordinary growth and prosperity of the literary profession, its wounds have been undeniably severe. Many novelists have suffered from the stresses of an uneasy individualism, and from a related compulsion to confess, if not to sin for the sake of confessing. Among their standard themes is the disgraceful vacillation or anguished choice between family duty and personal freedom of a character who appears to be a self-portrait of the author. Suicide is a frequent solution to such dilemmas, and novelists have been among the notable suicides of every generation since Meiji. Even the themes and tone of popular fiction, with its hopeless marriages, inevitably parted lovers, and conventional unhappy endings, create an atmosphere of gloom almost as impenetrable as that of the serious novel. Naturally these literary and social patterns often recall old configurations. It is not coincidental that the mid-Meiji enthusiasm for *Werther* was accompanied by renewed interest in the seventeenth-century suicide plays of Chikamatsu, nor that Japanese fictional counterparts of the frustrated heroes of Goncharov and Turgenev lapse into moods colored by the Buddhist melancholy of the theme of the medieval *Tale of the Heike:* "The temple bell echoes the impermanence of all things." That epic of defeat was to inspire many popular historical novels, first among them a sad, lyrical tale by Takayama Chogyū, who had already studied Chikamatsu and translated *Werther.* But most writers thought of their private or public agonies, their sense of impermanence and destructive change, as wholly modern phenomena. The literature of their own past represented a burden rather than a store of accumulated wealth.

To be sure, such leading contemporary novelists as Kawabata Yasunari and the late Tanizaki Junichirō have used the resources of their own tradition to advantage. Among younger writers none has done so more skillfully than Mishima Yukio, now in his early forties and the single new postwar novelist to have made an international reputation. Certainly Mishima owes much of his success to the enrichment of his otherwise unexceptionably up-to-date psychological fiction and drama by elements of traditional Japanese art. His "modern Nō plays," for example, brilliantly exploit the possession theme of the Nō, the dramatic inner conflict of a person haunted by the past. The ghosts may be only of the recent past, perhaps of the Meiji era, and may be evoked in a downtown Tokyo park, an antique dealer's showroom, or a mental hospital. But their power has its source in clusters of association that were time-honored long before Zeami used them, with a mastery of literary and dramatic techniques that were also the product of long tradition, in fashioning the classic Nō plays of the fourteenth century.

Unlike Tanizaki or Kawabata, Mishima seems to be drawn toward a theatrically self-conscious art. A discerning critic as well as novelist and playwright, he has stated that the heart of his method is to rely on the unconscious—and has explained in some detail how he controls it. Indispensable to the ritual of writing is a visit to a suitable setting for a work: paradoxically, in view of his skill at manipulating dramatic situations, Mishima says that he is more deeply moved by landscapes than by people. But these expressive landscapes, like the ones Kawabata has mentioned as the origin of many of his stories, are seen as symbolic metaphors of emotion in a manner already well established in Heian literature. Thus *Death in Midsummer* (*Manatsu no shi*) is a detached study in the French analytic vein of a woman mourning her two drowned children. What one remembers most vividly, however, is the ominous beauty of the setting—the "anger in the rays of the sun"—and the tragic irony of death in such a season. The epigraph is from Baudelaire (*La mort . . . nous affecte plus profondément sous le règne pompeux de l'été*"), and possibly the images of the sea have a glint of the Aegean or the Mediterranean. But the sensibility is of a kind that has been cultivated in Japanese literature in every age.

Touches of this sort enhance even the somber last novels of Natsume Sōseki, those in which he portrays with intense poignancy, but also with wit, drama, and profound psychological insight, a sense of loneliness and hopeless failure in human relationships. His memorably unhappy characters are realized through superb dialogue, dialogue heightened by analysis and by the delicately controlled tension of each scene; and they exist in a world that has its own sensuous reality rather than against a flat theatrical backdrop or in abstract detachment from their surroundings. As a novelist of alienation Sōseki has the Chekovian gift of depicting boredom and depression without being boring or depressing, but he has also the sensitivity to nature, the awareness of the changing seasons, of a *haiku* poet. (He took his literary name "Sōseki" when he began studying *haiku,* and he wrote distinguished poetry in Chinese as well as in Japanese.) Still, even this master, surely the greatest novelist of modern Japan, has been criticized both for insufficient skill at natural description (by the extremely high Japanese standards) and for undue skill in creating "fiction"—that is, imaginative writing that has a clearly defined structure and cannot be readily interpreted as autobiographical.

To purist critics in Japan, Western concepts of the novel have often seemed incompatible with the transcendent virtue of sincerity, a virtue that is thought to sanction both meandering reminiscence and confessionalist self-exposure. Insistent on the frank identification of author and protagonist, advocates of what is called the I-novel (*shi-shōsetsu*) have tended to equate fiction with falsehood, a Confucian prejudice, rather than with a means toward poetic truth. Novelists who disclaim autobiographical intent risk the charge of frivolity. Mishima and Tanizaki, among others, have been similarly criticized for their inventive talents, particularly after their novels began to attract attention abroad. Unfortunately, only a few of Sōseki's many novels have been translated, and only one of these (Edwin McClellan's version of *Kokoro*) into English of appropriate literary merit. But Japanese critics are inclined to regard with suspicion any novelist whose work has been admired in the West. Perhaps it is to be expected that writers in the discursive reminiscent vein of the I-novel should strike Western readers as so many wayward essayists, and that, conversely, novelists whose techniques are closest to those of the West are more likely to be read merely from an interest in their exotic subject matter. Yet in fact much of the appeal of modern Japanese novels abroad lies in the treatment of familiar themes—however unfamiliar their cultural setting. These themes have been explored most effectively by writers of verve and daring whose methods are in part traditional but who are also alert to the innovations that have transformed the literature of Japan since Meiji.

By far the most vigorous of the older Japanese masters whose careers survived the shattering Greater East Asia War was Tanizaki Junichirō, a novelist so prolific that one learns with surprise from his memoirs that he wrote very slowly. He envied Natsume Sōseki's capacity to dash off an installment for a newspaper serial in the morning, leaving the afternoon free for more lofty pursuits; he also regretted that his work had allowed him inadequate leisure for such pastimes as reading, travel, and love. Still, after more than half a century of dazzlingly successful industry, with all the re-

33

wards and honors due a pre-eminent literary elder statesman, Tanizaki remained as devoted as ever to his craft. His chief pleasure was writing, a pleasure which, along with his predilection for reading his own works, he modestly ascribed to weakening eyesight. But he also wanted to entertain, to enlighten, and to shock. In his flamboyant early stories Tanizaki seemed to be trying to naturalize the more outrageous literary ideas of Wilde and Baudelaire, but his later work makes it clear that these themes were indeed his own, and that the traditional elements in their expression —the Kabuki-like settings and atmosphere—were also important to him. Neither as a Westernizing bohemian nor, in the thirties, as a writer of beautifully finished tales in Heian, medieval, or Meiji styles did he use his virtuoso techniques merely to disguise the alarming implications of his art. From his debut in a literary magazine in 1910—he must have been chagrined that the issue was banned because of someone else's contribution—until his death in the summer of 1965 at the age of seventy-nine, he continued to devise new ways to reveal disturbing truths to a wide reading public.

Perhaps the most disturbing of all his novels, indeed of all postwar Japanese novels, was *The Key (Kagi)*, a spare, claustrophobic study of middle-aged depravity which appeared in 1956 when Tanizaki was seventy. The very style of *The Key* seems as shamefully naked as Ikuko, the professor's wife, in the scenes of bath and bedroom where she lies drugged with brandy, exposed under glaring lights to her husband's voyeurist scrutiny. The book opens with the New Year's Day diary entry of the aging professor (the reader never learns his name, and has only a hint of his apparently neglected occupation) and goes on with alternating extracts from the diary of his somewhat younger wife. Their diaries and their energies are concentrated on the stimulation of sexual passion, by whatever means and at whatever cost. For the husband, like the author a victim of high blood pressure, the ultimate cost is death. But his demure, respectable wife becomes an insatiable *femme fatale*, quite ready to destroy Kimura, the young man who is by then her lover and who is to marry her daughter. That her husband has carefully arranged the liaison, if not the engagement, seems a reasonable stratagem in this desperate battle. The two "secret" diaries, used as a deceptively guarded means of communication between husband and wife, permit candid though confusing glimpses of the process by which a cultivated, tormented man, presumably trying to recapture sexual vitality, sacrifices all the less exacting pleasures

34

of his highly civilized world in a blind effort to enact his persistent fantasies.

The two diaries stand in antagonistic contrast, different even as printed in their external form—the husband's written by fountain pen in the square syllabary used for official documents, the wife's by the traditional (and soundless) writing brush on thin rice paper in a feminine cursive script. Both diarists are wily, deceitful, intent on the life-and-death erotic struggle that culminates their two decades of unhappy marriage. We never know how far to believe these confessions, nor do we learn much, except indirectly, about the thoughts of the people who write them. At first Ikuko declares that she has no intention of reading her husband's diary, in spite of having been allowed to find the key to the locked drawer in which he keeps it: "I haven't the faintest desire to penetrate his psychology, beyond the limits I've set for myself. I don't like to let others know what is in my own mind, and I don't care to pry into theirs." Later she observes that most of that passage—all but the part about not liking to let others know her own thoughts—is untrue. Thus the reader has the privilege of enjoying intimate but suspicious revelations. The narrative method only hints at characterization; a few quoted snatches of dialogue delineate the student-accomplice Kimura and the disgusted, jealous, but conspiratorial daughter. The minds of the characters hold as many secrets as does the shadowy, silent old Kyoto house, the faintly sketched background against which the drama is played.

Rarely has there been such dramatic intensity in the modern Japanese novel as there is in *The Key*. The diary form, stemming from an ancient literary tradition in Japan, is usually a quasi-fictional genre, hardly differentiated from the novel. The novel itself is often considered "pure" only in the vein of autobiographical fiction of the I-novel, disguised very thinly if at all. The I-novel recommends itself as literature partly by stylistic beauty but mainly by the sincerity—whether of contemplative earnestness or confessional daring—of the author. Self-analysis is a frequent aim, though the results are seldom rigorously analytical. A mist of romantic or sentimental self-deception often clouds the supposedly pure I-novel. Tanizaki, however, was one of the few major novelists who used a wide range of Western fictional techniques without a trace of anxiety. He willingly defended the importance of fabrication, of plot, the "lie" that many Japanese writers have considered an obstacle in their search for truth. But Tanizaki also took whatever he needed from traditional literature. He adapted the style of the leisurely essay to a dramatic narrative, for instance, or blended the conventions of the diffuse, elegant *monogatari*—the "tale" in the sophisticated lineage of the eleventh-century *Tale of Genji*—with those of modern fiction.

In his last novel, *Diary of a Mad Old Man* (*Fūten rōjin nikki*, published in 1962), he used the diary form to create a sharp satirical portrait of an unruly though severely ill old gentleman whose tantrums and perversities belie the stock character of the elderly connoisseur of the arts. A man with tastes similar to those of the bland narrator of earlier novels (who revealed himself only discreetly, quoting a bit of poetry here or commenting there) has confided to this singular diary his most secret and ignoble thoughts, his curious remaining lusts, his childishness, his ill temper, his bitter humiliations and the perverse satisfaction derived from them, together with the richly orchestrated suffering and obsessive self-regard of a man whose sensibilities have for decades been attuned to art, to the nuances of sexuality, and to death.

Utsugi Tokusuke, the shrewd, Sybaritic Mad Old Man, seems to be a diarist with remarkable self-analytic insight, to say nothing of frankness, a model of psychological perspicacity in the service of a sincere desire for self-knowledge. He knows that he has a weakness for women with bad character and beautiful feet. When he observes his growing interest in the young Kabuki actors who play feminine roles, he calmly speculates on the relation of a youthful homosexual experiment to the sexual impulses that persist, at seventy-seven, now that he is impotent. He tends to dwell on his physical deterioration and other disagreeable qualities, much as he insists on removing his false teeth in order to show his daughter-in-law Satsuko exactly how ugly he is. He recognizes the masochism in his costly infatuation with Satsuko—a girl with a doubtful past who likes imported luxuries and who enjoys boxing matches, the bloodier the better. He is quite aware that his efforts to provide her with a lover have a selfish motive. Yet Utsugi is not merely shown to us in the unflattering glare of satirical illumination, nor as a more realistic (because more fully human) variant of the self-portrait of the I-novelist. Although there is no male-female counterpoint between diaries after the fashion of *The Key*, the comic, querulous, touching monologue ends abruptly and is followed by a quick succession of accounts from other points of view as the reader awaits with suspense the outcome of the gravest of the old man's attacks. All that is revealed of it, and of later events, is what is set forth in the nurse's slightly vulgar report, the doctor's formidable clinical records, and the notes by a daughter, sullen or shrewish in the diary, who is seen in an unexpectedly sympathetic light. Once again Tanizaki concludes his novel on a tentative note, the future in doubt and the characters somewhat more ambiguous than the reader had at times taken them to be.

Again the underlying themes are the relationship between love and cruelty, the necessary antagonism between Eros and Thanatos, between sexuality and the dark forces of decay symbolized by the medicines and appliances meant to combat them. The embodiment of these themes in character, action, and atmosphere is as spontaneously vital as ever. Utsugi's dream of his mother, recalled in all her classic Bodhisattvaesque beauty when he was a small child, is immediately associated with thoughts of the utterly different (though equally beautiful) modern temptress Satsuko. Far from shaving off her eyebrows and dyeing her teeth black in proper early Meiji style, Satsuko "has her hair set in a permanent wave, wears earrings, paints her lips coral pink or pearl pink or coffee brown, pencils her eyebrows, uses eye shadow on her eyelids, glues on false eyelashes and then, as if that isn't enough, brushes on mascara to try to make them look still longer." Utsugi's schemes to apotheosize Satsuko as a Bodhisattva engraved on his tombstone, or, better yet, to have Buddha's Footprints carved to the pattern of rubbings of her feet, supply a further, doubtless unconscious link between the usually isolated and antithetical images of woman as madonna or harlot, the sexually "pure" mother or the degraded, degrading seductress. In *The Key*, Ikuko, a respectable woman with an old-fashioned Kyoto upbringing whose body has "the gently swelling lines of the Bodhisattva in the Chuguji Temple," is corrupted from her stubborn feminine modesty as she takes to wearing earrings, lace gloves, and Western-style dresses that reveal her voluptuously curved legs. In *The Bridge of Dreams* (*Yume no ukihashi*) the images of mother and mistress are again fused, and the aura of incestuous guilt is particularly noticeable. Yet these mysteries, too, elude easy translation into pathological terminology. Such a tale may well be interpreted as a male fantasy of the sort described as "the most prevalent form of degradation" in Freud's first and second "Contributions to the Psychology of Love." But the novel's narrative subtlety, its indefinably complex characters, its nostalgic setting of a secluded Kyoto house and garden all suggest the atmosphere of *The Tale of Genji* (to which the title, the opening poem, and the plot itself allude) darkened by the influence of modern psychological fiction.

The cruel but irresistible temptress appears as the heroine of Tanizaki's first short story, and reappears, along with her willing victims, in nearly everything else he wrote. Sometimes she is set off against women of contrasting temperament, sometimes against a background from the lost world of the past. In *Whirlpool (Manji)*, the *femme fatale* is a beautiful young art student whose features are the model for a drawing of a Bodhisattva but whose actual character is perverse, deceptive, and destructive in the extreme, as she demonstrates in her seduction of a mild-mannered lawyer as well as of his rather aggressive wife. But the setting is Osaka, a city heavy with memories of the old Japan, in contrast to the shallow modernity of Tokyo. The entire novel is narrated in a lush feminine Osaka dialect, symbolic of the langorous charm of the traditional culture, a charm that softens the harsh outlines of this bizarre confession. Later the same year (1928) Tanizaki began serial publication of *Some Prefer Nettles* (*Tade kuu mushi*), in which the protagonist's romantic interest is divided between Louise, an expensive Eurasian prostitute in Yokohama, and the doll-like, solicitous O-hisa, his father-in-law's mistress, who has been meticulously groomed to suit the refined tastes of a conservative Kyoto gentleman. These two women provide alternative attractions to Kaname, a young man whose wife has long ceased to interest him. The rival claims of flashy Western-style Yokohama sensuality and the subdued, enduring appeal of an idealized Japanese beauty imply the cultural conflict between Western influence and the native tradition, between the new and the old, which has been such an engrossing problem in modern Japan.

As in *Some Prefer Nettles* the conflict is always sexualized in Tanizaki's fiction—one aspect of a single-minded devotion, unparalleled in Japanese literature, to the myth of the idolized fatal woman. Everywhere he stresses the sinister role of feminine adornment in working this transformation. Women have been drastically changed, corrupted but freed by those alluring Western garments that encase them in a glowing, resplendent skin, and yet, unlike the constricting trousers, coat, and tie (with stickpin) of European-style men, release their vital powers. And cultural change in general, while less absorbing, has for Tanizaki a considerable degree of morbid fascination. Of course such attitudes are not unknown among other Japanese authors, although most of them have a consuming interest in the predominantly masculine society in which they live. Relations between father and son, between brothers, between friends whose wives stay quietly at home, seldom visible, are at the core of most Japanese novels. Even the usual triangle consists of two men and, somewhere in the middle distance, a woman. But cultural conflict may be sensed in almost every modern Japanese novel—not because Japan has failed to assimilate any significant elements of Western culture, but because the process of Westernization (and modernization) has intensified a national self-awareness, a feeling of radical difference, ambivalently superior and inferior, from the intrusive civilization of the remote, inscrutable "foreigners."

In his longest novel *The Makioka Sisters* (*Sasameyuki*—literally, and more poetically, a term for thinly falling snow) Tanizaki depicts with nostalgic affection for detail the life of a once-prosperous Osaka merchant family between the years 1939 and 1941, when it was still possible to believe that suitably arranged marriages could preserve the heritage of the past intact. Most of the book was written during the war; the ironic ending (it appears that the family's future has at last been settled) is the final note of an elegy to a vanished era. A stable former generation has already disappeared by the time the novel opens, and the family continues to disregard even the few conspicuous signs of changing times, such as the austerity edicts and rationing of rice that are mentioned toward the end of the book. Yet within this narrow, decreasingly privileged circle there is still a tension between the old and the new: between the tastes and loyalties of all the sisters, and especially between the conflicting styles of the two unmarried ones, the elder of whom, so reserved as to seem inarticulate, resists marriage by conventionally genteel tactics, while the other, given to elopements and dangerous liaisons, has the independent spirit of a thoroughly modern young woman. Except in reference to some chance foreign neighbors, however, the ominous public events of the day seem unreal, hardly worth mentioning at all. They lack even the briefly noted reality of the student demonstrations (the 1960 Security Pact demonstrations, it may be assumed) in *Diary of a Mad Old Man,* where the blocked streets cause some inconvenience in driving downtown to a restaurant after the theater. And such an atmosphere of isolation from all but personal matters is not peculiar to Tanizaki's novels. Disillusionment and retreat from involvement with public issues have been important tendencies in Japanese literature since Meiji; they reflect a widespread anxiety, especially acute among intellectuals, over the political and social problems of modern Japan. Withdrawal into the world of the past or into the preoccupations of private life is not only a novelist's stratagem and a response to unsettling change, but a long-established mode of minimizing the pressures of a tightly organized society.

In his essays and memoirs Tanizaki often writes movingly of the past, and of the losses suffered in the course of Japan's headlong modernization. Through his own work he has done much to preserve traditional values, notably by his twice-revised modern version of *The Tale of Genji* and by his various stories and novels in a limpid classical vein. But he has no sentimental illusions about turning back from the doubtful, if not disastrous, path of Western-style progress, only a regret for what has been lost along the way. It is in the arts and in surviving customs and manners that one may hope to find some benefit from cultural continuity. Thus Tanizaki's historical tales are far from romantic escapism, just as those with contemporary settings always imply a living connection with the past. Throughout his fiction, problems of technique are solved with the restrained, sure taste of a craftsman in a well-defined tradition.

In characterization, for instance, Tanizaki's art has a closer affinity with traditional life and letters than with the practices of the Western novelists who have influenced him. Even *Some Prefer Nettles*, written in his more naturalistic manner, discloses its meanings delicately and tentatively, with a certain reticent decorum. Faithful to the texture of the life he deals with, Tanizaki shows a well-bred preference for hinting at feelings rather than seeking to penetrate the innermost mysteries of his characters. That is also true of *The Key*, and of such a massive realist novel as *The Makioka Sisters*, in which he might have been expected to use the privilege of omniscience to tell us far more than he does about the motives and reflections of his principal characters. After witnessing many incidents, being told of still others, and overhearing endless conversations, we may yet feel that we are only superficially acquainted with this declining Osaka family: the shadowy, idealized Yukiko, her scandalously impulsive younger sister, the ineffectual men, and even the central figure, Sachiko, who is portrayed without the tinge of fantasy that makes the others seem at home in Tanizaki's larger fictional world.

40

Perhaps, it has been suggested, so much attention to the surfaces of life results from the characters' own unawareness of any deeper feelings, their inner lives being governed by the same oppressive forces as their social behavior. Yet there is no lack of evidence, not least in literature and the drama, of the frequent Japanese failure to dam up "the spontaneous overflow of powerful feelings." What seems more likely is that such techniques of characterization reflect a preference for intuitive ways of knowing, whether in solitary thought or in interpersonal relations. From a slight gesture, a fleeting expression, a change in tone, or a verbal hint there may come a sudden revelation more significant than an overt act or declaration of sentiment. Once, in criticizing a novel by Nagai Kafū, Tanizaki commented wistfully: "Such things as psychological description, the expression of emotions and states of consciousness, the attempt to penetrate deep into the interior of a character, have come into fashion only very recently."[1] Often in his own novels Tanizaki preferred to rely on the reader's intuition to fill out a seemingly inadequate characterization. And other major novelists have used similar techniques.

In Kawabata Yasunari's *Snow Country* (*Yukiguni*) the climactic scene between Shimamura and the geisha Komako turns on a single word: after having affectionately called her "a good girl," and having been obliquely reminded that he once asked her to bring a prostitute for him, Shimamura feels a wave of sensual attraction and calls her "a good woman," which she correctly and despairingly interprets as marking the limit of his commitment to their love affair. As self-centered as he is, Shimamura soon comes to realize why his innocent remark provoked an outburst from her, but the Western reader may well find this a puzzling nuance. Even the Japanese, though finely attuned to just such faint implications, are often enough betrayed by their trust in intuitive understanding. For Kawabata, however, sensitivity to emotional nuance, the frequent misunderstandings that nevertheless occur, and the resulting possibilities for literary expression—all this fragile network of communication is at once an invaluable technical resource and a subject that illustrates his recurrent theme of loneliness and human isolation. Instead of analyzing his characters at length, he prefers to hint at their inner life by noting gestures, fragments of dialogue, momentary feelings. Thus, in revising the beginning chapter of *Snow Country* for book publication, Kawabata deleted several paragraphs describing Komako's first impression of Shimamura,

her past experience with men, her present uncertainty—and re-
placed the whole passage (following the sentence "She opened his
hand, and pressed her cheek against it") by the single phrase:
" 'This remembered me?' " In its context, it is sufficient.

To be sure, such economies are offset by a tendency to extend
the context, to add more and more episodes, each brilliantly
elliptical and evocative but joined to the others by the suggestive
illogicalities of Japanese poetry rather than as parts of an archi-
tectonic whole. Kawabata's novels rarely come to a decisive ending
—he has the habit of adding episodes from time to time over the
years—and their slow growth often seems to occur by a process
of natural accretion. Like several of his other novels, *Snow Country*
was originally intended to be a short story. The material stretched
over into a second installment, published the same month (January,
1935) but in a magazine with a slightly later deadline. Further
chapters were added—two more toward the end of the year, two
in 1936, and so on—until after numerous extensions and revisions
a presumably final version was published in 1947. This is doubtless
an extreme case of dilatory lyricism, but even under the journalistic
pressure of producing serial fiction for magazines or newspapers,
most Japanese novelists write without a plan or with only the
sketchiest of notes to indicate the way ahead. Mishima Yukio,
though unusual for his careful advance preparation of materials,
has remarked on the pleasurable spontaneity of a serial novel which
has proceeded without plan and has been enriched by unforeseen
complications. In his own work, once he has finished the prelimi-
nary stages and written a novel straight through, he makes it a
point to eschew revision. If few novelists are as close to the traditional *haiku* aesthetic as Kawabata, or as loath to revise as Mishima, many more share a preference for lyrical improvisation as
a working method.

Early in his career Kawabata wrote a number of very brief
tales—miniature *contes* were then in vogue—which he hoped to
make the prose equivalent of the Japanese poetic forms. He later
called them his "youthful poetry." But he continued to write occasional three- or four-page stories after others had abandoned the
genre; some of these remain among his favorite works. Often they
recount dreams, hallucinatory fables, curiously enigmatic anec-
dotes, but even the slightest of his sketches and vignettes convey
an emotional state with extraordinary vividness. Imagery of the sort
found in *haiku* may provide an essential element. Thus, the "Pome-

granates" (*Zakuro*) of the title of a story written in 1943 suggest the complex feelings of a girl toward her mother, her dead father, and her lover who is going off to war. Overnight the pomegranate leaves have fallen, dislodged in a strangely neat circle by a cold late autumn wind, and the suddenly revealed ripe fruit calls to mind the time of year her father had died, as other memories associated with pomegranates awaken a sense of guilt over her mother's empty life and her own secret joy. A tree in the garden or a wide, lonely landscape may be equally effective in expressing the awareness of time, place, and human feelings that is indispensable to the *haiku*.

Again, in *Snow Country* the natural setting not only creates mood and atmosphere but helps to define character. The mountain background, freshly green in spring, darkening in late autumn, then bright in snow, adds to the emotional significance of the work. Sometimes by poignant contrast, it heightens Shimamura's half-bored erotic longing, even his pleasure in Komako and his interest in her friend Yoko, but it also echoes the varying kinds of loneliness that afflict them all. Natural imagery in the *haiku* manner vivifies the foreground as well, with a symbolic relevance to the human situation that goes beyond fragmentary visual metaphor to help compose a harmonious world in which nature is neither adversary nor merely the setting for an unrelated drama. A sensuous, intuitive response to people and places may at times incline the Japanese novelist to create a series of beautiful but static pictures, like the *tableaux vivants* at moments of dramatic tension in the Nō and Kabuki, and to show various facets of his characters as if they had "suddenly and briefly caught his attention, not because of any personal quality they possessed in their own right, but because they seemed at the moment to be such an integral part of the mood of the scene around them."[2] Kawabata in particular often seems to construct even his more dramatic novels by linking one impressionistic scene to the next in the associative manner of *renga* ("linked verse"), the historical precursor of the *haiku*. Lyrical and imagistic, where Tanizaki would be drawn rather to the manner of the mellifluous discursive essay, Kawabata is another of the major Japanese novelists who have mastered Western fictional techniques without abandoning the resources of the native tradition.

Kawabata's career began in the early 1920's, and his writings are often directly influenced by experimental Western fiction. But his most obvious importations—of a "stream of consciousness" style, for instance—are his least successful. Only when an exotic technique has been fully assimilated to the needs of his essentially Japanese art is it adequate to express his own haunting themes of loneliness, the fragility of love, the cold, interstellar distances of withdrawal from human involvements. In the exquisite opening passage of *Snow Country* when Shimamura sees a girl's face reflected against the evening landscape in the window of the train, there is a cinematic movement to the scene—the heart of the passage is a flashback, and the novel advances by moving back and forth in time. But there is also a vision which accommodates surrealist imagery, pointillist detail, unusual camera angles, and the laws of optics to the familiar natural symbolism of the *haiku:*

The light inside the train was not particularly strong, and the reflection was not as clear as it would have been in a mirror. Since there was no glare, Shimamura came to forget that it was a mirror he was looking at. The girl's face seemed to be out in the flow of the evening mountains.

It was then that a light shone in the face. The reflection in the mirror was not strong enough to blot out the light outside, nor was the light strong enough to dim the reflection. The light moved across the face, though not to light it up. It was a distant, cold light. As it sent its small ray through the pupil of the girl's eye, as the eye and light were superimposed one on the other, the eye became a weirdly beautiful bit of phosphorescence on the sea of evening mountains.[3]

Somehow the effect is closer to the vision of a *haiku* poet (such as Issa, who observed "the distant hills mirrored in the eye of the dragonfly") than to Bunuel or Breton.

If Shimamura is a cold, withdrawn figure, one who prefers to witness life through an estranging window, Komako is depicted with all the empathy and mastery of feminine psychology that is characteristic of Kawabata's art. Frustrated women, subtly corrupted or disfigured women, especially very young girls who are destined to unhappiness—these are among the unforgettable portraits in his work. Youth is associated with lost love, with parting, with death. No doubt his elegiac themes may be traced back to his own childhood experience of the early loss of both his parents, followed not long after by the deaths of his grandmother, his only sister, and then the grandfather with whom he lived alone from the age of seven till fourteen. Funerals and separations occur in many of his earliest stories. Yet even his darkest fiction suggests a strongly sensuous response to life. Kawabata's eroticism is as much at conflict with death and decay as Tanizaki's, despite all the differences between them. In *Sleeping Beauty* (*Nemureru bijo*) and other recent works, these related themes become as explicit as in the late novels of Tanizaki. But Kawabata's "sleeping beauties" never awaken—they are heavily drugged young girls placed at the disposal of the old men who visit a special club. The single developed character, a man painfully sensitive to the anomalies of this sad pleasure, is left alone with his sensuous impressions of the girls, with his memories of other women, his dreams and nightmares, and, finally, with death. The novel offers a striking example of severe reduction in fictional paraphernalia, of poetic economy which increases the value of every glimpse into the interior world of a character.

For Kawabata, and also for Tanizaki and other perceptive Japanese novelists, even the microcosm of the family is no longer a secure refuge either from the menacing outer world beyond private experience or from the sorrows, frustrations, and bad dreams of the lonely, labyrinthine inner world. Like most serious novelists since Meiji, they have tried to explore that inner world; they have followed any path, old or new, which promised to lead into it. Gifted younger writers such as Abe Kōbō and Oe Kenzaburō are finding still newer paths, paths that often resemble those of their contemporaries abroad. These novelists are also interested in the larger world of political and social change, if not in the changing conditions of family life. Their journeys into the interior seem rapid, purposeful, and comparatively well-organized—perhaps at the sacrifice of random insight as well as of leisurely grace. But in their work, too, it is possible to discern traditional qualities that mark it unmistakably as Japanese. Fortunately, like the Nō and the *haiku*, the novel in Japan has been strengthened by a long literary tradition of economy, restraint, and poetic sensitivity. Without that source of strength, modern Japanese literature might well have been overrun rather than regenerated to new and vigorous growth by the aimless luxuriant tangle of Western-influenced writing which once seemed likely to obliterate the past.

REFERENCES

1. Edward Seidensticker, *Kafū the Scribbler* (Stanford, 1965), p. 131.

2. Edwin McClellan, "The Impressionistic Tendency in Some Modern Japanese Writers," *Chicago Review*, Vol. 17, No. 4 (1965), p. 58.

3. Translated by Edward Seidensticker. *Snow Country* (New York, 1956), p. 10.

ROBERT ALTER

The Israeli Novel

IN ORDER to make any sense of what is happening to the novel in
Israel, one must take full account of the stubborn and peculiar fact
that Israeli novels are written in Hebrew. Because of the unique
history of the language and the unique process of revival which it is
still undergoing, this has rather more complicated implications than,
say, the fact that American novels are written in English. The
anomalies of the Hebrew writer's linguistic situation play an important role in determining his relationship with other generations
of writers in his own literature, the lines of influence from the outside that are open or largely closed to him, and even, to some extent, the particular modes of fiction he will adopt. To understand
why this should be so, a few essential facts about Hebrew literary
history will be necessary.

The East-European intellectuals who formed the nucleus of
modern Jewish immigration to Palestine more than half a century
ago did not arrive in the new pioneering community and then as a
result begin to write fiction in Hebrew. Almost the opposite is true.
It is partly as a result of Hebrew literary activity in nineteenth-
century Russia and Poland that the fantastic idea was conceived
of re-establishing a Hebrew-speaking culture on the soil of Palestine. Short Hebrew fiction of a crude sort was being written in
Galicia by the 1820's, and the first identifiable Hebrew novel was
published in 1853, decades before people dreamed that anywhere in
the world toddlers would be prattling, cabbies cursing, professors
lecturing, in Hebrew. By the first decade of the twentieth century,
Hebrew literary centers in Odessa, Vilna, Warsaw, and elsewhere
had produced a surprising variety of writers of fiction—most of
them intent, imitative, and imaginatively limited, but among them
one novelist of real stature, a number of sensitive short-story writers,

46

and even a serious experimenter in a kind of stream-of-consciousness fiction. All of this creative work took place, it must be remembered, in a milieu where the common spoken language was Yiddish, not Hebrew.

The whole development, then, of the Hebrew novel, from its beginnings until the 1940's, went against the linguistic grain that has been one of the generic distinctions of the novel. For the general movement of the novel, as we are often reminded, has been to narrow the gap between literary language and the language of everyday experience; this is why the genre typically begins with, and frequently recurs to, fictional memoirs, letters, journals, "true histories"—fictions presented in the vocabulary and form of documentary fact. The earlier Hebrew novelists, however, were forced to work in exactly the opposite direction. By writing in Hebrew about people whose language was in fact Yiddish, or, occasionally, Russian, Polish, or German, they had to produce what was manifestly no more than an "as-if reality," in the phrase of the Israeli critic, Dov Sadan. Where the European novel often tended to camouflage its own status as invented literature, the Hebrew novel had little choice but to flaunt its literary nature, to find ways of converting its obtrusive literariness into an artistic resource. It is understandable, therefore, that the first Hebrew novel, Abraham Mapu's *Love of Zion*, is historical—an involuted and improbable romance set in Jerusalem in the time of Isaiah, written in a style that is a sort of impassioned pastiche of Biblical phrases. Mapu's language was hardly a suitable instrument for rendering contemporary realities with minute particularity, and when the Hebrew novel came of age toward the end of the century in the work of Mendele Mocher Seforim ("Mendele the Bookseller," pen name for S. J. Abramowitz), it was through a recapitulation of the whole range of Hebrew literary history, a bold synthesis of the language of the Bible, the Talmud, rabbinic legend, of the medieval exegetes and philosophers, of the prayer book and later liturgical poetry, of moral tracts and legal codes, even of communal records. Using all these materials, Mendele was able to recreate with remarkable sensuous particularity the world of Russian Jewry in which he lived, peopling his books with Dickensian caricatures vividly and lovingly rendered down to the last bristling wart on the nose and the last grease spot on the hem of the caftan. But Mendele was always highly conscious that the components of his style were traditional and literary, and his practice and achievement fully established the peculiar central tradition of the Hebrew novel in which the principal rhetorical device is literary allusion.

The novel in general has, quite obviously, taken as its subject the new problematic look assumed by the human condition in a secularized world where traditional ideals, religious or otherwise, no longer obtain. What sets the Hebrew novel apart is that its language, until fairly recently, has been to a large extent the language of piety, suffused with the associations of a religious tradition, so that, typically, a continual tension—usually a pointedly ironic tension—is set up between the reminiscence of lofty spiritual ideals in the language and the fallen nature of the world which the language describes. Today, this allusive mode of fiction is rapidly disappearing from the novel in Israel as an increasing proportion of the writers are native Israelis who have acquired their Hebrew naturally as a spoken language; the transition is itself one of the problematic aspects of the Israeli literary scene. Writers now in their forties or younger make only occasional and fragmentary use of the old allusive mode, while it continues to be a standard practice of the elder novelists who are still active, and who, for the most part, are European-born and thus have learned their Hebrew first from sacred texts. The result is that by and large there is no common artistic language shared by literary generations in Israel, and, as the younger writers have come to dominate the scene during the last two decades, they have found themselves in the unenviable position of initiating, tentatively and unsurely, their own "tradition" of the Hebrew novel, every five years or so.[1] This disparity is heightened by the fact that the older generation includes one figure who is indisputably a great novelist—the seventy-eight-year-old Shmuel Yosef Agnon—while the younger group has so far produced no more than some very interesting possibilities and uneven achievements.

Agnon, who was raised in a pious and scholarly household in a small town in Galicia, has a masterly knowledge of the varied literature of Jewish tradition, legal and legendary, moral and mystic; and his highly stylized language, with its predominantly medieval coloration, represents the consummate achievement of the allusive mode in Hebrew fiction. For this very reason, his books tantalize, exasperate, and finally defy translation; if the words can be more or less translated, their complex allusiveness must be almost entirely abandoned and with it much of the pointedness and poignancy of his artful, painstakingly polished prose. Let me try to show

how this distinctively Hebrew rhetorical strategy works by offering an extended passage together with some detailed comment on its allusive play of language. I shall quote the opening paragraph of Agnon's long novel, *Just Yesterday* (1946), set in Palestine around 1906, when Agnon himself first immigrated; the translation is, alas, my own because, as with most of Agnon's major work, no English version is yet available:

Like the rest of our brothers, the men of our redemption, immigrants of the Second Wave, Yitzhak Kummer left his country, his birthplace, and his city and went up to the Land of Israel to build it from its destruction and to be rebuilt by it. As far back as he could think, our friend Yitzhak had not let a day pass in which he failed to meditate upon the Land. Like a dwelling place of blessing the whole Land seemed to him and all its inhabitants like the blessed of the Lord. Its settlements were hidden in the shadow of vineyards and olive trees, all the fields were decked with produce, the trees crowned with fruit, the valleys covered with flowers, while forest trees swayed and the sky was all pure blue and every house was filled with song. During the days, people plowed and sowed and planted and reaped, plucked the grapes and picked the olives, threshed the wheat and tread the winepress. At eventide, each and every one would sit under his vine and under his fig tree, his wife and sons and daughters around him, all happy over their work, rejoicing in their repose, recalling the days past in the Diaspora, as one will remember in the hour of joy his days of sorrow and so take a double pleasure in the present bounty. An imaginative fellow was Yitzhak—out of the place his heart desired he would conjure up imagined things.

The placid progress here of Agnon's prose through the luminous details of a Zionist idyll to the final modest demurral is perhaps meant temporarily to disguise, but certainly not to dilute, the acid irony that saturates the whole passage. Some notion of the subsequent course of the novel will make the particular bite of this irony more palpable. The protagonist's name is Kummer—which, as the verbal noun in Yiddish for "one who comes" and as the German word for "grief," suggests both major aspects of his emblematic role. Kummer's first name is Yitzhak, or Isaac, and like the Biblical Isaac, he will be bound for sacrifice on "one of the mountains"—tradition identifies the vague phrase in Genesis with the temple mount, and he actually dies in Jerusalem—in a twentieth-century Land of Israel where there is no heavenly voice to cry out at the critical moment and revoke the senseless immolation. (It is worth noting that other Hebrew novelists have since used this same motif of the outrageous Binding of Isaac in a way that is precisely analogous to the mythic motif of the secular Christ, the meaningless

49

crucifixion, which so many modern writers in other literatures have
employed.) The fact that this Isaac is "one who comes" only emphasizes his permanent location as an outsider, a man who comes
from the outside and remains there. Though he "goes up" to the
Land, in the traditional Hebrew idiom, to redeem himself and his
people, his coming is actually much like that of Kafka's K. in *The
Castle*—nobody expects him, there is no clear place for him or justification for his presence. Like K., the land surveyor, Yitzhak tries
to demonstrate that he has a calling which connects him with the
land; but his attempt to become an agricultural worker is a pathetic
failure, and he ends up, ironically, as a house painter, covering natural surfaces with artificial substance, hiding realities with façades.
The Land itself, far from corresponding to Yitzhak's idyllic vision,
is a place of spiritual confusion, cynicism, moral cowardice, hypocrisy, fanaticism. The protagonist discovers, moreover, that there
is not even one Land of Israel but two: the new city of Jaffa, with its
rootless intellectuals, and the old city of Jerusalem, with its religious
obscurantists. Yitzhak is tossed between the two like a shuttlecock,
and, though he dies in one, the novel suggests that both offer but
different faces of the same inevitable destruction for the man who
has come.

By now, the general force of the irony in the opening passage of
the novel should be clear. But almost every phrase in the paragraph
is a telling one by virtue of some pointed ironic reference, and in
noting the allusions, which range from Genesis to Zionist catch-
words, we can see how precisely Agnon characterizes Yitzhak's
mental world and the quixotic nature of his ideals. Most of the
reminiscences of Biblical verses in the passage should be recog-
nizable even in the English version, and they need only be mentioned briefly. Yitzhak Kummer leaves "his country, his birthplace,"
like Abraham, but he will find no providential God in the promised
land with whom to seal an eternal covenant. He imagines the bar-
ren, strife-ridden Palestine in language recalling the visions of pas-
toral harmony in the Psalms and in the Prophets—"Like a dwelling-
place of blessing . . ."—and he mentally invokes the verbal formula
of the Book of Kings for perfect peace and prosperity—"each man
under his vine and under his fig tree." A less obvious Biblical reference is the initial phrase, which echoes "your brothers, the men of
your redemption" of Ezekiel 11:15, part of a prophecy of the return to Zion.

More of the allusions, however, are post-Biblical. The pioneer

families sit together "happy over their work, rejoicing . . ."—a parallelism that recalls a Mishnaic phrase from the Passover home-service
used in a climactic prayer for the restoration of Zion. Yitzhak
Kummer comes to the Land "to build it from its destruction," a
recurrent idiom of messianic aspiration in rabbinic legend. Moreover, this man who is to be utterly shattered longs "to build . . .
and to be rebuilt," in the words of a popular Zionist song, once
danced enthusiastically to the step-hop of the hora. Even the list
of verbs specifying agricultural activities is rich with associations
for Yitzhak; he would know these words from having studied the
agricultural tractates of the Mishnah, which preserve a vocabulary
intimately connected with farming in ancient Palestine, a vocabulary that reflects the Hebrew farmer's closeness to the soil in its
specialized verbs (of course, untranslatable) for the harvesting of
grapes, olives, grain.

What is most difficult to describe is the subtle kind of irony generated in the passage by what might be called the allusiveness of
tone. Through the amalgam of styles in the Hebrew, one gets the
sense of a pious narrator—or rather, "as-if" pious—assuming the
modes of address and the idioms of a traditional tale of wonders
wrought for God's glory. The terms, for example, connected with
"imagination" at the end of the paragraph are taken from the vocabulary of the medieval moralists. The use at the beginning of
"our brothers, the men of our redemption," though it is Biblical,
as we have seen, also suggests something of the assumption of de-
vout solidarity one finds in the language of the Hasidic tales. "Our
brothers" is a standard usage in this folk literature, and "men of our
redemption" recalls in form the common Hasidic idiom, "men of
our peace," so that the whole phrase becomes a kind of "translation"
into the language of piety of Zionist ideals. Since the novel will
show the terrifying emptiness of the new "redemption," the awful
lack of true solidarity, and much more, the ultimate effect of
Agnon's assuming this mask—it is his usual one—of traditional narrator writing for a God-fearing world is not only ironic but also a
little eerie. Through the ironic contrast, Agnon forces us continually
to feel the full nakedness of living in an inimical world shorn of the
innocence and wholeness of piety.

This consideration of the beginning of *Just Yesterday* should
indicate that Agnon's central achievement is not one that lends itself to definition primarily in terms of influences from European
literature. Agnon does know German literature well (he lived in

Germany from 1913 to 1926), and it would be surprising if he registered no response at all in his work to the exciting developments in German fiction of the earlier twentieth century. Many critics have noted affinities between Agnon and Kafka; Agnon has even written expressionist stories that are quite close to Kafka in form as well as theme. And, from the outset of his career, he has been so intrigued with the possibilities of building fiction around symbolic leitmotiv that he must have at least followed with great interest the experiments in symbol and motif of Thomas Mann.

Agnon's imagination, however, is too vigorously original, and his practice as a writer too deeply involved in the distinctive literature of Jewish tradition, to make any large aspect of his work unambiguously attributable to a European source. What one can say with certainty is that there are some significant affinities—as well as decisive differences—between Agnon and many of the European writers who in the first decades of this century created the literature we still think of as revolutionarily modern. Like Kafka, Mann, Proust, and so many writers of this period, Agnon experienced in his formative years the radical breakdown of an older social and cultural order that had seemed to him to be solid, protective, relatively harmonious. The fact that he grew up in a largely Jewish town around the turn of the century, at a period when the dissolution of the traditional values of old-world Judaism was advancing rapidly, had the effect of putting him at one of the symptomatic centers of historical change and cultural decay. Themes of tragic separation and collapse of values appear even in his earliest work, before World War I; but, like so many other writers, Agnon saw in the war the great symbolic embodiment of the modern reign of moral chaos, and so the war, destroyer of houses—an archetypal event for Agnon—of men, and of ways of life, became a recurrent presence in his work. He shares with Mann, Eliot, Joyce, and others a fascination with symbol and myth because for him, too, these afford a means of holding together imaginatively the pieces of a fragmented world and because he, too, participates in what Lionel Trilling has called the "spiritual" quality of modern literature—which is to say, he is always interested in relating individual experience to some ultimate order of significance, in setting man against the backdrop of eternity, and symbols help him to do this.

But if the symbolic and mythic aspects of Agnon's writing link him with the creators of the modern movement in European literature, they are also the hallmarks of his distinctiveness. His intimate acquaintance with the rich lore of Jewish tradition means that he draws many of his motifs, images, and archetypes from a body of "mythology" that is simply unknown to Western writers. His own symbolic inventiveness, moreover, is extraordinary, as is his interest in exploring a wide range of possibilities of symbolic fiction. Thus, while his work sometimes parallels the symbolic modes of other writers, it more often twists off in its own strange and fascinating directions. Agnon has written simple parables of consummate artistry and folk tales cunningly woven with strands of motif; nightmarish expressionist stories with recurrent symbols that break off, redouble themselves, flicker ambiguously; haunting lyric tales centered on sets of symbolic images whose meaning seems hermetic, perhaps finally private; elaborately structured poetic novels that transform social milieu into symbolic atmosphere and develop plot through variations on themes from traditional Hebrew legend.[2]

Over against the fiction of Agnon, with its symbolic impulse, its anti-realist experiments, its intricate stylistic implication in the Hebrew literary past, the native Israeli writers have generally committed themselves to a much more direct transcription of local reality. It is true that a few of the most interesting Israeli novels of the past half-dozen years have been parabolic or symbolic—at least two of them showing the clear influence of Agnon—but, for the most part, the work of the younger writers remains artistically conservative in its realism. There are, I think, good historical reasons for this adherence to realism, even to realism in some of its less imaginative, more colorless forms.

Linguistic considerations, to begin with, have made conventional realism a more challenging mode of fiction in Israel than it is likely to be anywhere else today. The writers who began to publish shortly before or after the founding of the State in 1948 were in part reacting to the avowed bookishness of the older writers' Hebrew. As the first adult generation of native speakers of Hebrew since ancient times, many of them felt a kind of responsibility to make the slangy, slurred Hebrew of the streets, the army, and the kibbutz function as a literary language. What is second nature to novelists in other countries was and to some extent still is problematic for Israeli writers because modern colloquial Hebrew is so new and so continually changing that it lacks much of the range and flexibility, and certainly much of the richness of associations, of a highly developed vernacular. Lengthy transcriptions of speech, because they were linguistically faithful to actual models, seemed to be a virtue in themselves—perhaps this is why some Israeli novels are still too talky—and descriptive prose, aspiring to a tough modernity, was often no more than a literary adaptation of Hebrew journalese. At the same time, there were attempts to build a new kind of poetic Hebrew on the structural base of the new spoken language.

The culmination of all these tendencies of linguistic realism will remain, I suppose, S. Yizhar's immense stream-of-consciousness novel on the Israeli-Arab War, *The Days of Ziklag* (1958). Long sections of Yizhar's book are made up of dialogue, as the young Israeli soldiers who are the only characters anxiously question each other about the cause for which they are fighting, the disturbing meanings of their identity as Jews and citizens of the new state; the stylistic dividing-line between these spoken exchanges and the interior monologues is sometimes hazy. In between monologue and dialogue are exhaustively descriptive passages in which Yizhar renders the most minute movements of the battle, the smallest details of the Negev landscape with all its vegetation, even the changing constellations in the desert sky at night. Because Hebrew is structurally so different from the Western languages, there have been no really significant stylistic influences from without on Israeli writers—with the partial exception of Yizhar, who in both *The Days of Ziklag* and in his earlier fiction tries, by a constant kneading and reworking of the language, to make it expand to the capacity of lyric plenitude of the prose of Faulkner and Thomas Wolfe. The results of this procedure in his long novel are both dazzling and fatiguing. He makes his Hebrew embrace particulars of experience and nuances of perception which the language hitherto had been unable to reach; sometimes this descriptive activity has strict thematic appropriateness; sometimes it seems merely like an overly intent exercise in absorbing as much reality as is verbally possible. Surely one of the reasons that Yizhar has written virtually nothing since *The Days of Ziklag* is that in it he had carried the linguistic impulse of exhaustive realism as far as any writer or reader would want, so that to grow as a novelist he needed to strike out in a dramatically new direction, something which, for a variety of causes, he seems still unprepared to do.

The very conscious and immediate involvement in history that has characterized the Jewish settlement in Palestine and Israel has also encouraged native writers to feel a responsibility to "report" the world around them. Yizhar's recurrence to the war, ten years after it, in the most ambitious of Israeli novels to date, suggests the general orientation of the novelists of the fifties toward recent collective experience. Every war, of course, brings after it a spate of war novels, but the young Israelis who fought against the Arabs in 1948–49 felt a special urgency to convey their experience not only because it was one that had shaken their private worlds but also because they were, after all, participants in the first armed struggle for Jewish independence since the second century A.D. This is not to suggest that the Israeli novel has been nationalistic or chauvinistic. On the contrary, many of the writers have acted as a kind of public conscience, questioning ideologies, raising the profoundest doubts about the moral and historical implications of public events. But some kind of commitment to public events generally persists, and that is a quality which tends to distinguish the Israeli novel from characteristic developments of the novel today in America, England, and France. The Zionist leadership, with an expectation of close connection between literature and politics that ultimately derives from East-European cultural traditions, would like the writers to "do" certain aspects of Israel—the great national project of gathering in and assimilating Exiles, the building of new industrial cities, the reclamation of desert land, and so forth. The fiction, however, that the younger writers actually produce is often a negative image of the glowing picture expected of them by the zealously patriotic, especially among their elders. Yet, ironically, the novelists generally have proceeded to "do" the various sectors of Israeli life; in traditional novelistic fashion, they have "brought the news," and of course it is hardly ever good news, of their own personal encounters with the realities of life in the army, the kibbutz, the youth movement, the bohemian milieu of the cities, the new immigrant towns.

If one can speak at all of a single theme in the Israeli novel over the past fifteen years, it would have to be disillusionment. In this respect, the position of the Israeli writer now is rather like that of the American writer of the twenties: After the shooting is over, he finds that a national dream has faded with the gunsmoke, and he feels cheated, disheartened, a little embarrassed ever to have been implicated in the naïveté of corporate dreams. Corruption and moral stupidity are not, one would assume, any more pervasive in Israel than elsewhere, but Zionism in its classic pioneering stage was moved by a passionate utopianism, and, after such visions, the confrontation with "normalcy" (itself a Zionist ideal for Jewish regeneration) was bound to be painfully disenchanting. This general sense of the passing of a heroic ideal which one finds in Israeli writers is nicely summed up by a striking moment in *The Living on the Dead* (1965), Aharon Meged's most recent novel. The protagonist, occupying the garret of a dead sculptor who, after enjoying a period of fame in the thirties, lived out his life poor and forgotten, discovers in the laundry room a junkpile of abandoned pieces of sculpture, all tributes fashioned in the old forensic style to the generation of heroic builders of the Land: "What pioneers there were in that bathtub and in those laundry pans! Hammer-swingers, wielders of hoes and rakes, bearers of rifles, working girls in kerchiefs, pregnant women, hora dancers, busts of leaders. Ah, dust has covered them all!"

The Living on the Dead provides some helpful insight into the problems of younger Israeli writers because that is its subject and because the artistic uncertainty of its execution is symptomatic of weaknesses found in the work of many of Meged's contemporaries. In general, one is likely to find Israeli novelists a fascinating and exasperating group to follow because, until now, they have shown so much creative and intellectual ferment and so little sustained achievement. Meged is one of five or six Israeli writers who at some point in their career have given promise of unusual talent, only to fall short of its fulfillment. His previous book, *The Fool's Case* (1959), is an imaginative attempt, faltering at first but finally quite impressive, to get to the moral core of Israel's maddeningly bureaucratized society by adopting the narrative procedures of a Kafka novel. After the misadventures of its anonymous clerk, a well-meaning weakling in a meaningless world of blind power, it was possible to hope that Meged would make this symbolic form more fully his own and go on to create an exciting new variety of the Israeli novel. In his most recent book, however, all that is left of Kafka is an unending trial—with symbolic implications, of course —that serves as a framework within which two counterpointed stories are told in conventional fashion, one rather schematically and the other at a pace that is at times dangerously pedestrian.

The protagonist of *The Living on the Dead* is a young writer named Jonas Rabinovitch—Jonas because, like the prophet Jonah, he flees from the responsibility of a message he has been chosen to bear. Jonas has been given a large advance by a publisher to write the biography of a certain Abraham Davidov, a recently deceased hero of the old pioneering period of the Palestinian community. The would-be biographer spends his days, more or less, interviewing people who have known Davidov and his nights at The Cellar, a hangout for artists and writers. The contrast between the two is striking, although, after a great deal of reiteration, it becomes a little tiring too: Davidov, in the images Jonas culls of his life from the 1920's on, is seen galloping on horseback against Arab marauders, building roads, draining swamps, ranging the countryside restlessly, singing wildly through the nights, passionately discussing Tolstoi and Gogol till the dawn; the denizens of The Cellar, on the other hand, sit slouched in an alcoholic haze, trying to impress each other with intellectual patter, striking off hollow aphorisms about Art and Reality, and capping verses from Baudelaire, Breton, Ezra Pound. Davidov, it should be said, for all his fire and energy, is seen to have his own kind of inner emptiness, but it is different from the bottomless ennui of Jonas and his friends, and Jonas finds the figure of the pioneer-leader, who is supposed to be a spiritual father of the State, so alien that he simply cannot write the book about him. The publishers take him to court for his failure to produce the promised goods, and, though his attorney tries to allay his fears by assuring him that the case can go on for years, Jonas knows he can write nothing else as long as the Davidov affair remains unsettled.

The argument of the novel is quite clear: Until the Israeli writer finds ways of coming to terms spiritually and intellectually with his immediate national past, he will not be able to function creatively in the present; if his roots extend only to the bottom of a shallow pool of contemporary intellectual life, he will not be able to plumb the unsettling and confusing realities of his own society, and, whatever his subject, that remains a precondition for his art. The idea surely has some validity, and the scheme of the novel might have proved to be a suggestive one if, say, Meged had developed a nuanced psychological comparison of the young writer and the old hero, or perhaps, alternately, if he had handled his whole scheme as parable and elaborated its meaning through a boldly symbolic mode of fiction. The novel he did write, however, could serve as a paradigm for the trap into which an uncritical devotion to conventional realism can lead. One senses that Meged is terribly bent upon *reproducing* bohemian café-society in Tel Aviv, upon reproducing the type of Jew represented in Davidov, and so we get a welter of details about both, but neither Davidov

57

nor the habitués of The Cellar can really develop novelistically because they are, finally, only composites of details, and rather predictable details at that. One reviewer of the novel, Ada Tzemah, has made this point trenchantly in noting how the narrator's eye stays at visual surfaces, seeing its objects cinematically, so that the language itself repeatedly falls into catalogues of typifying particulars instead of being worked into artistic patterns that can show forth the realities below the details. The serious novel elsewhere seems largely to have surrendered to the camera its function of merely reproducing milieu because film, with its rapid series of comprehensive images, can do the job far more completely and less tediously than words; but this distinction between media would appear to be one that many Hebrew novelists of the fifties and sixties have chosen to ignore.

Although I have focused on problematic aspects of the enterprise of the native Israeli writers, the general prognosis is by no means bleak. Several recent Hebrew novels have shown real artistic merit, despite flaws of various sorts, and there has been some intelligent interest in formal experiment. In this connection, the novel most worthy of mention is Yehuda Amihai's *Not of This Time and Place* (1963). Although some sections of the book bog down in symbolic contrivances, to a large extent overly conscious imitations of Agnon, Amihai's symbolic imagination is remarkably athletic; he is alert to the expressive possibilities of wrenching narrative form from its conventional patterns, and, in his central action, he renders erotic experience vividly with a genuine lyric freshness while firmly relating it to larger aspects of cultural consciousness.[3] *Not of This Time and Place*, like Amihai's earlier volume of short stories, could benefit from some rigorous editing, but it gives evidence of a talent that could yet enable this writer to become a major novelist.

In any event, the case of Amihai, who is worlds away from Agnon though strongly under his influence, suggests something of the special situation of the Israeli novel in general. It has been in a continual state of transition—a fact which makes generalizations about it unsafe—but the transition is not, as an outsider might suppose, from bare beginnings to a first maturity. Rather, the Hebrew novel has behind it a brief but distinguished tradition of mature achievement, and it has had to move down from the last, greatest pinnacle of that achievement and outward toward another kind of achievement. This fresh beginning is understandable and probably even commendable, but if the new Hebrew novelists are to take full advantage of the unique resources of expression indigenous to their language and cultural past, they cannot afford to turn their backs entirely on their own literary predecessors. Hopefully, as they move closer to the as yet unperceived forms of their own artistic self-realization, they will also find ways to incorporate in their work an imaginative responsiveness to what is extraordinary in the older tradition of Hebrew fiction.

REFERENCES

1. I have discussed in detail this whole problem of the gap between generations of Hebrew novelists in "Israeli Writers and Their Problems," *Commentary*, Vol. 34, No. 1 (July 1962), pp. 20-27.

2. Because of the range of Agnon's work, the brief account given here must necessarily be inadequate. Some of his important fiction is now being translated into English. Schocken House has just published two extremely interesting symbolic *novellen* under the title *Two Tales* (New York, 1966), and it has scheduled for publication early in 1967 a major novel, *A Guest for the Night*. I have tried to give a fuller sense of Agnon's *oeuvre* in "The Genius of S. Y. Agnon," *Commentary*, Vol. 32, No. 2 (August 1961), pp. 105-113. *Nostalgia and Nightmare*, a book-length study of Agnon by Arnold J. Band, will be published by the University of California Press in the summer of 1967.

3. For a full account of Amihai's novel, see my recent article, "Confronting the Holocaust: Three Israeli Novels," *Commentary*, Vol. 41, No. 3 (March 1966), pp. 67-73.

GEORGE N. SFEIR

The Contemporary Arabic Novel

I. *Evolving a New Medium*

THE NOVEL, unlike poetry, is a very recent development in Arabic literary expression. About fifty years old, the Arabic novel is largely the product of the modernization or Westernization that had begun some fifty or seventy-five years earlier. Its first authors were, in the main, young expatriates who suddenly found themselves face to face with the modern ways of Europe and America.

For the *émigré* and for the student in New York, Paris, or London, it was a time for assimilation and interpretation, without the constraints of a society that had no meaning for them save that they belonged to it. What Europe provided to the American expatriate of the 1920's, America provided to the Lebanese and Syrian *émigrés* of the same period. In the words of the last surviving member of their circle, Mikhail Na'imah, "a handful of men gathered in one place at the same time to deliver a message which was due to be delivered and they were equipped to do it." Among them were Rihani, Gibran, and Na'imah. Their message concerned new forms and techniques, new ideas. They had discovered a whole new world to convey through Arabic literature.

Who were better equipped than the returning students to tackle the intriguing, indeed inspiring, problems arising out of the confrontation of the traditional, conventional life by the alien, yet more rational, modern ways? To these nascent writers no problem was more pressing than the issue of social change and conflicting cultural values. Here was the breeding ground of the modern Arabic novel, an experimental, adolescent novel. It was declamatory in style, direct in its message, proudly and unabashedly autobiographical in its approach. Among the best of these novels are Yahya Haqqi's *Qindil Umm Hashim* (*Umm Hashim's Lantern*), Ibrahim Abd al Qader al Mazini's *Ibrahim al Katib* (*Ibrahim, the Scribe*), Gibran's

Al Ajnihah al Mutakassirah (The Broken Wings), Taha Hussein's Al Ayyam (The Stream of Days), Taufiq al Hakim's 'Usfur Min al Sharq (A Bird from the East), and Mohammad Husayn Haykal's Zaynab. The latter, which first appeared in 1917, was destined to become a literary milestone in modern Arabic literature. Critics later turned to it and said: "It is the first work in Arabic that one can really call a novel." Zaynab describes the life of the peasant and his village. This theme recurs throughout modern Arabic writing, but for Egyptian writers it assumes a national dimension that is unparalleled in other Arab countries. In Egypt, as in Silone's Italy, the village and the city have coexisted side by side, separate and distinct—like two different worlds, with no communication between them save in the silent dialogue of jealousy, distrust, and fear.

The most recent major novel treating this theme is Abd al Rahman al Sharqawi's Al Ard (The Earth). Its appearance gave Egypt's post-revolutionary critics a welcome work with which to compare and condemn pre-revolutionary writing. They claimed that novels such as Zaynab were static and bourgeois, that they sought only to record and perpetuate the feudal conditions of the Egyptian fellah.

Al Ard was published fifty years after Zaynab. During that half century, European and American literature was undergoing rapid change. Arab writers continued to be influenced by Western literature, but were also experimenting on their own. They have tried their hand at the conventional novel and the nouveau roman, partaking of romanticism and existentialism, indulging in socialist realism and in themes of the absurd. The generation of the experimentalists and the innovators of the decades following World War I were succeeded in the forties and fifties by a new breed of writers—writers who were more sophisticated in their approach to the social problems of their time and broader in their interests. Unlike their predecessors, these writers lacked a common cause and did not form a single group or school. They scattered in pursuit of the many and varied problems of modernization. Their awareness of these problems was only partly the result of their immediate experience; it also stemmed from their readings of such modern masters as Gorki, Dostoevski, Joyce, Kafka, Sartre, Camus, Mann, Silone, Hemingway, and Faulkner.

Although Arab writers readily employed and excelled in the short story, their development and perfection of the novel proved

61

slower. Not only is a half century a short time for the maturation of such a complex medium as the novel, but its progress is intimately tied to changes in society, to social and intellectual development. Furthermore, the dichotomy in the Arabic language between the spoken and the written word frustrates any realistic and genuine rendition of dialogue. This is perhaps the hardest problem which Arab writers face today—a problem they will have to struggle with for a long time to come. Nevertheless, the novel in Arabic, despite its deficiencies in technique and form, has now caught up with the times.

II. *Taufiq al Hakim with Some References to Taha Hussein*

This half century of literary development produced two Egyptian writers of great stature: Taha Hussein, a novelist and critic, and Taufiq al Hakim, a novelist and dramatist. Despite the partial parting of the ways in their literary careers, they present a strange similarity of themes in their fictional works. For both, the issue of social change and the conflict of cultures is paramount.

After qualifying for the bar in Egypt in 1923, al Hakim journeyed West to Paris, the intellectual and artistic center of Europe at that time. The rich literary life of France opened al Hakim's mind and heart to human associations unknown in his limited and restricted milieu at home. Out of this enriching encounter came *A Bird from the East*, a euphemism for Muhsin, a young man who journeyed from the Middle East to the West. Although this novel was written some ten years after his return to Egypt, in it al Hakim draws extensively on his personal experiences during his student days in Paris.

Muhsin's reaction to the superior and alien culture of Europe varies. Some times he is defensive; other times, understanding and receptive. His attitude reflects the passionate struggle raging within him—the struggle between the pride of belonging to a rich ancient culture and the recognition of the more rational and advanced ways of modern Europe. Stylistically it represents a dialogue similar to that in André Malraux's *The Temptation of the West*. The correspondence between A. D. and Ling in *The Temptation of the West* also focuses on several of the arguments that al Hakim allows to develop between Muhsin and his French woman friend, on the one hand, and between him and a Russian *émigré*, on the other.

Whatever its technical weaknesses, *A Bird from the East*, like most of the Arabic works of that epoch, dramatizes the experience of a new generation of Arabs who confronted European ways and concepts for the first time, with a freshness and youthfulness all their own.

Taha Hussein, who left the traditionalist Al Azhar University of Cairo to continue his studies at the Sorbonne, also draws upon his personal experiences in his novel *Adib* (*A Man of Letters*), published in 1935. Typical of the writers of the period, both al Hakim and Hussein record through their protagonists their own impressions of French life, their inner conflicts and outspoken arguments with European ways, and their love for a French woman.

The dialogue between the relative virtues of East and West (speaking in a cultural rather than a political sense) is recurrent in the Arabic writing of the past fifty years. It has assumed varying forms: soul versus mind, spiritualism versus materialism, humanism versus mechanization—with the East laying sole claim to the first of the contending concepts and the West (Europe and America) invariably identified with the second.

Al Hakim indulges in this argument in his major novel *Awdat al Ruh* (*The Return of the Spirit*, or *The Resurrection*). Here the dialogue is between two Europeans, a Britisher and a Frenchman, rather than between a European and an Easterner. It is almost as if al Hakim seeks to produce objective outside evidence to prove the superiority of the Eastern soul vis-à-vis the European mind, which, according to the author, is all that Europe can brag about. "Europe's strength lies in its mind, that limited instrument which one has to augment by will power. Egypt's strength lies in its heart which is limitless."

In *The Resurrection* al Hakim again sends his protagonist on a journey, this time into the national past of his own land in search of the spiritual and cultural sources of his national ethos. Al Hakim maintains that this ethos derives from the residue of the ancient culture and that it is still present and alive in his people's consciousness. "I do not have a recent past. I am compelled to penetrate the ancient past which is about to disappear under the sands of time," says al Hakim.

The protagonist in *The Resurrection* is the son of rich landowners. He fails both in mitigating his parents' contempt (particularly his mother's) for the peasants who work for them and in ignoring the suspicions aroused in him by rumors about the girl he loved. Eventually he finds satisfaction and fulfillment in revolutionary acts against the alien rulers of his land. In the revolution, al Hakim seems to be saying, Egypt finds her resurrection. He borrows his symbolism from the oldest known Egyptian script, "The Book of the Dead," and applies it to the modern reawakening of Egypt that the revolution of 1919 represents. In a frontispiece to his novel, al Hakim draws on "The Book of the Dead" by quoting Isis' pleadings over the dismembered body of Osiris:

> Rise up Osiris, rise,
> I am Horus, your son
> I come to bring you back to life
> You still have your heart
> Your heart of the ancient past.

Like *A Bird from the East, The Resurrection* is partly autobiographical, depicting much of al Hakim's experiences in his childhood and early youth. Like his protagonist, Muhsin, al Hakim spent his childhood on his father's country estate where his mother's contempt for the peasants working for them annoyed him terribly. He was later sent to Cairo to stay at his uncle's home while attending school there. It was in Cairo that he, like Muhsin, became involved with his uncle in the 1919 revolution and was imprisoned for a time.

Following the parallel that curiously exists in the fictional works of al Hakim and Taha Hussein, Taha Hussein's *Al Ayyam (The Stream of Days)* records his childhood and adolescent experiences in his village home and during his early schooling in Cairo. Over and above their contribution to the early development of the novel in Arabic, these works provide important source materials for an investigation of Egypt's social conditions during the first two decades of the twentieth century.

Al Hakim's use of mythology as a source for his themes on the human condition is particularly evident in his plays. *Ahl Al Kahf (The People of the Cave)* is based on the "Seven Sleepers of Ephesus" as related in the Koran. The sleepers come to life after three hundred years only to be disillusioned with what has happened to the world and the faith in the interval. They decide to return to the world of the dead because for them life in the present—without a living past—is, in any case, equivalent to death.

In both *The People of the Cave* and *The Resurrection*, al Hakim develops his outlook on Egyptian life. He explores the Egyptian's built-in resistance to disintegration, to the corrosive effect of time. In *The Resurrection* al Hakim, speaking through a French archaeologist working in Egypt, says that the Egyptian people continue until this day to harbor the spirit of the temple. In saying this he alludes to the symbolic significance of the pyramid in Egyptian life and history—the Egyptians' spirit of resistance and their need for an object of worship in times of crises. "Truly, Mr. Blake," the Frenchman admonishes his British friend, "you should not under-estimate this people. They have the potential strength. All they need is one thing—someone to worship. They need a man of their own who would personify all their passions and hopes."

Al Hakim resolved his earlier concern with the conflict of cultures as an enlightened liberal would: by the inevitable recognition of the unity of mankind. And if he concerns himself with the past, he does so only to enrich the present, never to deny the merits of progress. The condition of man here and now concerns al Hakim. On this issue he is in agreement with Taha Hussein, who, in *The Future of Culture in Egypt,* portrays the cultural make-up of his land as the result of the confluence of various streams of civilizations throughout its long history.

Al Hakim treats the cleavage that separates the life of the city from that of the village as a tolerant liberal would. His critique of the sumptuous but empty values of the vain aristocracy is devoid of the vengeful bitterness of the radical but is not unmindful of the outworn irrational ways of the fellah.

He evokes this attitude effectively in *Yawmiyat Na'ib fil Aryaf* (*The Diary of a Representative in the Country*). After his return from France, al Hakim was appointed Assistant Public Prosecutor in the Delta region where he spent five years; *The Diary* is based on a diary in which al Hakim recorded his experiences during those years. The protagonist of *The Diary* sets out to solve a simple murder case. But he is faced with apathetic villagers and reluctant witnesses. The day-to-day account of the Public Prosecutor brings to mind in smaller or greater degree a baffling comitragic paradigm of Kafka's *The Trial* without, however, its terror and enigma. Here in the world of Egypt's fellah, peasants are tried for crimes they are unaware of committing and according to laws they cannot possibly comprehend. Life is hazardous and puzzling, but there is a relieving sense of simplicity and jest that renders al Hakim's work no less amusing for being a stinging satire on the life of the judge and the accused alike.

Taha Hussein's treatment of this theme is also essential to his fictional endeavor. He is even more directly concerned than al

Hakim with the social and economic plight of the fellah. In *Du'a' al Kayrawan* (*The Call of the Nightingale*) and *Shajarat al Bu's* (*The Tree of Misery*), he exposes not only the vicious exploitation of the innocent fellah at the hands of the more sophisticated urbanite, but also the equally vicious social customs that retard the progress of the fellah. This is evident in both *The Call of the Nightingale* and *The Tree of Misery*. In the former a father kills his daughter to cleanse the dishonor she brought upon his house by her innocent submission to her employer; in the latter, an overly dominant father forces his son into a marriage of interest.

In his latest novel, *Al Mu'adhdhabun fil Ard* (*The Wretched of the Earth*), Taha Hussein directs his attack at social injustice in whatever quarter he finds it. Published in 1951 in Lebanon, this work remained banned in Egypt until the fall of King Farouk in 1952.

The image of Egypt's millions of toiling and disinherited peasants—the burden and the bearers of Egypt's long and tortuous history—is well embedded in the conscience of Egyptian writers. The theme is peculiarly Egyptian, which places many an Egyptian writer in the tradition of Russian authors from Gogol to Sholokhov. As al Hakim himself has pointed out, it is the fellah who is the true embodiment of the Egyptian soul, and it is he who symbolizes Egypt's eternal existence. Without an awareness and understanding of this consciousness, any critique of the work of Egyptian writers would remain incomprehensible and incomplete.

III. Nagib Mahfouz

Mahfouz belongs to the second generation of Arab writers concerned with the novel form. This generation followed that of al Hakim and his pioneering colleagues and was not uninfluenced by them. But, like immigrants to a new world, the generation of al Hakim labored under the divisive loyalties between a new and an old world, between a modern and a traditional life, between the here and the there that was their literary as well as their cultural and social experience. Mahfouz and his generation are more at home, more familiar with the adopted medium and ideas. Gone are the embarrassment, the self-consciousness, and the divided loyalties of the immigrant. Not only did Mahfouz avoid discussing the conflicts of cultures, he also steered away from the rural-urban confrontations. His subject matter is the city, his own city Cairo, to which he wholly belongs and where he never ceases to enjoy mingling with its people, frequenting its cafés, strolling through its neighborhood streets. His best-known works draw on the names of Cairo's neighborhoods for their titles—*Khan al Khalili, Zuqaq al Madaqq,* and *Bayn al Qasrayn* and its two companion volumes, *Qasr al Shawq* and *al Sukkariyah,* which form his celebrated trilogy. In these novels and others not mentioned, Mahfouz deals with the urban middle class during the period immediately after World War I until the decade following the end of World War II. In his mid-fifties, Mahfouz, not unlike Dos Passos, is the chronicler of his country at mid-century.

The trilogy, the first volume of which won the Egyptian state prize for literature in 1956, is a monumental work in the tradition of Galsworthy's *The Forsyte Saga.* In its theme and its treatment of changing times, however, the trilogy is closer to Thomas Mann's *Buddenbrooks;* Mann is Mahfouz's favorite author. It is the long and intricate saga of a middle-class Cairene family. Its head, Ahmad Abd al Jawad, symbolizes an age and a tradition, both of which die with him by the beginning of World War II. During his life Abd al Jawad manages to lead a dual existence. At home he is the conservative, domineering, unbending father; outside, the libertine, frivolous man of pleasure. His obedient and dutiful wife exists in a world that never extends beyond the walls of her home; his two daughters and three sons are caught in the web of shifting traditions, the uncertainties of values in a changing society. Their fate is typical of Egypt's youth between the two world wars. The eldest, Yassin, like his father outside the home, is frivolous and irresponsible, indulging his own selfish pleasures. The middle son, Fahmi, is a young patriot whose life is cut short by British bullets quelling a student demonstration. The youngest, Kamal, an introspective student of philosophy, becomes a writer; he leads an untiring search for a more meaningful existence in a milieu of shifting values. This is presumably a picture of the author himself. In fact, Mahfouz admits that the personality of Kamal reflects his own "intellectual crisis." Indeed, it reflects the crisis of an entire generation of intelligentsia who grew to maturity during the decade following the late 1930's. During this period Egypt was sovereign but not independent, enlightened with European ideas but dragged down by the weight of underdevelopment, aristocrats and ruffians, sumptuousness and suffering, fun and frustration. Many of that generation either identified themselves with the European Left or became resigned and stood aloof from the events of Egyptian life. Thus, when the revolution of 1952 broke out, they were taken by surprise and virtually left behind. Even the leftists among them could not find accommodation in the socialism of the new order. Mahfouz more than any other modern Egyptian writer fills us in on the background of what has occurred on the Egyptian scene since 1952.

The events in Mahfouz's trilogy fall short of the 1952 revolution. They follow an orderly chronological sequence from their original setting in 1914 through the 1940's. They move on a wide front, sweeping before them the entire urban community, sometimes dramatically and turbulently, sometimes softly and sensually. These events capture not only the lives of the personalities in the novel, but the conditions and the spirit of the entire neighborhood as well. They encompass two or three generations of these inhabitants. Time alone emerges as the true and lasting hero.

Time is cardinal to Mahfouz's literary themes and technique. But his is not the concept of time born of the stream of consciousness that one finds in the works of Thomas Wolfe or Marcel Proust, not time recaptured through subjective remembrance of things past. "Time," Mahfouz has said, "is apparent only in its historic sequence, and then through living social experience." The various protagonists of his novels are invariably caught in the ever-present life triangle of overwhelming circumstances, constrictive conventions, and endless time. But, despite the certainty of their failures and frustrations, they manage to marshal that last ounce of power necessary to make the ultimate gesture of rebellion. Mahfouz's heroes are driven by a burning desire not so much to free themselves of their temporal confines as to overcome their social estrangement and to achieve reconciliation with their milieu. This is particularly apparent in his post-neighborhood novels. It is the primary motivation of Sa'id Mahran, the hero of *Al Liss wal Kilab* (*The Thief and the Dogs*), who seeks to alter a despicable social reality and to make it conform to a more desirable social ideal. It is also the theme of *Al Summan wal Kharif* (*The Quail and Autumn*), in which the hero, 'Isa, is caught in a struggle between his reason which dictates an acceptance of the new order born of the 1952 revolution, and the yearnings of his heart for the old values which have been by-passed or deliberately destroyed by the new order.

The Thief and the Dogs is a Sartrian work of dark and lonely life. The hero, Sa'id Mahran, has just been released from prison after serving a sentence for larceny. He leaves prison intent on seeking revenge for the wrongs committed by his wife and Isma'il Hilmi, his friend and former schoolmate. His wife had abandoned him to take up with Hilmi, who is now a successful publisher. Hilmi had urged Sa'id Mahran to commit the crime by convincing him that, unlike stealing from the poor, stealing from the rich is not a crime. Sa'id fails in his efforts for revenge and only gets himself into trouble with the police. They finally corner him in a cemetery where he takes his own life. In the interval, Sa'id Mahran is abandoned and lonely. He tries to find solace and understanding in the company of an old cleric, but the holy man's purposes and ideals are not of this world. His sole friend and companion turns out to be a prostitute named Nur, which in Arabic connotes light. Although he treats her with disregard and disdain, she labors to provide him with food and shelter and remains faithful to him to the end. She refuses, despite police torture, to betray him. In Sa'id Mahran's world of depraved "dogs," only the prostitute Nur is human and understanding. This he realizes only toward the end. The narrator says:

He shall not see Nur again and felt himself strangled with desperation and was overtaken by sadness, not because he shall soon lose his secure refuge, but because he shall lose a heart, a compassion and a fellowship. . . . He now realized that his feelings for her were much deeper than he had thought, that she was an indivisible part of his life now torn and tottering over the edge of the abyss. He shut his eyes in the dark and confessed a silent confession of his love for her.

The prostitute is a familiar figure in many of Mahfouz's novels. In *Bidayah Wa Nihayah* (*A Beginning and an End*), published in 1942, her name is Sana', and in *The Quail and Autumn,* published in 1962, she is Riri. Invariably she is a woman compelled by dire need and unfortunate circumstances to accept this degrading fate. But at the crucial moment in the story the reader always discovers how loving, loyal, and uncompromising she can be. One wonders whether in the person of this downtrodden, contemptible prostitute Mahfouz is not chastising the state of morals in Arab society today where, in the face of stringent conventions, hypocrisy is not unknown.

Mahfouz is also vitally concerned with socialism and religion. "For some," he says, "socialism could be the elimination of obstacles that stand in the way of God's justice." In saying this, Mahfouz, the realist and the socialist, is reconciled with his religious background. To Islam and to Marxism, history and the building of the good society are important. Islam's acute consciousness of the transcendental imbues it, however, with a morality repudiated by the atheism of Marxism. Atheism has failed to establish itself in Arab thought and literature; God is alive in all his glory. When Rushdi 'Akef, Mahfouz's protagonist in *Khan al Khalili*, finds himself face to face with death as a result of an incurable disease, he seeks solace in the Koran, in the Word of God. And when Ahmad 'Akef goes to the Department of Health to obtain the necessary release for the burial of his brother, he is appalled by the cold routine approach of the government official who receives his request and processes the papers. "How could he," Ahmad 'Akef complains, "approach death in this nonchalant way when it is the greatest event in the world."

In *Awlad Haritna* (*The Kids of Our Neighborhood*) the religious theme is unmistakably present. In fact, the work is an allegory on the story of creation and the development of the prophetic religions. It is, in essence, the story of all neighborhoods everywhere; the setting is universal. The grandfather, al Jabalawi, who lives to be a hundred or more, resides with his family in a large garden mansion at the edge of the desert, a modern terrestrial garden of Eden. One day he calls on all his sons in order to select an heir and administrator for the estate. His choice falls on the youngest son; the eldest, bitterly disappointed, rebels against his father's decision and is consequently expelled from the garden. Eventually the youngest is also expelled for having connived with the eldest to reveal to him the text of the will. From then on, the family multiplies, and its members form an entire neighborhood. Their concern revolves around the property and al Jabalawi's "ten conditions, over which great debates have taken place and were the cause of all the conflict in our neighborhood ever since." One of the grandsons, 'Arafah, develops the power of magical healing in the name of al Jabalawi. He is sought by the usurper of the property, attempts to flee, but is betrayed by a woman friend and eventually killed. 'Arafah's body is raised from the grave by his civilian followers who refuse to believe the accusations leveled against him and fight against the usurper's partisans. "We have nothing to do with the past," they declare. "Our hope lies in the magic of 'Arafah and if we were given the choice between al Jabalawi and magic, we would choose magic."

The Kids of Our Neighborhood was the object of varied and contradictory comment. The religiously-minded condemned it as a work of profanity. They accused Mahfouz of committing the un-forgivable sin of personifying God, creation, and the prophets. To Mahfouz, the allegory merely presents a philosophical critique of the moral state of the family of nations. He contrasts his style in this novel to that of Swift in *Gulliver's Travels*. Swift, he says, uses myth to criticize reality, whereas he, Mahfouz, uses reality to criticize myth by giving myth the attributes of existing reality.

The Kids of Our Neighborhood also heralds the changes that have occurred in Mahfouz's technique and themes since the publication of his novels of the neighborhoods and the historical novels that preceded them. Leaving behind the techniques and themes of socialist realism, he began to deal with the experience and fate of man as man. He did this at a time when "socialist realism" and "socialist critique" were the forms of writing officially sanctioned in Egypt, and when many promising young writers, carried away by the new political winds, were promoting ideological commitment.

Mahfouz, however, rejects any categorization of his style and denies that it has undergone change. He admits that he is a realist. But realism, he explains, treats the realities of life in a particular period of time and in a way that reflects the social ideas dominant at that time. Natalie Sarraute, speaking for her colleagues in the French *nouveau roman* school, would agree with him completely.

The Quail and Autumn is the only novel by Mahfouz that uses the revolution of 1952 as a background. *The Quail and Autumn* is the story of 'Isa, a respectable upper-class politician in the old regime who suddenly finds himself deprived of his status by the revolution. He loses his government job and his socialite fiancée. He finally abandons his home and, turning his back on Cairo, on his past, moves to Alexandria. There he lives in the Greek quarter, where he hopes to lose himself among "you all who are strangers in an alien land." He languishes in idle despair, sitting in cafés and walking along the waterfront. By the seashore he watches "the bevies of quail swooping down to an inevitable fate after a tedious journey full of illusory heroism."

Eventually 'Isa befriends a simple streetwalker called Riri who, like himself, has abandoned her people and home town and dares not return. He sees in her life a reflection of his own condition, and, consequently, he is often brutal to her and coldly avoids her when he realizes that she is bearing his child. He refuses to go along with the plans of his friends who try to set him up in a job. Despite all his efforts, he is unable to escape the past. "The truth is that my

71

mind is sometimes convinced of the revolution, but my heart is always with the past. And the problem is whether there could be a reconciliation between my heart and my mind." He is finally pushed into a marriage of interest, which only leads him into deeper despair. He eventually seeks out Riri again and comes face to face with their child who is now a grown-up girl. This confrontation moves him to beg Riri to let him come back to her, but she rejects him and elects to stay by the side of the poor shopkeeper who sheltered her as his wife. The author leaves 'Isa's fate vague and undefined, shrouded in the early-morning mist of the story's last day.

Mahfouz's most recent novel, *Al Tariq* (*The Road*), is the story of the protagonist's search for a familiar but unknown image. After thirty years of uneasy and difficult life as an orphan, Saber discovers that his father is alive, but that his whereabouts is unknown. He sets out on a tortuous search to find him, knowing very little about his father, not much more than his name and his title which indicates a sort of religious eminence. Along the way he falls into many absurd situations and eventually into crime and imprisonment. His lost father, like Beckett's Godot, remains elusively beyond reach or recognition.

The Road is a companion to Mahfouz's two preceding works, *The Thief and the Dogs* and *The Quail and Autumn*. In fact, the similarity of the style and theme has led certain critics to view the three novels as another trilogy, one which employs the ideas of existentialism and the themes of the absurd.

IV. *The Political Novel*

The Egyptian revolution of 1952, the Algerian war of independence, and the ferment in Syria and Iraq helped to make the 1950's a decade of radicalism in the Arab world and set the stage for the contemporary political novel. The strong social pressures generated by these events forced writers to seek commitment to and involvement in the political issues of the time. As one post-revolutionary author, Abd al Rahman al Sharqawi, has said, "A writer in this age cannot be just a writer. He must adopt a message. His message should be to defend life, the future of mankind, and the spiritual heritage of our civilization."

When Sharqawi's first major work, *Al Ard* (*The Earth*), appeared, it was hailed by the new literary establishment as a model of revolutionary literature. It dramatized the dormant potentialities, suppressed aspirations, and usurped rights of the peasant. Above all, it expressed the possibility that the peasant, if he were only given a chance, might be capable of heroic acts. Sharqawi's style became known as "critical realism."

The Earth is a portrait of a village, the village where Sharqawi grew up and to which he periodically returns from Cairo. With a sharp realism reminiscent of Ignazio Silone, Sharqawi relates the life of the peasants, their joys and miseries, their ambitions and disappointments, and the role of the local tax collector, police, and sanitation officials, who represent in the village national authority, as symbolized by the distant capital of Cairo.

To the charge that his realism is dogmatic and springs essentially from a political commitment, Sharqawi replies with unmistakably dogmatic and dialectic fervor:

Realism is an outlook on life which helps the man of letters to understand the source of life and join in the battle of antithesis which is ever pushing toward progress. Realism makes man understand this contradiction, points out to him the nature of the motivating force and leads him eventually to the outcome of this contradiction which is the future itself.

It should be mentioned that the term *political novel* is used here as a convenient means of identifying a certain wave of politically inspired novels and short stories written during the 1950's, and not for purposes of rigid categorization. Practically all the works that can be labeled *political* have dealt with themes common to the contemporary Arabic novel. The new element, however, is the heroes' unmistakable awareness of the national community, a national interest or cause, and their loyalty to this cause. The writers often return to the past in search of political themes. But whether they treat past history or contemporary events, the end product has invariably been a literature of justification and of rehabilitation.

Following *The Earth*, Sharqawi wrote *Al Shawariʿ al Khalfiyah* (*Back Streets*), the story of Shukri Abd al ʿAl. An Egyptian army officer, Shukri was forcibly retired in 1925 following an argument with his superior, a British officer, over Shukri's refusal to open fire on Egyptian street demonstrators. The events of the story take place in 1935. Shukri, now a widower, lives quietly with his two daughters on ʿAziz Street, a back street of Cairo. He is suddenly recalled to active duty and reinstated in his previous rank, but his primary interest continues to be with the people who live on

'Aziz Street. He solves their problems, reconciles their differences, protects the weak, and finds jobs for the unemployed. He eventually organizes the inhabitants of the street into an effective action group that participates in the 1935 uprising against the British.

Mahmud Taymur, in *The Blue Lanterns*, goes back to World War I to tell the story of an Egyptian woman who leads a double life. She is both Na'imah, the prostitute to the British troops of occupation, and Bahiya, the good woman who tends a sick father and a fatherless son. She separates her two worlds successfully until she falls in love with a young man who visits her in her home as her fiancé and in her business as her lover. He sows the first seeds of revolt in her by reproaching her for selling herself to the troops. When her son is accidentally killed in an anti-British demonstration, Na'imah or Bahiya joins an anti-British underground group and is herself killed. The alternative between despicable self-enrichment through servility to the enemy and honorable self-sacrifice for the national cause is clear. These represented the only choices open to Egyptians at that time.

For Yusuf al-Siba'i, the use of the revolution as the apocalypse toward which his characters are inexorably drawn becomes almost a matter of duty. In the Introduction to his two-volume work, *Rudda Qalbi (My Heart Regained)*, he says: "It seems to me that the reason for my particular concern with this story is my belief that it is essential that a record be made of those contemporary events which have just taken place in our history."

The fighting in Port Said and the Suez Canal in 1956 gave Egyptian writers a more immediate historic act to treat in their works. The writers exalted the revolution, stressing the virtue of solidarity, selflessness, and sacrifice in the service of the national community. These writers maintain that the individual himself is powerless and insignificant; only by working with and through the group does he or she find strength, achieve self-realization, and rise above the petty to the heroic, a theme well expressed by André Malraux in his *Days of Wrath*. Unlike works by Malraux, the emphasis in the Egyptian novels is on the external, overt act of the protagonist, on his or her attempt to identify with the national cause, a war, a revolution, or merely a limited act of political resistance. The authors seem to be saying that a person achieves compensation for his sacrifices or redemption for his past sins against society through this identification. The most pertinent aspect of the political novel—the personal conflict and the internal tension

74

that arises out of this conflict—has somehow escaped these authors. The Egyptian writer, suddenly and unexpectedly faced with a historic act, felt that if he could not explain the act, he should at least try to justify it.

In failing to develop the dramatic possibilities of personal conflict in their work, the Arab writers also avoid the tragic. As Egypt's Yusuf Idriss has explained, the Arab is "unable to weep for a long time or laugh for a long time. Unlike the European, he cannot be completely sad in a moment of sorrow or completely hilarious in a moment of jest: In their eyes are always intermixed the tears of joy and those of sorrow." This is why, he says, comedy and tragedy are European concepts. The Arabs, by contrast, are sensitive to such concepts as honor, sincerity, and loyalty. The violation of any of these is tantamount to a social sin which a simple act of purgation can absolve. For the Arab, there can be no contest with fate. Destiny is preordained, and his soul is not free to violate the moral order that the faithful believe is ideal and complete. In such an order, an act of atonement can absolve the guilty socially, but cannot raise the transgressor above his guilt to a new moral order.

A work by Lebanon's Halim Barakat heralds the beginning of the Arabic political novel in the best sense of the term. Set against the Arab debacle in Palestine, *Sitat Ayyam* (*Six Days*) marks the approaching communion of the heroic act and the tragic experience in the Arabic novel. Halim Barakat weaves his novel around the inner sensibility and inner conflicts of his protagonist, Suhayl.

The six days represent the lease on life that the superior forces of the enemy grant the inhabitants of the small hamlet of Dayr al Bahr in their ultimatum to surrender or face annihilation. During these six days, Barakat, through his protagonist, portrays the crisis faced by the Arab intellectual of that period. The crisis is expressed in all its religious, social, and cultural ramifications. Suhayl defies destiny by struggling against insurmountable odds to uphold his ideals, to be true in his love, and to save his land. He experiences pain, torture, and despair. "It may be hard to commit suicide but it is even harder to face life. Suicide is a passing protest whereas life is a continuing act of protest," he declares.

He joins the partisans in an engagement against the enemy even though he harbors great doubts about the worthiness of their cause, for the partisans are defending a kind of life and society that he despises. He loves Nahidah, a victim of irrational and outmoded social and religious conventions. Winning her seems as hopeless as victory in battle. But he remains in the thick of both these battles. Why? That is what he asks himself and tries to resolve. "Why does he love her? To forget boredom. Why does he expose himself to death? To forget boredom. Why defy? To forget boredom. He did not mean what he said about the blessings of death. He wishes only to overcome boredom."

Suhayl is captured by the enemy. Despite the torture he suffers at their hands, he refuses to betray the defense plans of his hamlet. He thinks only of his colleagues and of Nahidah, who, toward the end of the novel, rebels against her parents and runs away to join him only to learn that he has disappeared and is believed to have been killed. The enemy attacks before the ultimatum has expired and takes the hamlet by surprise. Suhayl's colleagues, in a desperate maneuver to defend the village, are all killed.

Written in direct, staccato-like sentences, *Six Days* reflects the development of a new stylistic technique and a higher level of perfection in the Arabic novel. Barakat's work is comparable in craftsmanship and spirit to Marguerite Duras' *Moderato Cantabile*. It is a genuine work, fashioned out of the raw material around which it is woven—the sweet breath of nature that envelops Dayr al Bahr and the sweaty bodies of its inhabitants. The leading characters are tragic loners who, amid the ruins of their place and time, must bear the agony and conflict created by their acute sensitivity.

V. *The Female Revolt*

The cries of boredom and revolt in Barakat's *Six Days* are heard with even greater anguish in the novels of social protest by female Arab writers. The objects of this protest are the social and psychological barriers that continue to restrict the freedom of Arab women and prevent their emancipation.

The pioneer in this revolt was Layla Ba'albaki, a youthful Lebanese barely twenty-one years old. In 1957 she attacked both family and society in her defiant novel *Ana Ahya* (*I Live*). Since then the avalanche of female fiction of social protest has been tremendous. Colette Suhayl in Syria, Sofie Abdullah in Egypt, and many others have adopted a Flaubertian approach to social experience: They have pitted their heroines' lives and experiences against the life and experience of the community.

Colette Suhayl's *Ayyam Ma'ahu* (*Days with Him*) treats the reader to an especially frank statement of the heroine's struggle to consummate her relationship with her lover, free of the emotional repressions and social impediments of a conservative, closely-knit society and its incongruous, all-powerful, ever-present, devouring being—the People. The test of freedom, progress, maturity, and many other things seems to be a woman's ability to associate freely with men.

In *I Live*, Lena, the heroine, makes her position clear from the start. Nothing can restrain her in her quest for total and unfettered freedom to live and love. She tries to break out of her real and psychological chains. In the process, however, she meets and thinks she loves Baha, a fellow student who is himself the captive of a political ideology (he is a Marxist).

But Lena's concern goes beyond mere freedom of association. She yearns for a more meaningful relationship with her fellow beings in order to kill the terrifying sense of absurdity she sees and feels all around her, even in her home. "In my home, I am lost. I am neither Eastern nor Western, neither free nor enslaved." At school she endures the boredom of frustration, watches the meaningless motions of the teacher and students, and turns to daydreaming. At the office where she works, the ever-empty suggestion box she is in charge of symbolizes the emptiness of her life. She walks the streets in search of her identity. "I am an absurd creature cast out on these streets." Then she finds love and thinks she has found herself: "My consolation is that I am in love." But even this fails to satisfy her completely. "I yearn to be lost in the clash of the struggle in Baha's life . . . which would afford me the chance to establish a genuine relationship." Despairing that his loyalty to his politics is stronger than his passion for her, she finally leaves him. Love is lost, but the search goes on. "I want him to know that I alone will build my own future."

The last statement reveals the essence of the problem that the modern Arab woman faces. "I alone will build my own future," independently of him, the man she has traditionally been tied to and identified with—be he father, brother, husband, benefactor, or protector. These fetters on a woman's freedom have been considerably weakened since Egypt's Qasim Amin addressed himself to the problem of the emancipation of women in his controversial book *Tahrir al Mar'a* (*The Liberation of Women*), published in 1889. The Gordian knot of this issue, however, is an indefinable

77

psychological trait in the Arab male's temperament. The Arab male rejects a complete break from tradition and insists, if not on total possession, at least on a degree of submission from a woman. This is important to him since it involves his pride, honor, and manhood.

In France, where *I Live* appeared in translation, Layla Ba'albaki was acclaimed as the Arab Françoise Sagan. Although her lyrical style and decidedly youthful feminine social preoccupation put her work in the company of Sagan's *Bonjour Tristesse,* there remains a world of difference between the two. They are as different as French and Arabic social mores and especially as those mores affect the woman's place in society. Lena never finds the courage or the means to overcome her adolescent innocence. In an interview, Ba'albaki has succinctly expressed the difference between her world and that of Sagan: "The problem of a girl in Sagan's novels is how to live with a man in her own apartment, while the problem of an Eastern girl is how to go shopping alone." In her second novel, *Al Aliha al Mamsukha (The Disfigured Gods),* Ba'albaki resorts to the technique of a series of letters, a technique the French author Michele Perrein had employed in *La Sensitive.* Mira, the heroine of *The Disfigured Gods,* is, like Lena, searching for a more meaningful relationship between the sexes. But Mira, not unlike Perrein's heroine, is caught between two men: a middle-aged man who seeks her company as compensation for his unhappy marriage and a young man who, losing his existential bearings, finds in Mira's body the only sensual evidence of belongingness.

The correspondence between Mira and her lover's wife—who happens also to be her close friend—dwells on the subjects of love, manners, customs, the relations between men and women, and death. In *The Disfigured Gods* death is symbolized by a purple cloud that hangs over Mira's mind after she witnesses a man being hit by a car and watches a blot of purple blood form on the road by his side. The problem of death dominates the novel; Ba'albaki's other considerations gain definition only through their juxtaposition to her discussion of death.

The Disfigured Gods has not achieved the popularity of *I Live,* although in the former Ba'albaki shows greater maturity and deeper insight into the existentialist dilemmas of both men and women. In *I Live* she simply indulged in a declamatory self-pity which, in a society of traditionally silent feminine submission, sounded like a resounding protest. Lena's milieu is stagnant, weighted down by half-dead traditions. Only in her own agitated soul is there life. Only her experience matters. Lena suffers from the weakness that afflicts many protagonists in Arabic novels—the inability to face adversity. The community is dead and with it the hero. Nothing is left for Ba'albaki's protagonist to do but meditate about the idea of death; this is exactly what she does in *The Disfigured Gods*.

VI. *In Search of a Theme*

The heroine of the female novel of social protest is a vanishing heroine. She was utilized to plead for a cause that has already had its actors and encounters. What remains is the tedious effort necessary to widen and deepen the scope of female freedom. Time and technology will, one hopes, take care of this.

But if the protesting heroine is vanishing, the searching hero is here to stay. Camus' Meursault and Sartre's Roguentin have won a fairly large Arab following. *Al Mahzumun (The Routed)*, by Hani al Rahib of Syria, is a good example of attempts to create characters who fit certain existentialist ideas developed in European literature. As the author himself had been, Bishr, the hero of *The Routed*, is a student at Damascus University. He tries to extricate himself from an existence burdened by incompatible inherited values, social and moral chaos, estrangement, boredom, and absurdity. He solves his problem by marshaling sufficient freedom to decide of his own volition to become "committed" to the revolutionary struggle of the society he originally rejected.

Bishr is obviously committed to a struggle that promises change rather than a particular idea or program. In this he is not atypical of his generation which has been uprooted and is, therefore, searching for a new belongingness. Deprived of the security of the stable values of an earlier age, of the comfort of an identifiable code of absolute moral standards, this generation is searching for new values and morals. The value systems of their fathers and grandfathers are no longer relevant. For the writer in Arab countries today, as in an earlier epoch in the United States, this moral dislocation has resulted in what John W. Aldridge has called the "novel of the single consciousness." The writer, having lost direct communication with his environment, seeks "to impress his own assumptions upon his audience." The mood in contemporary Arabic fiction, not unlike that in Arabic politics, is one of the searching restlessness typical during a renascence.

COSTAS M. PROUSSIS

The Novels of Angelos Terzakis

WITH THE exception of the works of Nikos Kazantzakis and those
of one or two other Greek writers, the modern Greek novel is almost unknown in the United States. Yet, some outstanding modern
Greek novelists may be favorably compared with the most famous
novelists of other countries. In order to understand and appreciate
the work of any contemporary Greek novelist, some introductory
notes on modern Greek literature, and particularly on the development of the novel, are necessary.

Throughout the nineteenth century, modern Greek literature
attempted to find its way and to establish itself by depicting the
life and expressing the aspirations of the Greek nation, which was
gradually and painfully being liberated. But there were many obstacles to the development of literary and cultural pursuits: for
example, the long enslavement of the Greek people, the lack of
widespread education, and the poverty of the country. Moreover,
the awe with which nineteenth-century Greek writers and poets
sometimes viewed the literary glories of the Greek past hindered
the creativeness of modern Greek literature, and the glittering
achievements and fashions of contemporary European literature
very often overwhelmed modern Greek literature to the point of
blind imitation. Even the instrument of the literature's expression,
the modern Greek language, was a tantalizing problem that vexed
the Greek nation in general and modern Greek literature in particular. On the one hand, there was the archaic (*katharevousa*,
purist) language which was used in varying degrees according to
the erudition of the writer; on the other hand, there was the vernacular (*demotic*), the living, spoken language of the people. The
fight over them was long and bitter, but by the end of the nineteenth century the *demotic* was accepted as the language of crea-

tive literature. Since then it has steadily been adopted by other intellectual fields.

These problems did not prove insurmountable for poetry, as can be seen from the works of Solomos and Kalvos, and later Palamas and Kavafis, Sikelianos and Kazantzakis, Seferis and Elytis, to mention only the best known. But, throughout the greater part of the nineteenth century, prose, and particularly the novel, was less fortunate, although occasionally some glimpses of solid and genuinely Greek work appeared. During the last quarter of the century, however, there was a wholesome reaction against the previous sterile admiration of ancient Greek literature and the blind imitation of foreign literature. First, the studies of Greek folklore by Nicolaos Politis and, later, the language revolution initiated by Psycharis marked a turning point in the understanding of the real "Greekness" of modern Greek people. In a way it brought to them self-knowledge, self-respect, and self-reliance. As a result, the novels and short stories of the late nineteenth century began to use almost exclusively modern Greek themes, taken particularly from life in the country, for Greece had not yet developed a strongly characteristic urban life. But most of the writers of that time were content simply to describe faithfully the simple rural and maritime life of Greece. Thus their works (to which the term *ethographia* was given) are interesting documents describing a given life at a given place and time, but they usually lack vision and are narrow in their outlook. Yet writers like Papadiamantis and Karkavitsas are exceptionally important from many points of view; even today they are considered among the masters of modern Greek prose.

During the first decades of the twentieth century, life in Greece became more urbanized. The social, political, and intellectual milieu grew more complicated and more frequently appeared thematically in literary works. Of course, contemporary foreign influences continued to be clearly evident in the period's literature. Contemporary political, social, and philosophical trends (such as socialism and Freudianism) also made their appearance in Greek literature, but they were still undigested. As a result, there was a great deal of propaganda and didacticism in many novels and short stories of the first three decades of the twentieth century, although some of the writers turned to symbolism, fantasy, or escapism. The short stories and novels of that period, however, remained basically "ethographic."

Modern Greek literature was really reborn around 1930. While the prose writers and poets of that period continued to have their roots in the Greek literary soil, they also seemed to be nourished by the strong contemporary intellectual and artistic currents of Europe and to breathe in a more universal literary atmosphere. Of course, there has always been a considerable European influence on modern Greek literature, even to the point of open imitation, as mentioned above, but the Greek writers of the thirties were not mere imitators. Broadly educated, deeply grounded in the Greek tradition, and experienced in the demanding problems of contemporary Greek reality, these young writers opened new roads for Greek literature in both form and substance. They are Greeks, but their work can speak to and be appreciated by other people as well. On the one hand, they boldly broke with the narrow, local tradition of modern Greek literature—particularly with its provincial *ethographia*—and created something new, wider in range and scope, and valuable in form and substance. On the other hand, what they had received from the outside, they re-created, adopting it and adapting it, incorporating it organically, almost indiscernibly, into their own work, which was actually a new, realistic orientation in the postwar crisis of the Greek world.

After World War I, Greece, like all countries, underwent an intellectual, moral, financial, and political upheaval. Values "eternally" true were shaken. But, unlike other countries, Greece was not free from war at the end of World War I. For four more years Greece was at war with Turkey, a conflict that ended with the Greek catastrophe in Asia Minor and the flooding of almost 1,500,000 refugees into the Greek mainland, which could hardly sustain its own population, then a little more than 5,000,000. Greece, already plagued by military revolts and general political instability, faced new and acute social and financial problems attendant on the influx of refugees.

Naturally, the frustration with current conditions, the lack of a "central core of ideals on which all groups could agree," and the impact of the fast-changing social and political structure shook the area of letters and arts. Thus the literature of the twenties, when it did not docilely follow the established tradition, was pessimistic (especially in poetry, the best example being the work of Karyotakis), or individualistic and escapist, or even indicative of an attempt to express the new social doctrines. But, in the late twenties and early thirties, a new generation of writers reacted strongly against the docility of the past and the sterile escapism of the present. They also started from their personal, bitter experience, but, instead of escaping or condemning reality, they made the objective world a matter of personal concern. Perhaps they did not find personal salvation or offer concrete solutions to the many problems plaguing Greece. But they were able to see beyond the picturesque provincialism that had dominated earlier literary efforts and portrayed Greek life as a integral part of European, and even universal, life. That was the main task of the novelists. For, although poetry claimed some important new voices (Seferis, Antoniou, and Elytis, among others), and the short story, play, and essay suddenly came alive, the novel became the predominant literary genre of the thirties and the main outlet for expressing the new trends that were shaping the literary climate of the period. Myrivelis, Venezis, Terzakis, Theotokas, Cosmas Politis, Petsalis, and Karagatsis, to name but a few,[1] are dealing in their novels with the problems of contemporary life and with issues that are vital to modern man. Their works reveal perception and seriousness, originality and concreteness, frankness and concern, and, above all, the superior literary qualities that prove them masters of the art of the novel.

War—its actual process, its horrors, and its aftermath for individuals, groups, and the nation—was one of the great themes that fruitfully nurtured some of the creative novelists of the thirties. The works of these novelists are based on their personal experience, but they also reflect the bitter experience of millions of other people in Greece and other nations during World War I. The Greek *couleur locale* in them concretizes the war theme, thus giving the novels verisimilitude and certain distinct boundaries. Still, the Greek war novels could, *mutatis mutandis,* be easily understood and appreciated by any people who had experienced the war. These novels are basically against war. They oppose war implicitly by presenting its horrors and condemn it explicitly. The treatment of war in some of these novels also encompasses the problems of the refugees: the struggle of the uprooted to adapt themselves to a new country, or their nostalgic reminiscences of their earlier, peaceful life in their lost and beloved homeland.

Other novelists of the thirties, usually drawing on their personal experience and, consciously or unconsciously, including autobiographical elements, present the contemporary, or somewhat earlier, Greek reality. Some of them, working out a subject in consecutive volumes from its beginning to its end—like the trilogies of ancient Greek tragedies—give broad pictures of Greek life as it was experienced by successive generations of one or more representative families. Others treat specific aspects of contemporary life such as the problems of the modern Greek family, the acclimatization of foreigners in Greece after World War I, the sexual aspects of the life of extraordinary people, the life of adolescents, the escape into the visionary world of fantasy, the lyrical confession, the biography as fiction. Finally, the novelists of the thirties successfully cultivated the historical novel in its classical form and essence.

One of the best representatives of this restless and creative generation is Angelos Terzakis,[2] a writer of wide range and concrete accomplishments who is both Greek and European in spirit, endeavor, and achievement. Although his novels, plays, short stories, and essays have all enjoyed equal success, only his novels will be discussed here. In his novels Angelos Terzakis examines the uncertain, undirected, and unbalanced aspects of life between the two world wars. He is particularly interested in the social and psychological characteristics of the modern family, its problems and tribulations. In fact, he is a very acute social observer—descriptive, detached, and objective, although always involved in the problems of his day. But, instead of attempting to present the whole of society and its problems, Terzakis, especially in his early novels, centers his interest on one family or a few characteristic individuals who, unable to cope with their anguish, are doomed to failure—stricken by their personal "fate" no less than by the circumstances around them. His heroes are, as one critic wrote, "characteristic specimens of their times, condensing in themselves all the transiency, fluidity, and contradiction of the external world, that itself goes on blindly, without orientation, without justification, sometimes without any hope."[3] The wider social and political setting of his time looms only dimly in the background, while he relentlessly illuminates and emphasizes the narrow, but representative, society of a family. Thus Terzakis is able to delineate the misery and anxiety of his time much more clearly by concentrating on the microcosm of a family or of a group of persons than he could have by generalizing about the macrocosm of society. He is earnestly concerned with presenting specific problems rather than with trying to solve these problems by preaching in pious or angry generalities. And, because he is exceptionally adept at revealing the souls of his characters, uncovering their dark sides and unearthing their hidden indecision, despair, and failure, he is unusually successful in accomplishing his purpose.

This is evident even in his first novel, *Captives* (two volumes, 1932), a large, composite picture of a lower-middle-class Athenian family during the twenties. It is the sad story of Fotos Galanis, his sister Maria, and their sickly mother, who, impoverished after the death of their father, are forced to live in miserable circumstances and almost in seclusion. They fail in all their endeavors to improve their life, become depressed and despondent, and silently, through lack of mutual understanding, nearly turn against each other, although they love one another deeply and sincerely. Eventually Fotos becomes the unwitting cause of his mother's sudden death and the conscious killer of the girl he loves.

The technical structure of Terzakis' first novel is not exemplary, although the over-all plot is presented in simple, clear lines. Sometimes the chapters and subchapters of *Captives* are not well integrated, and the action in the first volume proceeds slowly and asthmatically. But Terzakis' power of analysis and characterization is evident as is his ability to create the proper atmosphere through covert symbolistic realism and to depict the depressing conditions of the period.

In *Captives*, Terzakis presents ordinary people in their everyday life, which, for them, is an oppressive adventure in continuous failure and despair. Fotos Galanis, a weak and unstable person, is suspicious of everything and everybody, morose and ineffectual, afraid of expressing himself openly, and even more afraid of acting according to his beliefs and desires. Yet his real self, his inner self, is capable of affection and compassionate deeds. Being sickly like his mother, he is the prey of his family's solicitous and exasperating care. Both figuratively and actually he is his family's captive. The family often tries to destroy his initiative and eventually reduces him to complete dependence. At times he revolts, silently or openly, against this burdensome care and imposed captivity. But he soon repents and hurries to make amends by conforming even more strictly to his "fate" of despair and servile obedience. And, because he fully understands his degradation, he succumbs to ever deeper despondency, defeatism, and disappointment. He has no illusions about his inadequacies and hopelessness; this self-knowledge is his most bitter reality.

Maria, his sister, is a gentle, thoughtful girl, prepared to serve her home and, with her common sense and energy, to buoy up the spirits of her mother and brother. She has clear ideas and strong beliefs that she is willing to express and follow. Without compromising her principles, she demonstrates by her example the way, if not to salvation, at least to the reconciliation of conscience with reality. Maria, surrounded by unstable and mutually suspicious characters, is the only balanced and trusted person in the novel. She is loving and lovable, a dreamer, but also practical and efficient. Her tenderness is not weakness, though it betrays her soft womanly substance; her power is not masculine, but the result of clear, balanced thinking and steady, lofty principles. Her confinement and other misfortunes at times make her nervous and irritable, stubborn and brooding; but soon she is sweet and compassionate again, ready for sacrifices, understanding, and leadership. Maria Galanis might be considered a redeeming conscience in a world of frustration, disenchantment, and resentment.

The mother, always sick and secluded, is preoccupied with a falsely glorified past and her narrow, unfulfilled ambitions. She accepts her misery with pretended dignity. But in her meek, motherly way, she governs her children's lives, silently but effectively restricting their desires and actions.

Many other persons revolve around the three main characters in *Captives*. Sometimes they comment upon the life of the Galanis family much as the chorus of an ancient Greek tragedy. But more often they appear as conscious or unconscious causes of the events that befall the family, as instruments of a dire fate that gradually and inevitably engulfs its victims. One may particularly note Kalotyhis, the sympathetic friend of Fotos, kindly, unlucky, and subdued, clumsy but heart-warming; Sarmides, the corrupt and discredited officer of the army, arrogant and lusty, impudent and fiendish; and Eva, the young girl of bewitching beauty, a kind of *femme fatale*, perhaps more fatal to herself than to the men pursuing her.

In writing *Captives*, Terzakis attained his basic intention, which was, according to one critic: "To express the decomposition of Greece's old patriarchal small-bourgeoisie that did not succeed in entering into the rhythm of the times and was dissolved, heavily wounded in its moral and financial life."[4]

After this impressive beginning, Terzakis consolidated his leading position among the Greek novelists of his generation with his second novel, *The Decline of Skleroi* (1933). It is the tragic story of the strange Skleros family, which consists of a mother and two sons who vainly strive to run away from self-destruction. The father, deceased many years earlier, had been a wealthy, aristocratic playboy in his time, who in his middle-age had married a rather rich girl of lower class, but had continued his dissolute life until his death, never caring about his family. The mother, a taciturn but ambitious and domineering woman, pietistic and superstitious, thinking that she alone embodies the "high and correct spirit" of the Skleros family, tries, unsuccessfully, to restore its past glory by instilling its aristocratic elements in her two sons. Her love goes to Andreas, the older son, and she subdues and almost despises Stefanos, the younger son, whom she keeps secluded in a room in their mansion. However, both sons revolt against their mother—Andreas openly and wildly, Stefanos meekly and in isolation. They are well aware of the profligate life of their dead father and are repulsed by it; however, they also sense that they cannot escape his eroding character, which still lives in them and governs their instincts. A specter of doom hovers over them relentlessly.

Andreas, a powerful but strange personality, moody and impulsive, spends his life aimlessly, first in the unfortunate Greek-Turkish War, and later in Europe. Haunted by a sense of guilt for his father's sins, he returns to Athens even more bitter and grim, erratic in behavior and self-consuming. The secluded Stefanos, wanting to assert his manhood, frees himself and elopes with a middle-aged woman. His mother, ashamed of the "scandal" and eager to preserve the "honor" and prestige of her family, proclaims him legally insane. Andreas, indifferent to all and submerged in his own moral agony and chaotic state of mind, at first does not pay any attention to Stefanos' affair; but, at the repeated requests of his brother, he visits him at his hiding place. There Stefanos, sarcastic, offensive, and self-humiliating, provokes his brother and insults him, calling him as rotten as himself, and as doomed and useless. In a moment of self-recognition and self-contempt, Andreas kills his brother, almost believing that he has killed himself, his inner, rotten self. Their mother, a respectable member of society, goes to the police and charges Andreas with the murder of her younger son. The decline of the Skleros family finally reaches its lowest point.

Plot is not the important element in *The Decline of Skleroi*. The events are few and serve only to underline the decomposition of soul, the disintegration of ego. Conflict is expressed not so much in deeds as in grudging behavior and repugnant disposition. And, as all the characters are wracked by their self-made woes, their self-respect and self-reliance disintegrate; they almost gloat over their self-destruction. For them salvation is their mutual annihilation.

From the technical point of view, the composition of this novel is flawless; its structure, solid; and its analysis and characterization, penetrating. Its depressing theme is presented in a clear, well-balanced, nearly captivating narration, which is filled with keen observations, profound thoughts, and poetical touches. The charming, though ominous, chapter on love, fittingly entitled "Symposium," is an interlude of lyrical realism and painful insight.

Angelos Terzakis analyzes the souls of his characters mercilessly, revealing their conscious and subconscious thoughts and feelings, and especially the uncontrolled hatred that corrodes their inner selves much more than those whom they hate. "Every man is an abyss, and you get dizzy looking into it," George Buechner once said. When that abyss is full of hellish flames and demonic afflictions such as those haunting the souls of the Skleroi, the dizziness becomes unbearable. Andreas Skleros is especially caught up in the degradation of his time and his family. He frequently abandons himself, in a stream-of-consciousness way, to piercing self-analysis; what he finds, or imagines he finds, within himself is horrendous. As he ponders over the world around him, he finds only the putrid and the repulsive. The child of his degenerate time and the wretched progeny of a perverted family that quickly deteriorates into moral and physiological decay, he inevitably heads for destruction, death, and annihilation. There are moments, however, when he is gentle and decent, when he longs for love and understanding, and is ready to reciprocate. But the evil circle into which he is drawn is too powerful to be overcome by short-lived sentimentalities. Andreas is a tragic, tormented conscience of inherited and acquired abominations.

In his third novel, *The Violet City* (1937), Terzakis again deals with family relations during the interwar period. Although he attempts to put his new story and its ordinary, unassuming characters in a brighter, somewhat more joyous light, he still cannot entirely escape the nightmare of the oppressive reality that weighs heavily upon them. The misery of lower-middle-class people, the drudgery of their everyday life, and the shallowness of their inner life do not create an appropriate climate for an affirmation and appreciation of life, much less for true salvation. Most of the characters of the novel are good but weak and ineffectual people, inclined to compromise their values and to be subservient; a few are arrogant souls, destined to blind calamity. Some let themselves become instruments for the desires of others, fully aware of their inferior position; although they maintain an air of painful indifference, they often display dignity in their degradation. It is as if they say: "What is the use of pretending to be a hero? . . . It is so destined for us by fate." But this fate is of their own making as much as a result of circumstances. They are defeated even before they start—and they realize this. They cannot react effectively because their reactions are spasmodic, unmethodical, and desperate. Their efforts to escape the iron cage that they have built around themselves are doomed to failure.

There is another element, however, in this novel: the lurking presence of the growing city of Athens, the violet city. Yesterday it was still a large village; today it is suddenly a huge metropolis, a cosmopolitan center of powerful and dangerous enticement. This new city looms in the background, dynamic and menacing, a symbol of the ever-changing reality that affects people in different and not always beneficial ways. For instance, one of the main characters of *The Violet City*, the naïve old lawyer Meletis Malvis, averred that the growing city of Athens was a witch who lured her victims to destruction. He had devoted his life to establishing a profession and raising a family. For decades he had remained almost fossilized, unaware of the multiple changes around him. Only when disaster struck him did he discover that the friendly small city of yesterday had been transformed into a vast, inimical space of unknown dangers. And, being simple-minded, he blamed the city for his predicaments.

The main story of *The Violet City* revolves around the Malvis family. Malvis had married a very beautiful, haughty girl who, yearning for the "great expensive life," eventually runs away with her wealthy lover. Malvis, deserted by his wife, strives to bring up their two children. The daughter is a sweet, plain girl, sensitive and sensible. But the son, Orestes, is arrogant and conceited. He constantly alienates and humiliates his father by his disrespectful behavior and excessive demands. Meletis Malvis patiently bears the humiliation, secretly hoping that one day he might win his son's confidence and esteem, if not his love, and bequeath him his law office. But when Orestes receives his law degree, he runs away from home to join his mother, who has just returned to Athens after many years of silence. Meletis, wrecked for a second time, tries in vain to win back his son. Sick and heartbroken, he withers away in pain and despair. On his deathbed, however, he has the meager satisfaction of seeing his faithful and loving daughter united with a young man who has recently become his assistant at the office. At least a pretense of family might live on.

The subplots of the novel accentuate the poignancy of the central story. The people around the main characters live their own drama, in sympathy or malice, in active participation or passive indifference. They are common people themselves, sharing as onlookers or participants the painful experiences of the Malvis family, which in one way or another mirror their own static life. Meletis Malvis desperately struggles to maintain a cheerful appearance before the searching eyes of malevolent or kind neighbors and acquaintances. But the silent drama of alienation of feelings and of the open hostility of his wife and son unfolds, heightening the futility of any endeavor for an agreeable and viable settlement.

Angelos Terzakis became a master of the art of the novel with *The Violet City*. The design, composition, and narrative craftsmanship of this novel are exemplary. The style, always lucid and plain when presenting present reality, becomes delicate, almost poetic at times, particularly in certain sensitive, suggestive scenes. The realistic symbolism that strongly permeates the atmosphere of his two earlier novels is much less intense in *The Violet City*. It recurs only intermittently in gentle tones of serene imagery.

Terzakis' first three novels are important landmarks in his literary career and a positive contribution to the modern Greek novel. From the very beginning, his genuine ability in creative narration, his compassionate understanding of the plight of his fellow man, his searching mind, his sincerity of purpose, and frankness of expression marked the seriousness of his endeavor. His constant efforts to eliminate the unessential and to concentrate on structure and characterization soon enabled him to master the technical discipline of the novel form. These efforts gave him confidence and impetus to explore new paths. His sensitivity to and awareness of the agonizing problems of his time—especially those affecting individuals in family groups—make his novels a mirror of his time and the voice of an almost ignored and deserted segment of the people after World War I. Common people, striving to assert themselves despite hostile and depressing conditions, roam vividly and colorfully through his novels. Contradictory and unstable characters accentuate the futility and frustration deeply felt by man during those uncertain and shaky years. Finally, the family constitutes the nucleus of his work. His main concern is to observe and analyze family problems in a rapidly changing society.

Terzakis' first three novels portray a segment of life in his time. This portrayal is certainly accurate and powerful, but of limited horizons. Thus Terzakis, at this high point in his career, seemed, according to certain of his critics, to be compressed between the agony of his time and the narrowness of his themes. But those who were eager to downgrade him did not take into account his perceptive mind, his power of renewal, and his ability to respond to the urgent needs of his times.

For this reason, in the eyes of his critics, his next step in fiction was, to say the least, unexpected: From his previous tormented viewing of a portion of contemporary miserable life, he plunged into the heroic action of the historical novel, which he also endowed with the burning issues of his day. Certainly, his interest in history had already been displayed in some of his plays,[5] but nothing portended his employment of history on such a large scale in the novel. Yet, he turned to medieval history for his next book, and the result of his endeavor was a vast, historical novel, *Princess Izambeau* (1945). This work proved to be not an attempt, but a great accomplishment, in historical fiction. With its publication Terzakis brought the modern Greek novel to the classical sources of the historical novel. It is an epic in prose, an objective (as far as any novel can remain objective) narrative of past heroic events that border on myth and legend. Thus, diffuse legend is interwoven with historical truth; a sequence of living pictures freely and imaginatively re-creates historically fixed life. Yet the writer of historical novels is not alienated from contemporary life. On the contrary, the good historical novelist projects current issues, problems, and aspirations into the types and forms of the past. Without losing its epic character and conception, a good historical novel speaks for its time and sometimes envisions solutions of current problems. Moreover, the modern historical novel forsakes the serene view of the world usually characteristic of epic poems. The novelist's lyrical tones and his experiential, personal inner world enrich the

91

historical novel. Trenchant realism mitigates the romantic element; fanciful legend enhances the realism.

In both subject matter and form *Princess Izambeau* fulfills these prerequisites of a historical, heroic novel. Numerous exciting episodes that sustain and enliven the main action and admirably widen and illuminate the period's setting enrich the novel's fine, interesting plot. Its structure is solid, well planned, and perfectly executed. Its people are clearly and vividly depicted in their gradual evolution as full-fledged characters that struggle to hold a constant position despite the fluidity of life. The period and place—the end of the thirteenth century in the Peloponnesus, which is under Frankish occupation—are imaginatively and faithfully depicted.

Terzakis states the central theme in a brief introductory note which he, like the troubadours of old, addresses to the indulgence of his readers:

I shall narrate to you a very old chronicle, the wondrous adventures of the young gentle-born Nikephoros Sgouros from Anapli: how he fled, a fugitive, from his native land, how he struggled with his fate on land and sea, and how he waged war against a woman. The times that I wish to revive are of long ago; the voices that sang their glory are silent, and not even dust remains from the bones of the people who lived then. But I, a scribe, poor and exiled in this savage era, shall do whatever I can to please you as I give speech to the soundless past. And so, my kind sirs, may your goodness and tolerance forgive my errors that have escaped me and the shortcomings that I understand but did not have the skill to correct.

The general plot is much more complicated than his introduction indicates; the picture he draws is much wider and more comprehensive. A whole world of individuals and groups moves, acts, and lives around Nikephoros Sgouros and his secretly beloved but open enemy, Princess Izambeau. They love, hate, fight, die, revolt, trade, conspire, work, play, cry, laugh, toil, and suffer. They are nobles and commoners, knights and serfs, peasants and seamen, pirates and rebels, heroes and cowards, rich men and paupers, laymen and clergy, men and women. They represent all classes and all professions.

Princess Izambeau offers a vast, lively, and well-balanced picture of the Peloponnesus—indeed of the entire Greek world—during the Middle Ages, when foreign conquerors and intriguers, Franks, Venetians, and others, were trampling the country. The passive and active efforts of the Greek people to shake off the brutal foreign yoke occupy a great portion of the novel. In a sequence of color-ful, dramatic scenes, the struggle, particularly of the *rovolatores* (the guerrilla fighters of the time), is vividly displayed. There are also many superb, though horrible, scenes describing the famine and plague that befell the unfortunate people of the Peloponnesus during the Frankish occupation. One may presume that the recent occupation of Greece during World War II (when the novel was completed) gave Terzakis the motivation to write his medieval novel and provided the fresh, firsthand material that he painfully but skillfully incorporated into it. Indeed, *Princess Izambeau* is a responsible act of the author commensurate with the urgent prob-lems of that time in Greece. The tragic and brave experience of the nation and Terzakis in facing the hardships of the occupation and the ensuing liberation is artfully channeled into the remote medieval period, warming it and making it alive and convincing. At times this historical novel not only provides the pleasure of a re-mote and curious past, full of romantic adventures and myth, but becomes a powerful and meaningful message for contemporary life. It accomplishes that without any adulteration of its artistic essence or degeneration into didacticism. Terzakis is too competent an artist to sermonize, and too human to stray far from life. Just as he is able to keep his reader's interest alive (a noteworthy achieve-ment in a book of 530 densely printed pages), so, too, is he able, without intruding, to keep the reader's mind awake by projecting into past situations those problems and ideas that occupy con-temporary man and demand solution. The epic latitude of historical fiction allows him to put some of those issues comfortably into the history of the past. *Princess Izambeau* is one of the truly felicitous examples of modern Greek literature, an unmatched masterpiece of historical fiction, a classic of its kind.[6]

Terzakis' choice for his next novel was perhaps somewhat curious, but not altogether unexpected. His *Voyage with Hesperus* (1946), an exquisite novel about the life, thoughts, and experiences of young people, is one of the best examples of a new trend then introduced by some of the leading writers of the thirties: the novel of adolescence, especially as reminiscences or objective observa-tion and reflection. Some critics labeled the novelists' preoccupa-tion with and turning to reminiscences, the reminiscences of child-hood and adolescence in particular, as an attempt to escape from the harshness of contemporary life. Perhaps this is true, but "escape" was not the only reason. Much more significant was the desire of these novelists to apply their creative powers to a field of life that had previously been used only occasionally in modern Greek literature. They sought to present adolescence in a poetical atmosphere in which dream and reality become inseparable. Critics have also suggested that Alain Fournier's *Le Grande Meaulnes* (which appeared in 1913 and was translated into English as *The Wanderer* in 1928) exerted considerable influence upon the Greek novelists. Again, this might be so. But each of the Greek novelists used his material very differently than Fournier had, and they eventually produced some of the best novels of modern Greek literature, poetical in substance and far-reaching in disposition. For example, Cosmas Polites' *Eroica* is an epic poem of adolescence; Elias Venezis' *Aeolia* is a nostalgic poem of youth longing for a lost country; and Terzakis' *Voyage with Hesperus* is "an anguished metaphysical poem"[7] of youth. It shows, among other things, the first baptism of adolescents into philosophical thinking through exposure to the harsh questions of life, love, and passion.

Time and circumstances limit the main action of the narrative in *Voyage with Hesperus*. But the novel's esoteric projection, its dreamy world of thought and feeling, and its dynamic symbolism transcend the events described. Glafcos, a sensitive and pensive youth, goes to a lonely country place for his summer vacation. There he lives as close to nature as he can, devotes a great deal of time to contemplation and dreaming, and cautiously makes some acquaintances of his own age. Through them he meets a strange, secluded family and becomes particularly attached to Danae, their oldest daughter, who is a very beautiful and self-assertive young girl. Glafcos and Danae are both strong personalities, intellectually and emotionally combative, and impetuous, but, when necessary, coolheaded and coldhearted. They fall in love, meet secretly under strange and dangerous conditions, and consummate their love in a wave of dreamy passion and unruffled consciousness, in bitter pain and celestial sublimation. With the end of Glafcos' vacation, their magic voyage with the evening star ends on a gloomy note of unfulfillment and bitter-sweet experience.

In *Voyage with Hesperus* Terzakis respects his youthful heroes, their life and thought. He does not handle them condescendingly as mere children, but as distinct human beings. All of them have their own clearly defined personalities, although they do not lose the fluidity of their formative adolescent years. Their thinking, es-

94

pecially that of Glafcos and his anonymous male friend, may appear much more mature than what is usually considered appropriate for their age, but it is presented with enough particulars that one cannot doubt its credibility. In any case, if we, the elders, transfer ourselves to that golden period, we will find that we had (or believed that we had) such or similar thoughts in our youth. Danae, Glafcos, and his anonymous friend in Athens with whom he corresponds fight both separately and together, and with rare seriousness and intensity, to formulate in words and deeds their ideals of life. They are searching and contesting their views. They experiment with them, innocently and gracefully, painfully and ruthlessly. With each turn, their life and thoughts crystallize, and the mystery of their exuberant existence becomes more acute. For instance, did the anonymous friend of Glafcos really live the life that he claimed to live, or was it only a figment of his feverish imagination? Was Danae really the friend's first fatal love or was it only after he became aware of Glafcos' love for her that he seized the opportunity to take her away from Glafcos, to make him "unwilling to live," as he cynically wrote and told him? Was he really a great expert on life, or was he simply living in a world of fantasy and illusion? The reader may fashion the peculiar, anonymous boy at his discretion, projecting him or shrinking him. This is the charm and poetry of this character. He substituted, perhaps, the dream of a fantastically rich experience and the seeming strength of an excessively solid and bold intellect for the bitterness of his reduced and miserable personal life.

The secondary characters, young and old alike, are also convincingly painted. Their lives and personalities harmoniously entwine with the explosive course of the young heroes' lives: Aunt Suzanne, with her affected aristocratic and cosmopolitan manners, her austere outlook and limited horizons; the Pitsilas couple, the mother, a naïve *nouveau-riche* peasant who vainly tries to imitate the delicate manners of the upper class, and her husband, a physician who confined himself in the province and falsified his life as well as his medical science; their children, accessories to the strong will of Glafcos; the long-suffering colonel who, petrified by his resentment against the outside world, lives a secluded, bitter life and nearly drags his children down with him, although his affection for them is great, sincere, and protective; the charming grandmother who has known and experienced a great deal but even now is alert and cheerful; and, finally, the death-stricken old Pigi, who

95

bears her grief stoically and treats the others with understanding, devotion, and kindness—a simple woman whose intuition is uncanny and whose heart is expansive. All of them, through their deeds and posture, affect the development of the psychological attitudes of the young characters and offer something, positive or negative, to their molding.

Vincent Starrett once wrote: "When some of the best writers in the world remember their childhood with, as it were, the eyes of youth, the result is invariably some of the world's best literature." In some ways, Terzakis' *Voyage with Hesperus* belongs in this category.

Without God (1951) is, in substance and character, very much akin to the first three novels written by Terzakis, but it is broader in scope and vision, covering unusually diverse groups and dealing with problems of general interest for the period. Again, it is a vivid, composite picture of the troubled years between the two world wars. But it concentrates on the disappointments and disillusionments of the young generation in particular, their lack of faith, and their vain search for something to believe in and to pursue.

The hero of *Without God*, Michael Paradisis, has a gentle and liberal interest in the amelioration of society, a loving heart, and a probing mind ready to analyze, criticize, and revolt against established ideas, conditions, and men. He is easily pulled into the hasty and hazy revolutionary streams of the twenties. At first Paradisis is fertile soil for the Communistic slogans of liberty and justice. He zealously tries to disseminate and apply them. His critical mind, however, is not fully satisfied; his penchant for independent thought makes him suspicious of and suspected by professional revolutionaries—a situation that is very painful for him. His moral and intellectual integrity is deeply hurt. This disappointment and his timidity and restraint in a love affair make him flee Athens. He moves to the country where he establishes a rather prosperous farm and lives peacefully for some years. But, when his brother dies, Paradisis feels morally obliged to return to Athens to become the guardian of his brother's two children. In Athens he devotes himself totally and unselfishly to their welfare and proper upbringing. But, just as all the efforts of the interwar period failed to find a faith, failed to create a lasting peace, all Paradisis' efforts to form these two young individuals into ideal, or even ordinary, human beings fail tragically. Paradisis, the unfortunate dreamer of happiness and dignity, falls under the vicious attack of one of the children the very day of the outbreak of World War II.

Without God vividly presents the social, political, and financial instability, the moral corrosion, and the intellectual agony of the generation of the twenties and thirties: a lost generation, angry and unforgiving, a generation without God—not only without the God of Christians, but without any god, any belief. As Robert Kiely once observed, the characters in some contemporary novels "cannot forgive their own weaknesses and therefore cannot conceive of a God who would. . . . Surrounded by beasts of prey and cast in roles they are unfit for, these men turn inward and seek in the mind an order and safety the natural universe seems not to provide."[8] But even those who professed belief in some current ideology soon became halfhearted in their enthusiasm for this ideology and felt misguided. The spiritual vacuum was terrible. In that disintegrating atmosphere, some people hunted chimeras, others fell into despair, and still others meekly conformed to the drudgery of a mediocre life. But all awoke one day to discover that they were living under an illusion. When the illusion vanished, it was too late for them to avoid failure.

Discontented yet active dreamers, repulsive opportunists, chaste and proud souls, greedy and lewd characters, sound, broad-minded but ineffectual men, indifferent and inactive fatalists, and the multicolored, vivacious, unpredictable masses all move and live naturally in this great picture of Greek life—indeed of life everywhere—during the years between the wars. Yet the reader understands that, as Kavafis said, "there is no ship for you, there is no road" for salvation. War is inevitable, but is it the proper solution?

In *Without God,* as in all his works, Terzakis depicts his characters with clarity and precision. He builds them gradually—often using the techniques of flashback and self-analysis—through their thoughts and deeds, in the process of life, in their dramatic conflicts with each other. They are neither black nor white; each of them is a subtle combination of contrasting ingredients. Terzakis is a master in revealing the different hues and elements that comprise the actual character of a person. He does not merely describe the surface of life, but dissects life with compassion and perception, and re-creates it with feeling, imagination, and insight. Perhaps this is the reason Terzakis felt the agony of his time so acutely, was so fascinated or, as certain of his critics maintain, so obsessed by it that he was compelled to depict it with such urgency in most of his works. Be that as it may, Terzakis is really the voice of his time: anguished, yes, but clear, provocative, and truthful.

A side issue in *Without God* is the total sacrifice of oneself in helping and protecting others. A poignant variation of this issue constituted the main theme of an earlier work by Terzakis, his powerful novella, *Affection* (1944), in which he examines in depth the moral issue of disinterested devotion and unselfish self-sacrifice. He did not attempt to solve it or to provide answers. He was primarily interested in presenting in sharp relief the psychological aspects of the problem as it is experienced by true-to-life characters.

In the six novels examined above, Terzakis generally follows the rules of the conventional "classical" novel, in both form and subject matter. He soon mastered those rules; thus he was able to create novels that are faithful to the genre but that also have his personal seal distinctly imprinted upon them. His first three novels are undoubtedly concrete achievements for the modern Greek novel. The next three, *Voyage with Hesperus, Without God,* and the incomparable *Princess Izambeau,* are mature works that transcend national boundaries and place Terzakis among the world's leading contemporary novelists. But Terzakis, the alert, observing, and daring writer that he is, does not acquiesce in his success. Always ready to try something new, he constantly strives to improve his art.

This is especially evident in his latest novel, *Mystic Life* (1957), which, from a technical point of view, is a different type of novel both in form and subject matter. At first glance, *Mystic Life* seems to lack a discernible plot, an over-all myth, or a conceived design. But the author planned it that way. This intentional departure from the established order, from the norms of orthodox form and composition in the novel, proved successful, as were similar attempts by other modern novelists elsewhere. *Mystic Life* is an exceptionally powerful work of free narration, an uninhibted creation of subjective and objective reality presented in depth and with insight. It is revolutionary in structure and contemporary in substance. In its seemingly disjointed form, it tries to mirror the fragmentation of modern man's conscience.

The story of *Mystic Life,* the hero's unfinished manuscript which was written at irregular intervals of time, is narrated in the first-person singular. Past and present events, thoughts, and feelings are intermixed and interwoven in a painful and charming fabric of scattered dreams and shattered realities. The anonymous hero frequently expresses himself in a stream-of-consciousness style, reveals the depths of his soul, and in an unorderly but psychologically natural fashion relates whatever comes from his conscious and subconscious world: real impressions from his early or present life as well as mere figments of his imagination. He constantly pries into his own self and into the general mystery of human behavior. Faced with inconsistencies and contradictions, he seeks ultimate answers to the phenomenon of life. As one critic has said in reference to other contemporary novels: "Instead of living for the immediacy of the moment or living with the concreteness of the real thing, he looks for comfort in ultimates and abstractions."[9] Sometimes he willfully abandons himself to the rudeness of actualities, but more often he retreats into painful self-examination and the poetical world of dreams and illusions. His fierce, almost agonizing, search for truth, his inability to communicate his real self to others, and his refusal to accept reality become the tragic and ironic toil of his life. His futile effort to assert his extreme position often turns into self-deprecation and irony, self-disdain and sarcasm, reflecting equally upon himself and upon contemporary society in general.

Yet there is an exceptional person who might meet his high requirements and fulfill his most cherished ideals. She is Vena, an extraordinary woman who can match him in intellectual and psychic capacity, in inner experience, in uncompromising principles and attitudes. She is a tragic, mysterious, almost sacred person, capable of affection but aloof from life—a striking combination of cruel logic and tender feelings. But, as one critic rightly observed:

The inability to compromise with reality leads to the inability to understand each other. . . . The culmination of the tragedy, is that the hero and heroine of this fiction, who are made for each other, did not succeed in finding their common point of contact, in catching that decisive moment that would lead them to the longed-for union.[10]

But these two exceptional characters are not yearning for ordinary happiness, which they deem an "unbearable" condition, but for expiation and salvation through pain. Thus they finally drift apart and must submit separately to their painful destiny of unfulfilled intentions.

The surrounding characters, with their personal problems and trivial interests, their intense conflicts and conventional ideas, underline the tragedy of Vena and the anonymous hero. The personalities of the other characters are gradually constructed and securely placed in context, although the fluidity and cheapness of their purposes betray their basic insecurity. It is primarily for this latter reason that the hero-narrator, in his vain attempt to comprehend and define the purpose of mankind, directs much of his searing sarcasm at them, although, as mentioned earlier, he does not spare himself. Moreover, through the adventures and misadventures of those ordinary people, and their entanglement with the two heroes, the social and psychological scope of the novel is expanded. Through them *Mystic Life* assumes a kind of concreteness that is not appropriate for the two leading characters. Indeed, the narrator and Vena would have been better suited to an environment beyond this world, a mythical creation of their own. The antagonizing presence of these conventional people forces Vena and the narrator into bitter contact with reality. Thus, the manuscript that started as the narrator's hazy personal confession ("secret self-confession," one is tempted to say) becomes a wide, lively picture of tangible reality as well.

The interchange and interweaving of regressive daydreaming, keen observation of life, psychological insight, and poignant actuality provide *Mystic Life* with a suggestive power that projects it beyond its boundaries as fiction. The author's brilliant, consummate craftsmanship and his skillful, artistic handling of the theme are evident throughout. The style is rich and accurate, lucid and suggestive, poetical and dense; but at times it becomes light and familiar, capturing the matter-of-fact tone of everyday speech.

Terzakis' *Mystic Life* is, in substance and form, a modern novel of the highest rank and merits the attention of a wide and well-informed audience.

K. Th. Demaras, a sober, cautious historian of modern Greek literature, made the following comments about Terzakis' technical achievements in the novel:

In Angelos Terzakis we find the most austere novelistic conscience of modern Greek literature. The will of narration in his work is first, and he excels in it. All the powers of the writer, images, descriptions, dialogues, tend exclusively to the same end: the creation of an atmosphere that justifies and imposes the plot's course. His inventions are wise, his characters are delineated in clarity and probability. His language is not shining, nor his phrase dense. But his works move in a consistent world that is tight and compact and attains aesthetic sympathy. His dialogue has realism, ease, and natural articulation.[11]

Another eminent critic and active participant in the regeneration of modern Greek literature since the thirties, Andreas Karandonis, summarized his opinion of Terzakis as follows:

The work of Angelos Terzakis, based as it is on the solid talent of a builder who knows how to fuse every element into a coherent whole, is a landmark in the development of the modern Greek novel. His extraordinary sensitivity is capable of analyzing itself and of suffering the trials of its heroes. His is the conscience of a deeply cultivated man who feels acutely the problems of his time. And he adds to this a psychological insight equal to the task of anatomizing the suffering, the unsatisfied, the divided humanity which constitutes, in many ways, the spirit of our century.[12]

Indeed, the two main characteristics of Terzakis are his mastery of the art of fiction and his intense and sincere interest in the issues of his time. Sensitive, soulful, compassionate, with a well-organized mind and a rare ability for creative expression, he became the genuine voice of his time, the conscience of his generation. He faced the challenge of his time with understanding and resolution. The wasteland in which humanity existed between the two wars and the psychologically and morally oppressive climate of that period were a reality that Terzakis could not and did not wish to escape. The agony and despondence that dominate much of Terzakis' work were the by-product of those confused years. Although he was constantly attacked by critics for his preoccupation with agony and despondence, Terzakis remained true to his time, understood its problems, and spoke clearly and sincerely, though painfully, about it in his novels. As Dorothy Van Ghent has said, "First, novels have their primary interest in the illumination they cast upon life, not life somewhere else and at another time, but immediately here, immediately now. And second, novels are able to cast illumination upon life only insofar as they are coherent works of art."[13] Terzakis' novels exemplify these simple truths. He does not profess, however, to be a social reformer. Having incorporated into himself the bitter experience of his heroes, he simply records his impressions with penetrating insight, clarity, and authority, and leaves the reader to reflect upon possible answers.

From time to time Terzakis has introduced innovations into his art, but these innovations in subject matter and form were not made for the sake of uniqueness and novelty, or for the purpose of serving the precepts of any literary or other "school." For him innovation consists always in an intentional effort to achieve a more accurate understanding and expression of reality. He has always done what he was convinced a dynamic novelist must do to keep pace with his time. In this regard, Terzakis recently commented to me:

My opinion about the novel is neither conservative nor revolutionary. I think that in *Mystic Life* I have made some evolution in comparison with my earlier works, but I still preserve the persons-characters and a very free, fluid myth. I believe that in the novel the person must have a delineation, be it even fluid—a delineation that differentiates the person from the shadows and the inanimate objects. I admit that in life there are no "characters" with absolute, unbending qualities; I have always propounded the contradictoriness of inner man; but I maintain that man, the individual, is a personality that is a concrete soul, determined by the coordinates of space and time. I believe that the contemporary dissolution of every form in the novel conceals an organic weakness in the purely creative area: Alien elements have invaded the novel—lyrical, theoretical, visionary, metaphysical—and have dissolved it so that they may appropriate it; and of course the spirit of fashion makes for great havoc. The result is that they have driven away the reader of literature, the genuine one, not the snob. The novel must have affability, humaneness; it must come to welcome the good reader, not distress him and repel him.[14]

Furthermore, Terzakis does not belong to any "school," nor has he created one. Of course, he is well acquainted with both old and new schools, but he has not been overwhelmed by any—even though some of his critics have spoken of Hamsun and Dostoevski, Voutiras and Hatzopoulos, and others as influencing him in either subject matter or form.[15] In any case, as Andrew Lytle wrote: "Realism, naturalism, impressionism, existentialism—all those . . . remain signposts, showing the way only towards the discovery of the individual talent, which is there to be read for itself, for its unique contribution, not as evidence of a school."[16] And Terzakis' work is, to paraphrase Lytle, eloquent evidence of his individual talent as a novelist who has made a unique contribution to the modern Greek novel in particular, and to the contemporary novel in general.

Terzakis is an extremely gifted narrator of stories that match the urgency of our times and thus are perfectly adapted to what contemporary life demands of an artist. Again, as Lytle has said, "Anybody with a narrative gift can tell some kind of a story: the successful artist tells the one story the circumstances and actors demand."[17] Angelos Terzakis has, as perhaps no other Greek novelist of his generation, the power to create a concrete, emotional, or suggestive scene, to dramatize sharp moral and personal conflicts, to reveal the insight and thoughts of his characters in the appropriate environment, to make the ordinary interesting, to employ aesthetic techniques skillfully in order to attract and hold his reader and to force him to live his heroes' experiences in a powerful narrative of sincerity, passion, and reflection.

REFERENCES

1. The famous modern Greek novelist, Nikos Kazantzakis, is not mentioned among the novelists of the thirties because he does not belong to their generation: First, he was much older than they were, and second, all his novels were written much later, in the years 1946-1957.

2. Angelos Terzakis was born in Nauplion in 1907. Although he studied law at the University of Athens, he has devoted himself to literature since his early years. When he was very young, he published two volumes of short stories and edited two short-lived literary magazines; since 1963, he has been editor of the monthly, *Epochs*. Besides his first two books, he has published two more volumes of short stories, one novella, seven novels, ten plays, one volume of essays, and one historical narrative. He has been regular contributor on literary themes to many magazines and newspapers. His plays were produced with great success by the leading theatrical organizations in Greece, and two of them by university groups in America. Since 1937, he has been in the service of the National Theater of Greece in various capacities, as secretary, director, instructor, and general manager.

3. I. M. Panagiotopoulos, *Persons and Texts*, Vol. II (Athens, 1943; in Greek), p. 124.

4. G. Theotokas, in a review of Terzakis' novel, *Idea*, Vol. I, No. 3 (March, 1933; in Greek), p. 199.

5. Of course, Terzakis' theatrical work cannot be discussed here—useful and enlightening as such a comparative study might be. But there is no doubt that Terzakis the novelist has profited much from the experience of Terzakis the playwright, especially in character delineation, in dialogue, in the dramatic handling of situations, in condensation of issues and scenes, and in creating atmosphere. It may also be added this his accomplishments in the theater equal his achievements in the novel.

6. *Princess Izambeau* has already been translated into Swedish, and is now being translated into Romanian, Russian, and Spanish.

7. A. Karandonis, *Prose-Writers and Prose-Writings of the Generation of the Thirties* (Athens, 1962; in Greek), p. 211.

8. Robert Kiely, "The Craft of Despondency—The Traditional Novelists," *Dædalus*, Vol. 92 (Spring, 1963), pp. 230-31.

9. Harry Levin, "Apogee and Aftermath of the Novel," *Dædalus, op. cit.*, p. 218.

10. Yiannis Hatzinis, *Preferences* (Athens, 1963; in Greek), pp. 47 f.

11. K. Th. Demaras, *History of Modern Greek Literature*, Vol. II (Athens, 1949; in Greek), p. 201.

12. From "A Critical Mosaic" about Terzakis in *The Charioteer*, Vol. I, No. 4 (1962), p. 54.

13. Dorothy Van Ghent, *The English Novel. Form and Function* (New York, 1961), p. vii.

14. From a letter of Terzakis, May 18, 1966. Terzakis has frequently written essays and critiques on the novel in general, on the modern Greek novel or individual novelists in particular. His early essay, "The Modern Greek Novel," published in consecutive issues of *Idea* (Vol. I, 1933), is still today of basic importance to the serious student of the modern Greek novel.

15. He himself in the letter mentioned above states: "I have always believed in the genuinely great novelists: Walter Scott, Dickens, Balzac, Flaubert, Zola, Tolstoi, Dostoevski, Proust. Perhaps Flaubert and Dostoevski have influenced me the most. But I have never imitated. I have always acted according to my opinion—only, you see, that there are organic affinities also."

16. Andrew Lytle, "Impressionism, The Ego, and The First Person," *Dædalus, op. cit.*, p. 281.

17. *Ibid.*, p. 289.

CZESLAW MILOSZ

The Novel in Poland

The Editor
Dædalus

Dear Sir:
 You asked me to write on the novel in Poland. I gave just an outline, no more than sketchy information. You may wonder why my piece is dry to the extent that one is unable to guess my own personal views on the subject. I feel I should explain my reticence.
 On the contemporary novel written in Polish or in any other language, I have very little to say. I am confused and would like to see people who are not confused. There are some portents that should not be overlooked. Starting with my own reactions, I have to force myself to read a novel as if warned in advance by the boredom emanating from the devices one knows so well. To my surprise, I have discovered that many young Americans, if I may judge by Berkeley students, avoid novels, even if they are quite zealous readers of poetry, essays, and philosophy. Is it not significant that the only fad in fiction on the Berkeley campus has been of late (besides Candy) *fantasies of Tolkien, which hardly fit what is generally meant by "a novel"? In Poland today, the novel is certainly not considered a dominating genre. I sense in this a curious parallelism, a sign, perhaps, of a too much scorned* Zeitgeist.
 Good luck to novelists. I have written two novels: one bad, hastily jotted down for an international contest (which I won); another, probably not quite so bad, praised by readers, who accepted it as a kind of autobiographical story of my childhood in the woods of Lithuania. It seems to me that my readers' penchant toward interpreting it as "authentic" (while it is rather an exercise in disguised metaphysics) should be a lesson. They yearn after Daddy Defoe. Is it not so, that he set the pace forever and that any attempt to go beyond a "true story" and a "true romance" is doomed to failure? In any case, if what is good in my novel (Dolina Issy—

Tal der Issa *in German,* Sur les bords de l'Issa *in French) is a result of my training as a poet, why should I write novels? I am interested in capturing whatever can be captured of a large Whole, not in inventing situations.*

Another confession. I like to read books on the novel, such as L'Histoire du roman moderne *by R. M. Alberès. Here, I touch upon a shameful, unconfessed spot in the consciousness of modern man. He prefers books on the novel, on poetry, or on drama, to the novels, poems, or dramas themselves. Is he wrong? Not necessarily. His meditation on the changeability of styles and beliefs, let us call it anthropological meditation, is more vast than what creative writers are able to convey. And in every creative writer today there is a certain shame, a struggle of his awareness, his intelligence, against his means, which are always obsolete.*

I agree with Camus when, in his L'homme revolté, *he defends fiction. We know that when a man tries to tell nothing but the truth about himself, in diaries or memoirs, he lies much more than when he invents characters and plots, calling a boy whom he loved Albertine. Thus, only through the falsity of a convention can he tell something about his life experience. He will not renounce that urge, which in a crude form reveals itself in drunken confessions mumbled to a barman. So fiction will exist. Unfortunately we look more and more on our (extraordinary) experiences as commonplace, something that happens to Everyman. And instead of a novel, we are writing a medieval morality play on the Sinner. Where is the place for our (extraordinary) affairs with Julia or Judith if we are all sad flesh soaring above our confines with a feeling of self-pity and universal compassion?*

Undoubtedly, the novel's strength stems from a curiosity about a reality that is veiled yet cognizable. All the work of Balzac tends toward penetrating the secret of the big city, of its mythical center where innumerable human fates crisscross at a given moment. Yet Balzac also needed an act of faith in the adequacy of his tool, and this is why he defined his goal in the Preface to his Human Comedy: *to write a natural history of society. The novel thrives probably in an intermediary zone between mimesis, which threatens it with an invasion of false or valid poetry, and argument, which beyond certain limits degenerates into publicism. Many people today make sour faces at the sallies of Tolstoi, the polemicist, in* War and Peace, *as something "unartistic." They forget that had it not been for Tolstoi's passionate commitment to unraveling events, commenting, exposing his opinions, his epic would never have been written. We live in a time when a defense of "purity" in art is already an automatic reflex. This means that genuflections before art are permitted under one condition, namely, that it keep within its own specific sphere. The meaning of the adjective* specific *varies, but nearly always it denotes "away from discourse." Poetry can cope with this situation and even find a way out. A friend of mine, an eminent Polish poet of the younger generation, said in a letter to me that poetry for him is nearly identical with the search of pre-Socratic philosophers and with Gnosis. That is, more or less, what I think too. Yet the principle of prose is completely different. Whatever might be advanced to the contrary, the severe, "bare," rational, Stendhalian sentence remains its ideal. A belief in rational cognition, not "specific cognition" through art, seems inseparable from any healthy prose. Unfortunately, contemporary thought is very complex; it discourages the novelist who once upon a time used to be an investigator in sociology, economics, and psychology. The creative writer is left with the enigma of existence as his only theme, with a gigantic commonplace. What material for a novel could be drawn out of* Ah, les beaux jours *of Samuel Beckett? I am not convinced by the poetry that is published nowadays so often under the label of "novels." Poetry has a discipline of its own; it should stick to its peculiar ways. Not that I am against mixing the literary genres, on the contrary; but poetry assimilates various prosaisms much better than prose tolerates injections of objective correlatives.*

Perhaps all my skepticism boils down to my view of the writer as a reasonable human being. As such, he is confronted by a reality that resists his attempts at rational ordering, both in the sense of cognition and action. His feeling of impotence in the face of man-created absurdity makes him jealous of the great novelists of the past, who trusted their vocation as pathfinders. There is one, quite unpopular, truth that should be pronounced aloud even if it is just saying that the king is naked: a man paralyzed in the exercise of his intelligence and of his will cannot write good novels. Today, he is tossed around by mechanisms endowed with an inhuman logic of their own so he looks for more cryptic means of taking revenge— intellectual acrobatics of essay or images of poetry with their multiple layers of meaning.

You may be surprised by my dichotomy: poetry and prose. To put it simply, I believe poetry is more sturdy, better rooted in the tradition of innumerable millennia, and probably better prepared for protean transformations. Fiction will exist, but as for its present status we seem to have returned not to the "true adventures" of Eulenspiegel, but to that phase when a sermon, a poem, a dramatic poem on the stage, a wary and circumspect confession of a Montaigne found themselves on the borderline separating the known from the unknown. C.M.

THE TREMENDOUS new reading public that grew up in Poland as a result of the elimination of illiteracy finds that contemporary fiction only partially satisfies its nostalgia for interesting plots. Novels of the past, either in the original language or translation, that preserve the art of narrative in its traditional form constitute the fare of most Polish readers. Memoirs and diaries also enjoy great popularity— which is easily understandable in a country with many centuries of turbulent history. As for Polish novels of the nineteenth century, the very names of their authors are often completely unknown in the West—for instance, that of Ignacy Jòzef Kraszewski, whose works are avidly devoured by masses of unsophisticated readers looking mainly for fast-moving action. Kraszewski, a prolific writer of novels that dramatize various phases of national history beginning with pre-Christian times, provides the reader with a feeling of continuity, with a link between modern Poland and the Poland of the Middle Ages or the Renaissance. Other beloved novelists are also unknown in America—for example, Aleksander Glowacki, who writes under the pen name of Boleslaw Prus. In his major novel, *The Pharaoh*, he uses ancient Egypt as the setting for a metaphorical study of the state—its structure and its internal power struggles. In many ways this novel is unique in world literature; it is a pity that there is but an obsolete and forgotten English translation entitled *The Pharaoh and the Priest* (1902). Another of Prus's novels, *The Doll*, depicts Warsaw during the 1870's; many consider it the best of Polish realistic fiction. Although *The Doll* has been translated into several languages,[1] it has not yet appeared in English— perhaps such an exotic subject has discouraged American and English publishers. Two Polish prose writers have won the Nobel prize: Henryk Sienkiewicz in 1905 and Wladyslaw Reymont in 1924. Sienkiewicz, who wrote *Quo Vadis* (which certainly cannot be rated as great literature), is primarily a skillful reconstructor of the seventeenth-century language preserved in Polish memoirs; the peculiar charm of his yarns fades in translation. Reymont's epic of village life, *The Peasants*,[2] occupies a more modest place in the mind of the Polish public than the works of Reymont's contemporary, Stefan Zeromski, who was, for a few generations of progressive intelligentsia, a true model of "commitment." Zeromski's major novel, *Ashes* (1904),[3] deals with Poland's struggle on the side of Bonaparte throughout all the *desastres de la guerra*—a theme of crucial significance to the Poles.

If the public turns, thus, to old-fashioned fiction, it is because in Poland, as everywhere else, an objective narrative with the author acting as an omniscient, detached observer has been disintegrating. In spite of many works of fiction that continue the nineteenth-century method, perhaps the last representative of an ordered, "mirror-of-life" type of prose was Maria Dabrowska. Until her death in 1965, she was recognized by the Polish literary community as a leading moral authority. Dabrowska's main contribution to fiction was her *Nights and Days* (1932-1934), a *roman fleuve* written more or less at the same time that Roger Martin du Gard was working on his *Les Thibault* in France. *Nights and Days* is the story of a family whose internal conflicts and tragedies parallel the changes in Polish mentality from the last decades of the nineteenth century through the years preceding the outbreak of World War I.

During the interwar period, Polish fiction groped for new techniques and felt much less sure of itself than did poetry or the sophisticated literary essay. With the exception of some excellent short stories, such as those of Jaroslaw Iwaszkiewicz (who exerted, perhaps, greater influence as a poet), the most significant fiction turned its back on "lifelike" characters and realistic situations. The two novels of Stanislaw Ignacy Witkiewicz, *Farewell to Autumn* (1927) and *Insatiation* (1930), exemplify this development. Witkiewicz, a philosopher, a theoretician of art, and a playwright, refused to call the novel an artistic genre. Unlike music, painting, poetry, and drama, the novel for him was simply a catchall for the exposition of an author's personal obsessions and his quarrels with his contemporaries. His novels are a kind of grotesque *opera buffa*. The characters bear fantastic names, eat nonexistent dishes—the names of which Witkiewicz invents with relish—and mix their pansexual interests with long discussions on Husserl or Carnap or their drug experiences.[4] In both works, the action takes place in an indefinite future. They are novels of anticipation which in their somber vision belong to the genre initiated in our century by Zamiatin's *We* and continued by Aldous Huxley and George Orwell. Both novels reveal Witkiewicz's obsession with the modern dragons,

Collectivity (devouring the individual) and Ethics, or happiness for all (devouring metaphysics). In *Farewell to Autumn*, a victorious revolution of the "levelers" destroys relics of a decaying bourgeois society, that is, creators of dissonant music and nonobjective painting; in *Insatiation*, distributors of pills developed by a Mongolian ideologist, Murti-Bing, offer to all those ridden by metaphysical anxiety a means of achieving a feeling of harmony and fullness of existence—a painless preparation for a Chinese-Mongolian invasion of Europe. In the final chapters of *Insatiation*, the commander-in-chief of the unified European army submits to the Chinese before the decisive battle—for he cannot oppose "historical necessity"—and is beheaded with all due ceremony. It is impossible in this short essay to do justice to the complex thought of Witkiewicz, or to his originality which parallels, in some respects, the important undercurrent of historical pessimism in Western European intellectual life during the 1920's.

That well-defined characters, possessing their own essence, were disappearing from fiction can be proved also through an examination of a novel which was published shortly before World War II. In Witold Gombrowicz's *Ferdydurke*,[5] the characters are no more than their constantly changing gestures and poses; their behavior is not determined by any "inside" principle but is forced upon them by situations created by others. The hero, a man of thirty, is transformed by a malicious magician into an adolescent. He is forced to go back to high school, and his double consciousness does not save him from assuming all the idiotic attitudes typical of immature males. In his desperate search for authenticity, Gombrowicz constantly returns to the theme of adolescence. For him, the adolescent, despite his stupidity, still presents a certain hope because of his malleability, while the adult provokes sheer horror, imprisoned as he is by a definite form and by his complete dependence upon social ritual. Since the summer of 1939, when he left for a trip to Latin America only to be caught in Argentina by the outbreak of the war, Gombrowicz has been living abroad; but he is unofficially recognized in Poland, and justly so, as one of the most important prose writers. In his novels published abroad (*Transatlantic, Pornography*, and *Cosmos*), he has continued to develop his existential philosophy. Gombrowicz is fascinated by what he calls the "interhuman church"—a constant game of provocation and response, a kind of "one-up-manship," so that our unattainable true substance eludes all grasp and may be nonexistent. In *Cosmos*, we stand before a terrifying universe very different from that made by the wise Clockmaker of eighteenth-century philosophy. There are no laws and no universal structures—only relationships between things, arbitrarily contrived by our mind. Gombrowicz can perhaps be best understood in the light of a similar exploration going on in Polish poetry, as well as in the novel, long before he started to write. For example, Karol Irzykowski's *Paluba* (1903) attacked the very concept of "the character," discovering along pre-Freudian lines that the hero's consciousness is just a set of masks fabricated by his subconscious in response to external challenges.

The prose of Bruno Schulz was also shaped by the atmosphere of the early decades of our century. Schulz won recognition just before the last war and is now regarded in Western Europe as a figure of great stature. Born in 1892, he was the first to translate Kafka into Polish; but he cannot be called an imitator of the Kafkaesque style. Rather, he represents a parallel groping for self-expression. More inventive in his language than the author of *The Trial*, more poetic, and, in addition, more humorous than solemn, Schulz (who was killed by the Nazis during World War II) transformed his native Jewish town in southern Poland into a phantasmagoria where the most common objects are particles in a magma submitted to the constant movement of matter in a state of budding and exploding, assuming incongruous, bizarre shapes. Whether or not Schulz's tales[6] (*Cinnamon Shops, The Sanitarium Under the Hourglass*) should be called novels is an open question. They are, rather, attempts to build a personal cosmogony based upon the myth-making function of the language.

The last war found Polish prose in a state of flux. There is no necessity to remind anyone of the country's fate in the years 1939-1945. In any event, it probably afforded more opportunities for experiencing "limit situations" than did any other area in Europe. Neither traditional forms inherited from realism nor a refined satirical investigation accessible only to an elite fitted a reality that was reduced to a naked choice between life and death. This is why, immediately after the war, a leading literary critic, Kazimierz Wyka, foresaw an impotence of fiction. Anything invented by fiction would be pale compared with what every reader had seen and touched. He advocated a "borderline" novel, and he was not mistaken. The most poignant images of concentration camps, guerrilla warfare, escapes, and migration came from the pens of writers who barely fictionalized events—balancing on the limit of artistic prose and factual report. The stories of Tadeusz Borowski (a former inmate of Auschwitz and Dachau), published in Poland under the title *Farewell to Mary*, are an example of this technique. Narrated in the first person, they are perhaps the most durable work in world literature on Nazi concentration camps. It is curious to note, however, that Borowski's study of Hemingway, whom he admired and read in the original, enabled him to build up the figure of the narrator as a "tough guy" in contrast to all the passive victims in the camp. Thanks to a self-deprecating identification with his hero, he achieves effects of cruelty uncommon even in books dedicated to that macabre subject.

But where was the novel? The most ambitious attempt to capture postwar actuality was made by Jerzy Andrzejewski, whose literary debut occurred before the war. In *Ashes and Diamonds* (known abroad through translations and Andrzej Wajda's film),[7] he tried to combine a realistic description with a moral parable. The complexities of Poland in 1945 were such that probably few non-Poles can extract all the innuendoes from the novel or the film. At that time there was a guerrilla "Home Army," which had fought against the Nazis but maintained a reprehensible loyalty toward the exile government in London. Confronted in 1945 by arrests and deportations, it went underground, and its members were faced with the choice of remaining loyal to their soldier's oath or erasing the past by committing what was, in their own eyes, an act of betrayal to a cause. This moral problem is the central theme of Andrzejewski's novel. The hero, a young boy from the underground "Home Army," who receives an assignment to kill a local secretary of the Communist Party, is treated with no less sympathy than his Communist antagonist. Since "socialist realism" had not yet been imposed when the novel was published in 1948, this equilibrium was still possible. Andrzejewski's novel, in spite of its strictly Polish theme, deals with crucial conflicts of the twentieth century: How can one choose between an obsolete social system and an obsolete mentality, on the one hand, and a rule of terror, on the other? Obviously, every choice must be a tragic one, for it is a choice between two evils.

Bourgeois intellectuals, who felt that the victory of the Red Army happened in accordance with the "laws of history," sought to resolve their internal conflicts in a prose style that, immediately after the war, was designated "literature of taking account." Nothing is more typical of this literature than *Sedan* by Pawel

Hertz, a half-novel or rather several stories bound together by the person of the main character. The hero, psychoanalyzed in a Viennese clinic before the war and a prisoner in a labor camp in the Urals during the war, returns to Poland after the cessation of hostilities. Later he travels to Paris, where he observes the same self-perpetuating folly he had known in his youth. Disgusted, he goes back to his Communist country, but without nourishing any illusions about Communism. (He thus differs radically from Western admirers of the Revolution.)

Because his main effort in *Lake of Constance* was directed at puncturing all the national clichés and the search for authenticity, Stanislaw Dygat can be called a follower of Gombrowicz. His anti-heroic narrator relates a stay in one of the mildest Nazi camps, one for interns who, because of their passports, failed to fit any category of the German bureaucracy. A Pole with French citizenship, the narrator desperately tries to communicate to his inmates of various nationalities the essence of the "Polishness" which engulfs him despite his ambiguous and rather reluctant attitude toward it. Dygat, with his humorous detachment, is no exception among Polish writers of the postwar years. They approach even the most hideous reality with a typically Polish mixture of the jocular and the macabre. The "literature of taking account" was highly sophisticated. It programmatically sought its models in the works of the French ironists of the Enlightenment, and it possessed theoreticians associated with the literary weekly *Kuźnica* (The Forge). For some writers this was a school preparing them to become full-fledged standard-bearers for the Party. This is the case with Kazimierz Brandys, whose auto-ironic *Wooden Horse* was a novel on the bankruptcy of liberal individualism.

The crime of genocide committed by the Nazis upon three million Polish Jews has been one of the traumas marking the literature of postwar Poland. Here the inadequacy of traditional narrative again finds confirmation. Even the most gifted prose writer, Adolf Rudnicki, who dedicated himself almost exclusively to the subject, did not manage to convey the tragedy in the form of a novel. His voluminous work consists of long stories where reportage and memoir mingle with fictional devices. The feeling of responsibility for the Jewish fate and the intelligentsia's "taking account" of itself are closely connected. This question recurs under the pen of Rudnicki in his portraits of those liberals of Jewish origin who, entrenched in their nineteenth-century heritage of lofty ideals, felt protected until the end from sharing the fate of the Jewish masses. The long stories of Rudnicki[8] or of Arthur Sandauer (*Death of a Liberal*) may, incidentally, answer some questions posed by Hannah Arendt about the behavior of the Jewish elders in the ghettos.

In 1949 the Party imposed the doctrine of socialist realism, making it obligatory for all writers. In terms of the novel form, socialist realism was both an attempt to go back to the nineteenth century and an enforcement of a goal prescribed from above. The themes allowed in 1945-1949 were either looked at askance or forbidden. The only models that were approved by the Party were the Soviet novels of the late 1930's and 1940's. Published in large editions, Polish socialist realist novels at first provided the officials with confidence as to the influence of literature upon the masses. In fact, they were bought under compulsion by a network of libraries, where they gathered dust on the shelves and were known as "bricks." The almost total failure of socialist realism in Poland (only one prose writer of value, Igor Neverly, succeeded in maintaining his standards within its framework) led in 1955-1956 to the outburst of tendencies far removed from that stifling trend. This time a new "taking account" occurred. The literature of the years immediately following October 1956 reminds one of Pandora's box: Once the lid was raised, repressed hatreds, despair, and complete disillusionment with the tenets of the Stalinist (and often Marxist) creed were liberated. For a few years Jerzy Andrzejewski was a zealous orthodox writer with meager artistic results. Yet, in the short story "The Golden Fox," he was one of the first to denounce the inner emptiness of the so-called "new man." He left the Party and resumed his meditations of a moralist (which had been interrupted by his somewhat strange role in the time of terror). His novels, translated since into English, probe the intricacies of moral decisions that lead man to embrace the most ugly causes. Thus, in *Darkness Covers the Earth*,[9] he depicts a nearly amorous relationship between the Spanish Inquisitor, Torquemada, and a young monk, Diego. Understandably, Dostoevski has been avidly read in Poland, and Andrzejewski's novel is related to the "Legend of the Grand Inquisitor," though re-interpreted in the light of the author's own experience. The novel is typically Polish because it turns toward a philosophical parable where settings of remote epochs and countries are but a frame that permits the author to step back and examine his own time. Andrzejewski's *Gates of Paradise*,[10] written in a free-flowing, stream-of-consciousness style (no chapters and no punctuation except commas), takes place in medieval France, and has the making of an excellent film scenario. At the time of the Children's Crusade, a group of adolescents, motivated chiefly by their mutual friendships and loves, join the movement; the individual's libido thus appears to be a primary motor of social upheavals. In 1963, after a prolonged stay in Paris, Andrzejewski published *He Commeth Leaping Upon the Mountains*,[11] a novel about an old painter curiously resembling Picasso. It displays the writer's bravado, and parodies the styles used in Western European novels; but it also confesses indirectly a belief in the interdependence of sexual virility and creativity.

While Polish theater audiences after 1956 vibrated to *Hamlet*, who, as a man surrounded by secret police, reminded them of many things, and to *Richard III*, who acquired all the features of modern tyrants, the field was also opened for novelists using historical allusions. Jacek Bocheński's *Divine Julius* presented Julius Caesar as a vain, unscrupulous politician, a master of deceit; Caesar's conflict with his adversaries took on the familiar outlines of the permanent conflict between intellectuals and the bureaucratic establishment.

During the past ten years, translations of Western novels which had been forbidden between 1949 and 1956 have been appearing. Camus, Faulkner, Hemingway, Sartre, Steinbeck, and Salinger (to name only a few) became widely known in Poland, as did the re-edited works of Kafka and new versions of "classics"—for example, Krystyna Tarnowska's translation of Laurence Sterne's *Tristram Shandy*. Yet censorship of original works has been growing tighter, especially since 1960. A tug of war between censors and a sophisticated literary milieu characterizes the literary scene of Poland today. This, perhaps, explains to some extent the success of science fiction, particularly that of Stanisław Lem, who combines his scientific training with a historical and psychological approach to a degree rarely achieved in the West. For instance, Lem's *Solaris* is much more than the adventures of a young astronaut on a remote planet. In its sheer terror, it can match the thrill of reading Edgar Allan Poe for the first time. This is a man's encounter somewhere in the universe with a form of life incomprehensible to him. The ocean covering the surface of the planet Solaris behaves like an immense brain. It registers the inner experience of man and lends his nightmares tangible, three-dimensional form. When flying over the ocean, the hero finds in the compartment of his spaceship a girl in flesh and blood with whom he had been in love several years ago on earth and who had committed suicide. In this way, existential analysis, practiced by Polish writers since the end of the war, merged with science fiction.

Yet it is not the novel, but poetry, the philosophical essay, the theater of the absurd, and shorter narratives, usually in the first person, which score the points in the new race toward literature on the borderline of philosophy. An interaction of cinema and fiction further complicates the situation. Many talents find an outlet in both media. From these crisscrossing influences was born one of the most significant novels of the 1960's, Tadeusz Konwicki's *A Contemporary Dreambook*. In his early career Konwicki wrote several novels that toed the Party line; he later revealed himself as a gifted film director. The main character of his novel suffers from the sense that he has committed a crime and has not been punished for it. Since punishment cannot come from the hand of God, he must take it upon himself. At the end of the war the protagonist had fought in a guerrilla unit against the Soviet Army. Afterward, because of his feeling of guilt, he enters the Party. As the reader may guess from a tangle of symbols, the protagonist finds himself guilty again of crimes committed in the name of a political ideal. Finally, in a stagnant provincial town inhabited only by human relics of the past, he attempts suicide. While he is recovering, his past returns in a series of flashbacks intermixed with scenes showing the miserable existence of backward, small-town folk. This would be a powerful novel except that the title conveys its content all too well. It is a nightmare where reality loses its consistency and is transformed into metaphors for the subjectivity of a defeated man, and where love affairs in which all men prove to be sexually impotent evidently have symbolic meaning. One may ask whether this does not weaken the impact of those aspects of the novel that make it akin to such investigations of moral attitudes as attempted in France first by Malraux, then by Camus and others.

The goal of the Communist Party in Poland has always been to encourage works of fiction that would unfold a realistic panorama of social changes brought about by the Party itself. It was too early, immediately after the war, to pursue this goal; the richness of historical experience was such that no writer could have conveyed it in a satisfactory fictional form, especially since censorship pronounced many themes taboo. There was room for a critical appraisal of prewar Poland, and an example of it is Tadeusz Breza's long political novel, *The Walls of Jericho*, which deals with the

Warsaw milieu of the extreme, fascist-oriented Right. But the compulsory introduction of the doctrine of socialist realism doomed the political novel to failure. It would not be an exaggeration to say that the Party thereby thwarted its own goal. An honest reevaluation of prewar political and social issues became impossible because of the Party's mania for centering attention upon the activities of Communist heroes in all spheres of public life, even in those where they had been conspicuous by their absence. In addition, since the Polish novel had, even before the war, moved away from nineteenth-century techniques, the obligatory revival of these techniques according to the recipe of socialist realism made the new novels sound false to readers; neither characters nor plots seemed plausible. In 1956, the Party renounced its role of directing writers' consciences. The rule of one doctrine was supplanted by a chaos of contradictory opinions on what literature in a socialist country should be. This does not mean that the Party has ceased to favor a certain kind of fiction or that it has been averse to maintaining its standards through controls at the disposal of a monopolistic owner of all the publishing houses in the country. Yet to reduce published novels to those that are concerned directly with building socialism would be equivalent to keeping the printing presses idle. A whole crop of young novelists made their debut after 1956, but, for the most part, they write very subjective prose concerned with relationships between human beings and not with large pictures of society. The passion with which they tear apart the shibboleths of the so-called "bygone era," however, has provoked uneasiness, if not anger, in the Party. One of these writers, Marek Hlasko, had his passport withdrawn while he was on a trip abroad, and became an exile to the relief of officials who had been wringing their hands over his bad influence upon the youth of the country. Hlasko's quick-paced narratives are obviously influenced by American authors, even by those who in America are regarded as phenomena of "mass culture." Apart from his stories, his novel, *Next Stop—Paradise*,[12] which was published only abroad, can be considered a socialist realist novel in reverse. In it, a group of truck drivers who haul lumber over dangerous mountain roads, far from being socialistically minded workers, hate their jobs and try to mitigate their fear of death by heavy drinking; they perish one after the other in crashes caused by faulty machinery. Hlasko, after he found himself abroad, spent some time in Israel, where he was attracted by the large part of the population that still speaks Polish.

His stories and short novels dealing with life in Israel focus, as is usual for him, on the underworld or on the social margin between proletarians and the underworld.

The puritanical standards of the Stalinist era were broken in 1956. Since then Polish prose writers have been competing with each other in frank and brutal descriptions of sexual behavior. A certain morbidity in this respect makes one think of a neo-Manichaean duality, noticeable not only in Poland. Such prose reflects the young generation's way of life. Disillusioned by the unfulfilled promise of the "Polish October" (1956) and by a strict professionalization of politics, this generation has withdrawn into a sphere of friendships, loves, and private careers "between the jaws of the leviathan," as a Polish poet has remarked. Ironic and brilliant representatives of this generation shy away from ideology, which is an old bore to them. Interested as they are in new linguistic theories and anthropology, especially that of the Lévy-Straus brand, they apply to literature a structural analysis. A new type of pressure is created, and this time not from the Party but from the literary café. Consequently, some exponents of socialist realism, such as Kazimierz Brandys,[13] have put on an existentialist cloak. Brandys' somewhat too skillful profundity, though it won him applause in France, is beyond the scope of the present essay since, along with the crumbling of the doctrine, he has dropped the novel form and has been employing only the shorter genres of fiction. In general, the climate does not seem to augur any panorama-like novel. In his voluminous *Glory and Vainglory,* Jaroslaw Iwaszkiewicz, a senior writer, conducts a multitude of figures through several decades of social change. But the book makes difficult and rather tedious reading, confirming our skepticism about the possibility of returning, let us say, to the art of Courbet in painting or of Tolstoi in writing. The popularity of diaries and memoirs can be explained not only by their content, but also by their search for an authentic "I" of the narrator. Experimentation with a presumed "I" of a witness extends also to historical novels. Teodor Parnicki is quite widely read in spite of or, perhaps, because of his highly exotic themes and style which testify to his taste for the deliberate obscurity of fictional diaries and confessions ascribed to historical personalities. Even before the war, in his *Aetius the Last Roman,* he showed his interest in epochs of chaos and transition—in this case, Rome in the fifth century A.D. Deported to Russia during the war and later a resident of Mexico for many years, he has recently returned to

Poland. His huge novel, *The End of the Covenant of Nations*, delves into political intrigues of inextricable complexity in the Hellenistic empire of the second century B.C. in Asia Minor. His *New Fairy Tale* introduces eleventh-century Poland a few decades after its baptism, also treating Kiev, Denmark, Constantinople, and England during this period. His *Only Beatrice* is set in thirteenth-century Poland.

A wealth of material, hardly encompassed by the existing fiction on contemporary themes, awaits Polish writers. Possibly it can be tackled only with completely new tools. Two major subjects can be distinguished. The first is war, but war as approached by those who were children in the years 1939-1945, who have but vague recollections of facts and thus are free to shuffle them while introducing the fantastic and the grotesque. The short novels of Stanislaw Grochowiak, a gifted poet, are an example of this. But even more important is the subject of the Polish village, for Poland until the end of the last war was, in the main, a peasant nation. Many intellectuals who are now teaching, writing, or directing theater productions come from villages where their parents were illiterate or semiliterate. For these young people, memoirs of childhood mean a return to the countryside. But because they are now city-dwellers, they can see the peasant in a double perspective. Moreover, the village itself is changing and differs greatly from what they recall of their early years. If war takes on a somewhat mythical shape in the narratives of some young writers, the same may be said of the village. These writers see folk songs and peasant rituals as an intimate part of themselves, but they look at them with the eye of an anthropologist. One of the most appealing novels of the village, Urszula Koziol's *Stations of Memory*, makes no pretense of going beyond the subjectivity of the main character and verges on a memoir, though it is written in the third person. This novel tells the story of a little girl in a family of village teachers. It conducts the heroine from her first discoveries of the prewar world through the hard war years to her high-school studies in People's Poland. The peculiar warmth and charm of a primitive existence obeying the rhythm of the seasons is conveyed through folk songs heard by the little girl and innumerable names for plants, animals, and peasant's utensils. Although the equivalents of these names can be unearthed in English or French dictionaries, for urban readers they have become dissociated from the tangible objects they represent. If we have mentioned the lack of large fictional panoramas, we come upon one unexpectedly here—although it is unintentional, at least in appearance; the reader himself pieces together the heroine's sensations and impressions and deciphers in them the fate of a whole community. While the author does not aspire to a sociological treatise, her novel catches the village in a period of transition. In the last chapters, when the heroine is a high-school student, her classmates, the sons and daughters of peasants from her village, are visited by their fur-coated mothers who display permanent waves and lacquered fingernails. Thus, the novel is a kind of dirge for the traditional peasant life destroyed by the Revolution in the name of an urbanized, industrial society.

The difficulty inherent in an outline such as the one presented in this essay consists in shifting prerogatives: that of a literary historian and that of a literary critic. It may happen that as a literary critic I fall victim to my doubts and biases. In spite of certain limitations imposed by the Party, literature in Poland follows its own, though sometimes quite unexpected, paths. It would be risky to foretell the future of Polish fiction, especially because so many question marks surround fiction in world literature. Perhaps the most significant feature of young Polish prose writers is that they are neither enthusiastic supporters of the existing order of things nor rebels. Reality for them is what it is; ideological formulas seem to them a property of the older generation. For the young generation, what exists is both established and lasting. In this respect, they do not differ very much from young writers in Western European countries, which does not mean, of course, that the society with which they are confronted is of the same type.

REFERENCES

1. There are two versions in German, one in French.

2. Wladyslaw Reymont, *The Peasants* (New York, 1924-25).

3. Stefan Zeromski, *Ashes*, trans. by Helen Stankiewicz Zand (New York, 1928).

4. Witkiewicz took peyote for the first time in Moscow during World War I; his book on his experiments with drugs was published in 1932, several years before similar books were written by Aldous Huxley and Henri Michaux.

5. Witold Gombrowicz, *Ferdydurke*, trans. by Eric Mosbacher (New York, 1961).

6. Bruno Schulz, *The Street of Crocodiles,* trans. by Celina Wieniewska (New York, 1963).

7. Jerzy Andrzejewski, *Ashes and Diamonds,* trans. by D. Y. Welsh (London, 1962).

8. Adolf Rudnicki, *Ascent to Heaven,* trans. by H. C. Stevens (New York, 1951).

9. Jerzy Andrzejewski, *Darkness Covers the Earth,* trans. by Konrad Syrop (New York, 1960).

10. Jerzy Andrzejewski, *The Gates of Paradise,* trans. by James Kirkup (London, 1962).

11. Jerzy Andrzejewski, *He Cometh Leaping Upon the Mountains,* trans. by Celina Wieniewska (London, 1965). The American title: *A Sitter for a Satyr* (New York, 1965).

12. Marek Hlasko, *Next Stop—Paradise,* trans. by Norbert Gutterman (New York, 1960).

13. Karimierz Brandys, *Sons and Comrades,* trans. by D. J. Welsh (New York, 1961).

VALÉRIE KOREK

The Hungarian Novel in the Last Fifty Years

"WHY SHOULD only that in which we differ from others be of value, why not also that in which we are one with them?" asked the poet and critic Ignotus, and Antal Szerb, the literary historian, stated that "Hungarian literature is an instrument in the orchestra of European civilization. . . . Acceptance is as vital for Hungarian literature as creation is." These are problems of authenticity versus influence, problems involving parallels and contrasts, that are legitimately matters of literary science. They will be kept in mind while passing in review some of the Hungarian novels written since the First World War.[1] What looms in the background is, however, a less rewarding problem that transgresses the frontiers of art, the political intention behind writing or judging novels.

Good novels have seldom been written with preconceived intent, political or otherwise. But a system that denies individual liberty even to the most spiritual of personal acts—artistic creation—is apt to have a shotgun influence on works in the process of being written. Indeed, a whole apparatus of blurbs, jackets, prefaces, and a new literary history is busy evaluating and re-evaluating works of the present and the past.[2]

Take, for example, the story of Tibor Déry (b. 1894) as divulged in *The Revolt of the Mind: A Case History of Intellectual Resistance behind the Iron Curtain* (1959) by two ex-Communist authors, Tamás Aczél and Tibor Méray, who fled to England after the Revolution of 1956.[3] Are we reading a chapter of Koestler's *Darkness at Noon*, or merely a straight, eyewitness report on what the Minister of Education did to Déry, a card-carrying Communist since 1919, while "talking over" the problems of his forthcoming novel *Felelet (Answer)*? Déry's previous novel, the rambling, uneven *Befejezetlen Mondat (Unfinished Sentence*, 1948), was considered to be, by the omnip-

122

otent George Lukács, "one of the greatest works of our century" and given the highest literary award; but the manuscript of *Answer* apparently was not up to standards. Could it have been—as the authors, in a somewhat psychoanalytical manner, hint—that Comrade Révai, the Minister of Education, who was roughly Déry's age and a frustrated writer, gave vent to jealousy while tearing apart, indeed, practically, rewriting on the spot, Déry's *Answer* till it met the requirements of "socialist realism"? This spine-chilling meeting, which lasted into the small hours of the night, took place in 1952. In 1956, Déry wrote *Niki* (translated into many foreign languages), a story of a dog that keeps a woman company while her husband is a political prisoner. The day he is released, Niki dies. Because of the dog or because of the Revolution, Déry himself got a ten-year prison term, but was set free in 1960. In 1964, he gave a better answer to his Communist lords than his novel *Answer* had been, by writing the nebulous Kafkaesque *G. A. Úr X-ben* (*Mr. A. G. in X*). Would the night-marish country "X," and the eerie Hotel Astoria, with its new electric bulbs but no switches, bathrooms without water, and never-halting elevators symbolize the old, "reactionary" Hungary, while "abroad," whence Mr. A. G. came, symbolized the new one? Or is it the other way around? "One cannot catch reality in *flagranti*. The only way to get to know it is to turn one's back on it," announces a judge while presiding over a murder trial (or over "socialist realism"?). If it was socialist realism, no one caught Déry this time. He added a double-somersaulting introduction to this curious travelogue, which, if nothing else, is an amazing exercise in intellectual vigor.

Is the answer, then, to outwit the cultural regime? Or do the regime's requirements grow more subtle as the years go by? (The year of Déry's ordeal, 1952, marked the high point of Stalinist terror.) It would seem, for example, that another talented novelist, Magda Szabó (b. 1917), enjoys popularity as well as approval because of a literary attitude that merely suggests her rejection of the "old system." Her stream-of-consciousness novels are about small-town petty intelligentsia mingling with the simple and the poor. Obviously, as in *Freskó* (*Fresco*, 1958), the minister drinks and beats his children, while the half-illiterate old servant is honesty in person. Her protagonists—invariably youngish females, father-oriented, hard, and without self-pity—could well be interpreted as good builders of socialism. Judged on the basis of her best novel *Az Őz* (*The Fawn*, 1962; translated into English), her writing is expressive as she spins a dramatic plot through the mental processes of remembering and associating. As for some of her other novels, one wonders whether her occasional disregard for grammar is part of the smoke screen to ward off critics. The fact that ten consecutive sentences have no subject makes reading difficult, and her practice of introducing dozens of nicknames that are more ridiculous than amusing, while reserving true Christian names for dogs and cats, is puzzling. Could pumping the oxygen of "people are not much good—why feel sorry for them?" into the poverty-infested air of Communism be subconscious misanthropy? Possibly the inborn pessimism of the author found a good sounding board in the politically determined gloom of her country.

Iskola a Határon (*School on the Frontier*, 1959; translated into English) by Géza Ottlik (b. 1912) appeared in a well-cut jacket that praises the author's "elegant style . . . which reminds one of the best writers in English prose. . . . [It is] about the education of future officers during the Horthy-period . . . the inhuman discipline the young were submitted to in order to teach them, through cruelty, how to torture others . . . that is, to make the victims of an immoral society into the defenders of it." True, *School on the Frontier* is a boarding school story, the prototype of which are the novels of L. P. Hartley or Graham Greene. But since a military academy is hardly a finishing school for genteel young ladies, there are rough goings-on and rough language in the school, which is located in western Hungary, near the Austrian border, independent of any specific political system. It is the world of turbulent adolescents sharing classrooms and bedrooms and suffering under discipline, a world in which "there was no plotting, lacking someone or something to plot against . . . except the inner structure of the world. . . . We lived in a tangible reality, not in the abstraction of laudable ideas or well-rounded stories. . . ." This tangible reality is mirrored in Ottlik's well-rounded story. As for the laudable ideas, the reader does not need prompting from the novel's pseudo-literary advertisers in order to find them.

On the premises of an industrial plant in Budapest, a man, having been hit during a violent argument by his brother-in-law, stumbled into the debris of a junkyard below and was killed instantly. "His judges will exercise clemency," says the author, Endre Fejes (b. 1923), of his hero in the introductory chapter of *Rozs-*

datemeto (*Junkyard,* 1962), as he sets out to unfold a story of two generations, beginning in 1918, when János Sr. comes home from the wars. János Jr. was the killer. *Junkyard,* short and brilliantly constructed, portrays a changing world in which the fortunes of the working-class man were much the same whether he lived under a Habsburg king, Count Bethlen, or Comrade Rákosi. For forty years, whether they went to cafés-on-the-green to listen to Gypsy bands on Sunday afternoons or, decades later, formed their own jazz orchestra and packed sandwiches in nylon bags, they lived in the same room-and-kitchen apartment. Another impressive symbol in the novel is a lean, hard-working, loud-mouthed mother, whom the author never fails to call by her full maiden name. She sings the same self-made ditty at the cradle of her children and grandchildren, and invariably rises to occasions of christenings, engagements, or national events by "scouring the room, chalking the kitchen and frying fish." Is it possible that, fishing season or no, one can serve such meals in impoverished Budapest? Or did Fejes, at this specific point, ignore the requirements of socialist realism? In any case, with a truly epical, consistent characterization, he certainly made this proletarian *reine mère* unforgettable.

Few of the writers have been talented enough to avoid the issue of politics by letting it remain on the sidelines, like Ottlik and Fejes (no matter what their interpreters read into their novels). Some blatantly fell in line and, as people with little to offer, relied on their ancestry and became imitators, not always successfully. One of their father-images was Lajos Nagy (1883–1954), illegitimate son of a servant girl, and "a socialist," though (in his own words) "not a socialist writer, just: a writer." His two-hundred-page *Kiskunhalom* (name of a fictitious village on the Hungarian Plain; 1934) was described as a "sociographical novel." The opening page of this truly successful hybrid reads like a copybook: "Population 2687, territory . . . can be reached by rail . . . by water . . . ." As the pages turn, windows open from which figures emerge, a puppet show is set into motion, and behind the stage a voice relates not a story, but the everyday life of Kiskunhalom. The mailman goes on his daily round, the doctor calls, gossip spreads till the air thickens but then thins again in next morning's mist. Statistics get turned into individuals, while men are blurred back into data, through a good balance of detached words about people and facts that seem to carry emotions. Nagy has not overridden his device. In *Három*

Boltoskisasszony (*Three Shopgirls*, 1938), for example, he kept the village setting, but brought a dramatic plot into full bloom, as he did in his later novels as well.

A better social order had been much desired by the best ot Hungarian storytellers, even if they did not adhere to any specific political movement and used no other means than artistic. This may be one of the reasons why politically well-connected art critics of the earlier period failed to appreciate them. In his autobiography, *Életem Regénye* (*The Novel of My Life*, 1939), Zsigmond Móricz (1879–1942), son of a peasant and a village minister's daughter, hammers away at the problems of social justice. It becomes obvious, however, from his prolific novelistic output that, above anything else, he was interested in the human individual: the family, for example, the tragic entanglement of man and wife. Even his historical trilogy *Erdély* (*Transylvania*, 1922–1935) shows that his eyes were always on people—a perspective that made a novel about such an individualistic epoch as the sixteenth and seventeenth centuries into authentic history. His *Rokonok* (*Relatives*, 1930), which tells about small-town nepotism and is hailed by today's critics as debunking the rotten administration of old Hungary, is really one man's story. Its hero, just risen to higher office, becomes innocently involved in illicit doings through a web of suddenly emerging uncles, brothers, and cousins, and is driven eventually to suicide.

"The freezing atmosphere of Hungary between the two World Wars was portrayed with the utmost authenticity in three masterpieces: Móricz's 'Rokonok', Milán Füst's 'Advent', and Dezso Kosztolányi's 'Édes Anna'," states the opening lines of a preface written to a 1963 edition of the last mentioned novel: *Édes Anna*. Dezso Kosztolányi (1885–1936), one of the greatest lyric poets of the century, wrote *Édes Anna* (*Anna Édes*) in 1926. Like *Relatives*, *Anna Édes* also begins with the male protagonist being elevated to a high position, and, just as the first novel ends with suicide, *Anna Édes* ends with a double murder, committed by a nearly illiterate servant girl. But if Móricz's high-strung hero rides through tension-filled pages, Kosztolányi's translucent, simple style produces a realistic world "presented, with its many grotesque little features, entirely from the outside," as Antal Szerb remarked. Anna's own feelings are revealed but once, in the last chapter. She takes her low wages, long hours, and cot in the kitchen (on which she is seduced by the visiting nephew of the household) without complaint. Indeed, the reader is caught as unaware as the victims when Anna enters their bedroom with a kitchen knife. Not until the policeman tells her, "Thou knoweth, m'lass, this means the gallows," does she awaken, for the man has a broad, peasant's face, he might have been from her village, he called her "thou." Here the intimation of a message flashes through the reader's mind: the village as opposed to the city. But it is not easy to agree with the further elaborations of the 1963 preface and to read *Anna Édes* as "a social novel . . . hot with political emotion . . . in which Kosztolányi definitively turned his back on the inhuman system of gentry-Hungary." Instead of turning his back on anything, Kosztolányi faced the world with his poet's eye, and he had no comment, just a twinkle in that eye when Anna eventually escaped the gallows.

The third novel, Milán Füst's *Advent* (1920), could pass, perhaps, as one written with preconceived political motives, although not in the broad sense of "Communist versus old Hungary." Nineteen-twenty was the year of the "White Terror," an extended, cruel reaction to the "Red Terror" of 1919. In *Advent*, 1920-Hungary is cloaked as Catholic-persecuting England of the seventeenth century. Füst (1888–1967), according to his preface to a 1958 edition of his novel, "decided to awaken those who in the name of Jesus Christ practice inhumanity" by telling, in the first person, the story of a Catholic aristocrat in hiding: a timid young man, given to sobs as he trembles for his friends who have to face the unbending judges of the Church of England. Füst, as he states in the preface, "had shed bitter tears that year," which shows how well he situated his allegory: at a time when tears were not considered unmanly. Characteristic of Füst's writing is a firm hold on a single basic analogy to transpose the content of his story from that vantage point, stepping out of one reality in order to create another. His style carries full conviction with its mixture of stilted elegance and outspokenness, its *démodé* tone to suggest time-distance and, by the same token, detachment, and a mimicking of what seems like the translation from a foreign language. This is the technique of his five-hundred-page *A Feleségem Története* (*The Story of My Wife*, 1942). The narrator is a Dutch ship captain, a big, uncouth man of little education and a fatal passion for a volatile, pseudo-intellectual *petite Parisienne*. The theme of his being cured and succumbing again runs in cycles of calmly-taken agonies and droll adventures, until the

127

woman, loved through seven seas and seven hells, evaporates into an eerie mirage—death. By adhering to crisp, chronological story-telling and keeping his distance from firsthand reality, Füst has written an "arty" novel marked nowhere by deliberate effort.

Begetter of a peasant-hero who today is interpreted as having revolted against the "wrong" society, Józsi Jeno Tersánszky (b. 1888) has remained, like Füst, *persona grata* in Communist Hungary. His series of picaresque novels, *Kakuk Marci* (could be translated as *Marty Cuckoo*, 1923–1937), are products of a boundless imagination that never trespasses on the grotesque and of a style that is un-matched in wealth and vigor yet never degenerates into folksiness. Marci is an ingenious village vagabond who fools everybody, in-cluding the *gendarmerie*, while fighting, cheating, and wenching his way on a grand tour across the country. This lovable rascal is a practical anarchist of the Romantic school, ready to outwit "right" or "wrong" society at any time. Tersánszky, author of countless good novels, was a native of Nagybánya, in Northern Transylvania, called "the Hungarian Barbizon"—an artists' colony where Hun-garians and Rumanians, the well-to-do and the petite bourgeoisie, lived side by side in the picturesque foothills of the Carpathian Mountains. Such is the setting of *Rossz Szomszédok* (*Bad Neigh-bors*, 1926). A son of the intelligentsia and a daughter of the lower classes live next door to each other. Fate appears in the guise of topography as the girl gets seduced at the fence which divides the two houses. She moves to Budapest and for a while is submerged in the *demimonde*, until eventually she wiggles her way up into a suitable marriage. But after some years, it is again the uncanny power of location, rather than love, that, on a visit home, lures the woman from her parents' dilapidated porch through the closed doors of the neighboring mansion. The denouement is literally around the corner as she gets caught in the act and thereby loses her hard-earned position—this time, for good. Although amusing details authentically reproduce the petty life of the small town and the soothing gaslights of irony shine over it, *Bad Neighbors* is never-theless a dark story. Flaubert might well have helped to write it, but the prankish whistle of Kakuk Marci also lingers on its pages. According to *M. I.*, this novel has a message: Society forgives the well-to-do, while the poor remain guilty. If—and only if—there must be a message, is it not rather that men get away with more than women?

Another native of "the Hungarian Barbizon" was László Németh (b. 1901), playwright and novelist, now as before a major literary figure in Hungary. His most impressive novel, *Iszony* (*Revulsion*, 1947; translated into English), relates a woman's story in the first person, and conveys the conscious processes of a devilishly efficient, intelligent, loud, and tyrannical husband-hater. The story concerns two neurotics, a frigid woman who is essentially an inverted man, and a lazy, boisterous, oversexed weakling whom she kills, at the end, "accidentally" and without any regrets. *M.I.*'s thirty-page chapter on Németh hails *Revulsion* as one of the great novels of world literature. And this psychological double-portrait, achieved through minute descriptions of everyday life is, doubtless, a triumph in realism. But since Nellie has ecstasies (which she misses, rather deliberately, in bed) while preserving fruit, chalking the house, humiliating her husband in public, and indulging in soliloquies of scorn and self-pity, the style becomes overheated, as if her voice were declaiming lines from an outmoded tragedy.

Transylvania was the cradle of a specific civilization, with a spoken and written language richer, more original, and more pungent than the language elsewhere in Hungary. An independent principality for almost two hundred years, headed by great leaders, and also by clever men of political flexibility (some immortalized in Móricz's *Erdély*), Transylvania was able to save such values as were trampled on in the western parts of the country. Believers in individual freedom (predominantly Protestants), isolated in a far corner of Europe between high mountains and still cosmopolitan because of the region's foreign-language minorities, they went their own way in literature. The novels of József Nyiro (1889–1953) and Áron Tamási (1897–1966), for example, depict a beautiful, strange existence of shepherds and beasts, with the ever recurring drama of nature faced by the man who fights the elements and outwits everyone alive. Sometimes they almost create the one-dimensional world of the folktales, with its humorous peasant hero and a nature that yields to him, if need be, by miracle—a world that does not fail to impress readers who can sense, beyond a simple story, a very individualistic human consciousness.

The story of the clever mountaineer turned into tragedy in the late forties when Count Albert Wass (b. 1908) wrote *Adjátok vissza a Hegyeimet!* (*Giveth Back My Mountains!*, 1949). How the silent union of man and his native landscape becomes articulate during a long, historic manhunt is echoed by the linguistic crescendo of this Transylvanian writer, who shared the fate of his hero, and eventually fled the country.

Indeed, not only are the heroes' destinies noteworthy but also the authors' are as well, especially in times such as those decades in Hungary. Irén Gulácsy (1894–1945), in *A Fekete Volegények* (*The Black Bridegrooms*, 1926), told the story of the heroes who fought against the Turks in the Battle of Mohács. As Géza Ottlik in his *School on the Frontier* wrote concerning the four-hundredth anniversary of the disaster: "We got so used to celebrating lost battles that we survived. Perhaps because we consider defeat as made of denser fabric, as more important than victory—at any rate, it is more genuinely ours." After reading *The Black Bridegrooms*, however, one wonders whether Hungary could have ever recovered from 1526, such is the tragic impact of this book. Gulácsy was named, for her accomplishment, "the adopted daughter of Transylvania," and was killed on the streets of Budapest by a bomb.

The year 1945—with its bombs, battles, and persecutions—marked the death of many intellectuals: poets, historians, writers. Antal Szerb, the literary historian, fell under the rifle butt of his labor camp warden. A prolific scholar of Hungarian as well as foreign literature, he was also the author of two novels. *A Pendragon Legenda* (*The Pendragon Legend*, 1934; translated into English), an entertaining parody of the English detective story, was followed by *Utas és Holdvilág* (*Traveler and Moonlight*, 1937). Although the title would suggest another take-off, perhaps this time on the Romantic novel, *Traveler and Moonlight* was conceived in a more solemn mood. True, the hero's road to Italy is paved with hilarity and paradox, but it eventually turns into a nostalgic path in the search for undefined ideals, half-felt and suppressed desires of the past. With his story of almost-forgotten memories that acquire life during a wildly adventurous journey, Szerb wrote a truly neo-Romantic novel in 1937. Two years later, World War II broke out and interrupted the era of an undecided dispute as to whether spirit or matter, individual liberty or compulsion, is predominant in human affairs. While *Traveler and Moonlight* is a farewell whispered to one of the many eclectic times of history, it is, being of the thirties, the closest to us. Like swinging in a hammock, far from heaven but still slightly above earth on a fall afternoon, reading this book gives the feeling of a minute rendering of every atmospheric friction that marks a sunset in autumn. Indeed, Szerb's story reminds one of Fitzgerald's *The*

Great Gatsby and Erich Kestner's *Fabian:* What they had to tell about the twenties, Szerb says of the thirties. All three of these short novels have lively plots in the Romantic sense, rather than personal comments intended to revive a *Lebensgefühl.* Perhaps none of them will prove eternal classics, but they are the clearest-hued rainbows on the near-past's horizon.

Irén (1939) by András Hevesi (1902–1940) is a *roman à clef*, a day-by-day account of the author's short love affair with a girl who stepped out of his life with the same suddenness as that with which she entered it. The novel is written at the same ecstatic speed at which things happened to this sophisticated intellectual when he met a visitor from Transylvania—a plain girl, outlandishly dressed, but his equal in learning and appetite for adventure. The girl, however, was his superior in shrewdness, a true daughter of those hardy people who figure in the novels of Nyiro and Tamási, accustomed to outwitting nature and its creatures. Thus she went as she came, and the regrets were not hers. Anger and hurt male pride have seldom fathered a better story.

As a soldier in the French army, Hevesi died in 1940. Indeed, destiny took both Szerb and Hevesi at an early age. And destiny— of course, the fate of books is proverbial—somewhat earlier played a strange game with two Hungarian novels, when the first prize of two separate international contests were given to each respectively, before their authors were so much as known in Hungary. (Both emigrated later.)

Jolán Földes (1903–1960) wrote *A Halászó Macska Utcája* (*The Street of the Fishing Cat,* 1936, which was translated into twelve languages and sold one million copies in the first six months), a bittersweet story of post-1918 emigration. It was not the loss of country in any political sense, but poverty and unemployment that drove a Budapest working-class family to the picturesque slums of Paris. In telling her story, Földes lived up to the best nineteenth-century tradition by subduing sobs and laughter in the streets where simple people of barely articulated emotions lived. Thus absence of tragedy or comedy makes this short novel a paradigm of emigration's timeless tale.

A few years earlier, also in London, the first prize offered by another international contest was awarded to Ferenc Körmendi (b. 1900) for his *A Budapesti Kaland* (*The Budapest Adventure,* 1932). It is a long novel with a full cast and war-torn, bleeding Budapest as its stage. The story opens at a class reunion of disillu-

sioned, unemployed young men, mostly veterans of World War I—
a sordid evening, which brings the opening chapter of Werfel's *Abi-
turiententag* to mind, as one of the men advances the idea of luring
home an absent classmate who had emigrated and made good somewhere in Africa. The classmate might lend them money; he might
also help them to leave the country. Subsequently, we learn the full
story of the hero's hard-won success abroad up to the day when he
accepts the invitation to spend a long, hot, and emotional summer in
his home town: his tragic adventure in Budapest. Since a too readable plot frequently prejudices critics, only a few saw the psychological mastery in the follow-up of a love game, played by two with
desperate consistency—for different aims—or, as the novel closes,
the step-by-step account of a subconsciously planned suicide. True,
the atmosphere of the book does not elevate the spirit. On the other
hand, this meticulously executed picture shows a society whose
despair stems from economic hardships that often override ideals.

A few months later, this time at home, Körmendi had a second
novel published, *Ind. 7:15 via Bodenbach* (literally, Lv. at 7:15
through Bodenbach, referring to the schedule of the Budapest-Berlin
express, 1932; published in English translation as *Via Bodenbach*).
While the clear, to-the-point style of everyday life, tinged with
Budapest slang, is the same as that of the first novel, the elaborate,
detailed realism of voluminous *Budapest Adventure* is limited in
this short work to the supporting cast; otherwise *Via Bodenbach* is
interior monologue in which free association, psychological flashbacks, and dilemmas of conscience thicken into a web, but without
ever strangling the narrative, which reaches its climax through an
utterly unexpected turn. It is not only the outer coincidence that
recalls another story of a train ride, Michel Butor's *La Modification*,
written thirty years later, but also the complex presentation of stream
of consciousness. Moreover, Körmendi's protagonist remains just
"he," with a minimum of features as compared to the other figures,
who are clearly seen through a realist's eye, a device not far from
Butor's innovation of the second-person narrative.

Eventual emigration was also in store for the two most read, most
talked about, most compared, and, in short, most important novelists
of the interwar period: Zilahy and Márai. Lajos Zilahy (b. 1891), a
born storyteller and gifted with an inexhaustible imagination, continued in the tradition of the nineteenth-century novel of action,

battle, and passion; a man who knew his ancestry, indeed wrote about it, and lived by the advice of his literary forebears. Also playwright and poet, Zilahy is a versatile observer of things and an avid reader of people's minds. His short *Halálos Tavasz* (*Deadly Spring*, 1922) is the story of a suicide the inevitability of which is so closely reasoned that it convinces more than a factual report ever could. The reader is first cajoled into believing in the perfect idyll between a lovely, highborn girl and an attractive, wealthy young man. Then clouds begin to form in this almost too-blue sky, and at first are only petty intrigues. But they subsequently gather momentum in an abyss of the human soul from which there is no exit. *Két Fogoly* (*Two Prisoners*, 1927) is a long novel about World War I, which separates a honeymoon couple forever. The wife becomes the prisoner of her own youth, her valiant but vain effort to remain faithful, while her husband is taken captive by the Russian Army. The privations of men thrown together in a Siberian camp, the hero's calvary from near-madness to frozen resignation and his eventually going native, are portions of the book that are worth rereading after forty years. The hero of *A Lélek Kialszik* (*The Soul Dies Out*, 1932) is a boy who comes to the United States. Since Zilahy's forte is the emotional, the ups and downs of homesickness lend psychological depth to an adventurous story of emigration.

Before leaving Hungary after World War II, Zilahy set about writing an epical work concerning a wealthy, absentee, unpatriotic family of aristocrats. *The Dukays* and *The Angry Angel* (both of which first appeared in English in 1949 and 1953 respectively) were on the best-seller list in New York. Later Zilahy reversed time and wrote *Century in Scarlet* (1965, directly in English) about an ancestor of the Dukays, a novel in the best style of the nineteenth century, with a hero far more lovable than the modern Dukays. Although in his journalistic work he was an alert critic of the regime that governed Hungary in the twenties and the thirties, Zilahy was not kindly treated by *M.I.* The pseudo-literary reasoning of such literary historians is not overly articulate, and their whimsical judgment of writers who emigrated—such as Körmendi, Zilahy, and Márai—should not be considered to be any more than sour grapes.

Sándor Márai's vast literary output, as it evolved, became the multiple target of Communist criticism. *M.I.* admits the impact Márai (b. 1900) had on the intellectual reader as the thirties went through a veritable "Márai-fever," but he says further that the "famous-Márai-sentence" just "camouflaged reality and tricked the reader into an ecstatic acceptance of fiction." Is this sentence, which conveys a mood through clarity, with no poetic overtones but still satisfying the reader's emotional expectations, really a "trick"? Or is it rather Márai's own predicament, evoking a wish for feelings in which he cannot participate and perceiving only the outside of the complexity he has shown to others? What makes Márai's writing into novels is not boundless imagination or the rhythm of an inborn epic temperament but the mood of his sentences, his way of intoning feelings by a seemingly rational device—the atmosphere of some particular period conveyed by a single, archaic adjective, or that of comedy by a single, deliberate anachronism. *Béke Ithakában (Peace in Ithaca,* 1952) is typical of Márai's work. In this retelling of the closing parts of the *Odyssey,* Márai has Penelope begin her confession in the best style of a Budapest woman-of-the-world. 'The consciousness of the human race never readily accepted the idyllic end of the epic," states Márai in the epilogue, after having added the twist of Ulysses' murder on his homecoming. The idyll in *Peace in Ithaca,* a sad-funny compromise, is contrived by Penelope, Telemachos, and Telegonos, another son and the killer of Ulysses. These three are first-person narrators of the novel, who chronicle, with admiring irony, the deeds of the ineffable traveler. Márai's travesty does not hit at them or the Homeric work; rather, it is against the social order, human and divine; against the law, which gets stricter as its purpose becomes more idiotic. "Was there ever a war that made sense? They rally to a rag, whether a banner or a petticoat . . . a delusion for which one has to die." Those grave words are Ulysses'; the storytellers themselves keep aloof from judgment and despair. "Behind the friendly surface of human and divine order there lurks a dark intent: madness . . . the best protection for us is to feign insanity as well . . . ," the hero advises his wife, though the narrators feign only detachment, which turns into the most pungent taste that ever spiced the Homeric story.

Another famous wanderer, Casanova, is the hero of Márai's *Vendégjáték Bolzanoban (Guest Performance in Bolzano,* 1940). Not unlike *Peace in Ithaca,* this novel is also merely an added incident to an often-told story. "You-alone-and-forever- . . . write these words with hyphens, will you?" dictates the hero to his manservant-scribe as he leaves the room for the yard to have his horses harnessed. The servant, alone in the room, bursts into a belly laugh. So ends the novel—a copybook sample of Romantic irony, an ending meant to lift the mask from the story, no matter how convincingly it had been told. *Guest Performance* is a torrid account of a passion that the "great lover" had nourished for long years and never consummated, reaching a dead end at a masked ball and in a long letter. The late baroque, a departing mood of life, is symbolized by the forty-year-old traveling salesman of love, who had just been chased out of another town. Márai's pithy, almost tongue-tied language triumphs in this novel and suggests the design of the baroque which was able to hold its overwrought ornaments—in other words, the impeccable proportions of its architecture—without the turbulent colors of its painting. The last passion of an adventurous time (the French Revolution was not far off), a farewell to a relentless and daring chase for personal happiness, was caught in one breath and exhaled in the last sentence of *Guest Performance*. The reasons for Márai's preoccupation with the lonely adventurer, the wandering exhibitionist admired by others but facing his own conscience uneasily, are obvious; and his denouement technique suggests his well-adapted knowledge of Romanticism.

Márai's *Az Igazi* (*The True One*, 1942), like *Guest Performance*, also concludes on a note of Romantic irony. As in Németh's *Revulsion*, a woman's story is related in the first person. As if the author's feigned sex would allow him to be more talkative than usual, it is a deluge of words, conveying to a friend the fateful passion that the protagonist has for her husband, who, in turn, loves "the true one." A fascinating plot reveals "the true one" as a person without breeding or education, but while the narrator gives up her man, who is now united with the other woman, it is suggested that his attainment does not promise to be more than the mere outcome of a successful hunt.

A year later Márai wrote *Szindbád Hazamegy* (*Sindbad Returns Home*, 1943), which achieves a merger, indeed, a mystical union, of his own, crystalline style with that of the impressionist novelist Gyula Krúdy, whose last days he evokes. However, he did not manage to unite his mood with his hero's in *San Gennaro Vére* (*The Blood of San Gennaro*, 1965, the somewhat briefer and smoothed out German translation of which appeared before the original: *Das Wunder des San Gennaro*, 1957). Was the death of an unnamed foreign transient in a southern Italian village an accident or suicide? Those who knew the man speak up, but their long monologues fail to paste the crumbling pieces of this narrative together, as question marks weigh heavily on the skeleton plot of a futile sacrifice. The Romantic irony of Márai's endings gives way to a skeptical double-split as one begins to suspect that the author does not believe his hero a savior any more than he believes in the recurring miracle of the Italian shrine. With the story, out went "the Márai-sentence," clipped to the bone, reversing every move of the story, and disappearing behind the wall of a self-conscious style. And still: "Unsteadfast, he went down the narrow gangplank, tottering, as people always do when they cross over water," relates the priest-witness of the accident, "but then again, he appeared, in the dark, as someone who walks *on* water." This could have been said about the author, as well.

The last word should be given to the first personage of this section, Lajos Zilahy, who greeted the poet-writer Gyula Illyés in 1962, on his sixtieth birthday, with *Vers Libre*, four lines of which are:

> Exile did not help Ovid or Turgenyev,
> Nor Zweig—to name just a few;
> Many a banished writer perished
> Of rantingly denied homesickness' cancer.[4]

Zilahy's pessimism, of course, takes the long view. But if we consider 1956, which marked the last exodus, a remark of Kerényi's seems apt. Károly Kerényi, classicist and collaborator of C. G. Jung, said that exile might even add a new dimension to being a Hungarian. Indeed, newly-gained freedom of expression, fantastic experiences left behind, anger and indignation, all combined into a fictional explosive for some talented refugees. But just as explosives leave dregs, political manifestos and journalistic or autobiographical glossaries began to parade as novels, of tremendous interest to those engaged, but of ephemeral literary merit.[5]

Unless it is thought cynical to judge works of art built on the horrible bloodshed and the destruction of an old city (for the second time in twenty years), two novels should pass as achievements of the Revolution. The first, *Tatárok a Széna Téren* (*Tatars on Széna Square*, 1963) by Péter Halász (b. 1922) begins as a Communist judge condemns a young girl to death, a judge who, just a few days before, had hidden her after she had killed a notorious member of the political police. *Tatars* is the brief tale of an opportunist who, through the revelation of a god-sent, wondrous love, grows into a noble human being, but subsequently falls when he is terrorized into carrying on from where he had left off those few days ago. The judge's destiny was that of the Revolution, his road from redemption to renewed condemnation that of the country. Perhaps the ecstatic suddenness of all that happened made the horror of the situation bearable to man and the country as a whole, for no time was left them to grasp the triumph before tragedy hit again—a meager consolation, but part of the atmosphere in which this extraordinary novel was conceived.

The thread of *Tatars* comes to an end in November, 1956. *Nyugodt lehetsz Elvtárs* (*Rest Assured, Comrade*, 1959) by István Eszterhás takes place a few months later, in early 1957. Those were the days when a wave of terror had swept away the last vestiges of the Revolution and hit a crescent-shaped, dead-end street in a workers' district of Budapest, where about a dozen families lived, practically on top of one another, with adjoining backyards and windows that let glances slant in all directions. Suddenly one afternoon, a rumor began that the political police were about to raid the street. Most of Eszterhás' five hundred pages reproduce the ever-mounting electric shocks of hurried dialogue as men and women pass on warnings: flashbacks of their political pasts are given, while broken fragments of hatred or attraction are mended or torn apart in an effort to face the inevitable with precarious dignity. With the descending night, a murderous chase begins, and killed are the hunted and the hunters alike. "Rest assured, Comrade," says the villain-protagonist, a police captain to his superior, "it will never happen again." Richly spiced with the newest, Communist slang of Budapest, a powerful language complements this original narrative. As doorknobs change hands on the crescent, events move as if on a spiral staircase. Indeed, the technique recalls a revolving stage; the brevity of time and the staccato of the conversations add elements of drama to the novel. But the warmth with which its many characters smolder accounts for the best epic qualities of *Comrade*.

Leaving behind these novels, which were published on free soil, and picking up the thread of political intrusion in Hungarian literature, certain books bordering on the pure novel should be mentioned. The thread, lucky for their authors, gets thinner as novels such as the juvenile and the historical, as well as the autobiographical, are, by their very nature, less susceptible to political analysis. The juvenile novel in Hungary has a distinguished tradition, since works by the greatest novelists—Mór Jókai (1825–1904), Kálmán Mikszáth

(1847–1910), and Géza Gárdonyi (1863–1922)—were "clean" stories and inspiring favorites with the young. As for current products, *Bogáncs* (*Thistle*, the name of a dog; 1963) by István Fekete (b. 1900) is a charmingly-written adventure story, and Magda Szabó has also a few successful juveniles to her credit.

Historical novels enjoy somewhat of a common ancestry with the juveniles, since almost all of Jókai and Gárdonyi's works deal with the past. Although Zsolt Harsányi (1887–1943) was practically slaughtered in the pages of *M.I.*, this branch of writing thrives mostly unmolested. Harsányi, who specialized in biography, recounted in *És Mégis Mozog a Föld* (1937) and *Magyar Rapszódia* (1936) the lives of Galileo and Liszt respectively, the English translations of which—*The Star Gazer* and *Hungarian Rhapsody*—were at one time widely read in this country. He also wrote about the Hungarian King Matthias, the painters Rubens and Munkácsy, and several Hungarian poets of the past. Without too many personal speculations and comments, the habit of many biographers, the heroes' lives yield their psychological portraits. One learns from Harsányi's books the easy way, but one learns, nevertheless. Transylvania-educated László Passuth (b. 1900), with his rich style and astonishing knowledge, is concerned with chapters in history rather than individuals, and whether he takes his reader to Spain, Mexico, Italy, or Transylvania, his intrigues and romances of the past are presented in full panoply. Most of his work is translated into foreign languages.

Rózsa Ignácz (b. 1910) crossbred the historical novel and history in *Toroczkó Gyász* (*The Mourning of Toroczkó*, 1958). A legal battle fought by a mining village and its ruling family, which denied the community's exemption from serfdom granted to them by a medieval king, comes to a murderous conflagration in 1702, as the Unitarian church is surrounded by the landlord, aided by foreign militia, while the minister is performing a wedding ceremony. The *mémoires* of the minister's seventeen-year-old tubercular daughter is the fictional part of the book, and after death wrests the pen from her hands, Clio takes over and the story is brought up to the present day. *Toroczkó* is proof of the view that historical novels are best when their action reaches back only to the point at which the author can relate to his ancestral background. Ignácz, for example, was able to lean on the folklore and archives of her native Transylvanian environment, even on the oral tradition of her family. With versatile talent, she also wrote about the stream of consciousness of an old woman in *Titánia Ébredése* (*The Awakening of Titania*, 1964), and in *Róza Leányasszony* (*Damsel Rose*, 1942) immortalized Róza Laborfalvy, the great tragic actress of the nineteenth century who became the wife of Mór Jókai. Thus the author leads the way home to Mór Jókai, the foremost Hungarian storyteller of all times; and an essay on the modern Hungarian novel should perhaps end at this point, were it not for two autobiographies that are still worth mentioning.

Both were written, not by novelists, but one by a painter, Aurél Bernáth (b. 1895), and the other by a painter and poet, Anna Lesznai (1885–1966). They kept interesting company in historic times and were bent on revealing themselves only through others, while their artistic temperaments made them, although newcomers, masters of prose. *Igy éltünk Pannóniában* (*Such was Our Life in Pannonia*, 1958) and *Utak Pannóniából* (*Roads from Pannonia*, 1960; Pannonia was the ancient Roman name of Western Hungary) were the two volumes of Bernáth's reminiscences about the vineyard-bordered shores of Lake Balaton. This landscape, a favorite of artists and writers, is drawn by Bernáth as antiquity already knew it, a geographic reality which is likely to withstand more millenniums of political earthquakes.

Anna Lesznai was born in northern Hungary. Her *Kezdetben volt a Kert* (*At the Beginning Was the Garden*, 1966), a third-person narrative, is a three-generation story of two neighboring families which runs parallel to that of the villages that flank the two manor houses. The lives of poor Slovak peasants were—through their work, their subordination and its consequences, their loyalty or hatred—fused with those of the protagonists around the turn of the century. Doubtless the landowners set their hearts on improving the lot of the people, but they became involved in their own turbulent affairs and concentrated on Budapest, where the heroine and her family remained for over a decade. After these years, during which Hungarian intellectual life was fermenting and was crossed at many points by the catastrophe of World War I, the family returned to the estate, which had been lost in the meantime, but was still overlooking the village, asleep in poverty and indifference, as before. The early twenties, *le temps retrouvé* in these thirteen hundred pages, brought a moment of atmospheric peace that only true artists are able to convey, although that time marks the dawn of the uneasy period during which the novels, reviewed here, were written.

REFERENCES

1. Hungary, small and landlocked, has come to be known to many as an exporter of talent, perhaps mainly in music, mathematics and the mathematical sciences, but is productive also in less exportable arts, e.g., literature. Today, about a dozen periodicals are published, abounding in poetry, short stories and "criticism." By mentioning twenty-eight authors and less than fifty novels, I cannot pretend to have done justice to the output of novels in the past fifty years. I had to be selective because of limited space; I tried to say something about a few rather than a little more than nothing about all who could have been listed. In part my selection was inevitably arbitrary, and it reflects my personal preferences.

Also, I am defining the period of fifty years as one beginning with the ending of the First World War. Should an initiated reader find fault with my omission of a truly great novel, I remind him that Szinek és Évek (Hues and Years) by Margit Kaffka (1880–1918) appeared in 1912. (Though just the story of a beautiful girl whose failure in life was rooted in a superficial upbringing typical for her class, the impoverished but still reactionary gentry, between the lines Hues and Years is heavy with the doom of a rigid regional administration which stifled Hungarian life. Together with her small son whose first steps she described in a lovely poem, Kaffka perished in the Spanish epidemic which followed the First World War.)

2. My main source of information concerning these interpretations is A Magyar Irodalom Története (History of Hungarian Literature, Vols. 5 and 6, Budapest, 1965–1966). In the text I will refer to this work as M.I.

3. I was using the Hungarian version of the book Tisztító Vihar (Purifying Tempest, London, 1961).

4. The translation is mine.

5. I am greatly tempted to mention Hungarian-born Christine Arnóthy's (b. 1929) Dieu est en retard (God is Late, 1956), although, having been written in French, it is not Hungarian literature. But this story, which takes place in the worst years of Stalinism in Hungary, ends on an exemplary psychological question mark; was its hero, a composer-conductor, doomed at the performance of his latest work because his fall had been decided, as the narrative suggests, or was his composition a failure because inwardly he could not get along with the Communists any longer? It is a good novel and has a smooth English translation.

SEYMOUR L. FLAXMAN

The Modern Novel in the Low Countries

In the seventeenth century, Dutch literary influence extended to England and Germany, and several important German poets traveled to the Netherlands to perfect their art there. But that was long ago, and today Dutch writers complain about the frustrations of working in a language that is not a world language. They feel that they write for a limited audience, a disadvantage both artistically and economically. (Du Perron, one of the most important novelists of the thirties, once complained that he wrote "in a secret language.") Some works get translated, of course, but these are few and not always the best. The economics of publishing being what they are, an adventure story has a much better chance of publication abroad than a philosophical novel. The result, when viewed by the non-Dutch reader, is a kind of literary iceberg, with a small part showing at the top, but with the weightiest part still submerged.

Editions are small, and it is difficult for even a successful writer to live on his royalties. Besides, the educated Dutch reader usually knows at least one or two foreign languages, and Dutch bookstores regularly display books in these languages, which compete for his attention. Also, some intellectuals in the Netherlands suffer from a literary inferiority complex; they pride themselves on reading only books published outside their mother country. Yet Dutch literature does have an audience of some seventeen million people, which is much larger than that in certain other small countries, such as Norway or Sweden. About twelve million of these people live in the Netherlands. Some of the remaining five million consist of the Dutch Diaspora in South Africa and Latin America, but most of them are Dutch-speaking Belgians, whose language is commonly called Flemish. The differences between Dutch and Flemish appear mainly in the spoken language, being largely dialectal in nature, while the written forms are almost identical. For all practical purposes, these Belgians form a literary continuum with their neighbors to the north. Some critics even speak of the Dutch literature of Belgium as coming from Zuid-Nederland or "the Southern Netherlands."

Readers accustomed to thinking of Holland as a picturesque little country of windmills and tulips may also suppose that it has a somewhat quaint and provincial literature. It would be an unfortunate error in our understanding of contemporary civilization, however, not to recognize that Dutch literature fits into the main stream of modern European literature.

The modern period in Dutch literature begins with the literary revolution of the 1880's, when a group of young writers rebelled against the clichés and fossilized rhetoric of the older generation. The patriotic poetry of the previous generation was scorned as they turned to the lyric, which remains the most vital literary genre in the Netherlands today. The usual difficulties of translating poetry have combined with the "secret language" to throw a veil of obscurity over modern Dutch poetry.

At the end of the nineteenth century, two important literary influences entered Holland from abroad, English Romanticism and French Naturalism. It was at this time, too, that socialism began to have an impact on Dutch literature, and it found expression in the naturalistic novel.

In Belgium, Guido Gezelle brought a new voice and spirit to Dutch poetry. This gifted priest understood the power that lay in the words and rhythms of the Flemish language, and he created an influential poetic idiom. The Flemish language has long carried overtones of nationalism with it in Belgium, and it is still a burning political issue today. The Flemings thus have a different attitude toward their language from that of their Dutch neighbors to the north, and this also creates other psychological relationships.

In the novel, the realistic tradition has dominated both the Netherlands and Belgium for almost a century. Beginning with Multatuli (Douwes Dekker) in 1860 and continuing to World War II, this style has prevailed over Romanticism, Impressionism, and Expressionism. *Max Havelaar,* the novel of life in the Dutch East Indies that brought Multatuli immediate fame, contains several elements which reappear in the great novels of later writers.

First of all, it is about the Indies, an area of the world that was of great importance to the Dutch until shortly after World War II. Many an ambitious young Dutchman went there to earn his fortune, and then returned to live a life of respectable retirement in The Hague. Couperus, a master of the social novel, has depicted the lives of such men and their families in his realistic fiction. That is all gone now, but the mystery and spell of the Indies are occasionally evoked by a modern novelist, such as Maria Dermoût, whose *Nog pas gisteren* (*Yesterday*) and *De tienduizend dingen* (*The Ten Thousand Things*) appeared in the fifties.[1]

As a commercial people, with worldwide interests, but without a world language, the Dutch are not easily moved by nationalism; they have a cosmopolitan spirit, which has often found its way into their literature. In the thirties, especially, some of their best novelists stressed the importance of European culture and looked upon themselves as essentially Europeans. In his novel *Het land van herkomst (Country of Origin)*, du Perron re-examined European civilization against the background of Java, the country of his birth. He had a skeptical attitude toward the colonial authorities and a strong affinity for Multatuli. Although he was a European writing in a European language, he was able to recreate the colors, sounds, and sights of the Indies, remembering not only the Dutch, but the Malays, the Sundanese, the Chinese, the Arabs, the Belgians, and the Germans. A whole heritage was thus transferred from one world to another.

Arthur van Schendel, the greatest novelist of the period in the Netherlands, produced a number of realistic works which are also thoroughly Dutch. This does not mean that they are chauvinistic, but rather that they convey the essential elements of Dutch life: the uneasy alliance with the water, the moods of the landscape, with its changing light and moving clouds, and the religious ideas and conflicts that have animated Dutchmen. The Dutch are a seafaring nation, and a good part of the country lies below sea level. One of the greatest national programs today is the Delta plan, a vast new system to control the sea and save the land. Thus the Dutchman who reads *De waterman* (*The Waterman*) now has no difficulty in identifying himself with the hero, who lived his life on the water and died in it.[2] The light on the water and the clouds scudding by are as familiar to him today as they were to the artist van Ruysdael three centuries ago. They are a part of daily life and will never change.

The Waterman lives in harmony with the water, but he is in conflict with his family and fellow men. Religion and the question of an established church determine some of the most important events in this novel. The influence of pietism and social idealism as forces in Dutch life appear here. The Waterman seeks the ways of God and finds them not in a church, but in a brotherhood living apart from society. He possesses the virtue of *caritas*.

The Dutch have long had a reputation for religious tolerance. With the population almost equally divided between Protestants and Catholics, there have been tensions, nevertheless, and these have been reflected in Dutch literature. There are still critics in the Netherlands who speak of Catholic poets and Protestant poets. The Jews, who contributed much to the cultural life of the country, were destroyed by the Nazis. This tragedy is still resented in the Netherlands, which was occupied by the Germans in World War II.

Calvinism and the idea of predestination have been influential in the literature of the north, while anticlericalism has been a theme of some of the Dutch writers in Belgium. It is worth noting that two contemporary writers, Vestdijk and Mulisch, who represent different generations and different points of view, do not profess any religious belief, yet both have brought religion into their work.

Multatuli was an effective and angry critic of society. Although its direction or scope may have changed, social criticism remains a significant element in the Dutch novel to this day and is often given a sharp edge by satire. Until the end of World War II, Dutch society remained very stable and relatively immobile. It was conservative, and the middle class was strong. The Dutch have an old culture, and Holland has been a prosperous country with a high standard of living. But provincialism was frequently a danger. It was a society in which merchants, rather than artists, were respected. Many writers hid their identity behind pseudonyms, as they still do, for privacy is regarded as important.

Since the end of World War II, a number of young rebels have appeared whose attitude toward the novel and the world differs radically from that of the older generation. There is a greater awareness of international events and a stronger hostility to traditional views. Using the end of the war as a boundary line to delimit a period of contemporary literature, this article attempts to give an account of the Dutch novel, both in the Netherlands and in Belgium, during the last twenty years. I have selected a few of the most significant contemporary writers, drawing upon their outstanding and representative novels, to illustrate the main features of Dutch fiction today.

Simon Vestdijk, who was born in Harlingen in 1898, is easily the most prolific and influential novelist writing in Dutch today. Only a few years after getting his degree in medicine, Vestdijk gave up his practice in order to devote himself completely to literature. He began his career by writing poetry. In the development of Dutch literary life, magazines have played an important role, and Vestdijk was one of the writers who gathered around *Forum*. Since then he has written some one hundred books, including novels, essays, poetry, and criticism, and covering such diverse fields as music, religion, and astrology. The novels alone form an impressive *oeuvre;* they range from *Meneer Vissers Hellevaart* (*Meneer Visser's Descent into Hell*), his first novel, which employs Joyce's technique of the interior monologue, through the Anton Wachter series, to *Juffrouw Lot* (*Miss Lot*), which appeared in 1964. Vestdijk approaches the novel autobiographically, a trait characteristic of many Dutch novelists, including Multatuli. His first novels are based on a complete description of his early years, a manuscript of almost a thousand pages, which has never been published.

Continuing the tradition of social criticism in the Dutch novel, Vestdijk has mocked small-town society and scorned Dutch provincialism. This has angered some of his fellow citizens; but in a country where industrialization and urbanization are proceeding at an accelerating rate, the accuracy of his vision has been widely recognized. By capturing the structure of society, be it in an unnamed provincial town or in Amsterdam, and delineating the essence of its leading social types, Vestdijk has laid bare the social prejudice prevalent in a conservative and stratified society. In *Meneer Visser's Descent into Hell*, for example, Vestdijk draws a merciless picture of a petty tyrant in the little town of Lahringen, which no one had any difficulty identifying as Harlingen, the author's native city.

It is not a difficult matter to follow the autobiographical vein in Vestdijk's work and to identify characters in his novels as particular persons in his life. But it would be wrong to imagine that Vestdijk the man and Vestdijk the writer are one and the same. Although he is a social critic, he is, like other modern Dutch writers, interested in individual lives and individual problems. His own life has served him as a source of material, which he has reinterpreted to serve the purposes of fiction.

Vestdijk's mastery of psychological technique and his knowledge of psychoanalysis appear repeatedly in his novels, not only in his analysis of the relationships and actions of mature adults, but in his characterization of children and young people. He is particularly adept at probing the world of the adolescent, with its early sexual experiences and the pangs of unrequited love. In *Terug tot Ina Damman* (*Back to Ina Damman*), he reveals a son's relationship to his father, and his changing relationship to his mother after his father's death.

The father-son conflict is not a new theme in Dutch fiction, and it has been treated by other modern Dutch novelists. Bordewijk portrayed it in an outstanding novel, *Karakter* (*Character*), in 1938. Vestdijk makes it one of the motivating forces for the hero of *De koperen tuin* (*The Garden Where the Brass Band Played*).[3] It should be noted that Vestdijk "murdered" his own father on the ninth page of *Sint Sebastian* (*Saint Sebastian*, 1939), the first of the eight Anton Wachter novels. At that point in time in the novel, Vestdijk was only twelve years old, but actually his father lived to be eighty-one.

In *Saint Sebastian*, he explores the psychology of the very young child, and the book opens with the weaning of the infant. Vestdijk takes a Freudian point of view, and weaning, like birth, is interpreted as a traumatic experience. The life of Anton Wachter is then portrayed up to the age of four. *De redding van Fré Bolderhey* (*The Salvation of Fré Bolderhey*) is the story of a schizophrenic boy, and there is *Angst* and something of Kafka in this novel. Writing from his autobiographical vantage point, Vestdijk is able to infuse technical skill and knowledge with the immediacy of personal experience, for he himself has suffered from serious depressions.

In *The Garden Where the Brass Band Played*, Vestdijk presents the boyhood and young manhood of Nol Rieske, the son of a prominent judge, who is in conflict with his family and the conventions of narrow-minded small-town society. Nol meets Trix Cuperus, the band conductor's daughter, in the garden. Although an enormous social gulf separates them, Nol falls in love with Trix. He returns to the garden in thought and deed again and again.

Nature plays an important role in this novel, and the garden is a very special kind of garden, where some of the most important episodes in Nol's love affair with Trix take place. Here he recalls scenes in which he was moved by powerful emotions. The garden and its foliage have a strange surrealistic quality, and when Nol remembers the musicians playing on their brass instruments, he realizes that it is a brass garden. That is the real meaning of the Dutch title *De koperen tuin.*

Dutch literature is often said to have a pictorial quality, a characteristic that is related to the Dutch interest in art. Some critics have found such descriptive passages static, but there are typically Dutch relationships that can be seen in proper perspective only against a landscape in the Netherlands. A modern steel mill may lie within sight of a medieval castle, but some things, such as ice skating, never change, and probably never will. That is perhaps what gives a certain stability to the Dutch character. In *Back to Ina Damman* one of the crucial scenes in the novel takes place while Anton is skating with Ina. When Nol and Trix meet while skating in *The Garden Where the Brass Band Played,* the burghers in the background form a characteristically Dutch scene as they skate past in their own particular styles.

Old friends and enemies, rivals and lovers, cuckolds and philanderers looked round at each other with surprised smiles, and nudged their wives to smile and wave too. Groups of yelling youths, hands linked, separated to streak, one by one, under helplessly protesting arms. Hunched-up veterans of all ages sped towards an invisible objective that was nothing more than speeding past everyone else over and over again. Barge captains jovially followed the pipe-smoke trail of other barge captains. Billowing females, sturdy farm-women, hands on each other's shoulders, formed sinuous rows, some grey, some colourful. Local ladies who couldn't skate were being given dangerous instruction by strong and eager gentlemen.[4]

For Vestdijk nature is not always benevolent; it can be indifferent, even hostile. When death brings an end to Nol's tragic love for Trix, the "emptiness was filled with the unreasonable sunlight of a late summer's day." Vestdijk the physician sees nature within man too. He does not consider man a purely moral being, but a physiological creature as well. Social pressure and ostracism alone do not destroy the bandmaster. Vestdijk portrays with clinical accuracy the bandmaster's decline into fatal alcoholism, describing all the pathological symptoms and the horrors of his delirium.

Death recurs thematically in Vestdijk's novels; as in the work of other modern writers, the religious overtones of death have practically disappeared. Vestdijk does not connect death with sin or punishment, nor does he suggest a life hereafter. He describes pure physical decay and disintegration—objectively, almost brutally. When Nol is shaken by the sight of his mother dying, he admits:

My mother suffered, I suffered. But she couldn't get up and run away. I could. My chest was tight with despair and grief, my head spun with boredom and guilt, my stomach throbbed from hunger, thirst, the need for alcohol, life's bitterness and sweetness, sublime wisdom, the profound insight of the intestines.[5]

The old religious basis of morality in sexual relationships has also been challenged in contemporary Dutch literature; both the Catholic and the Calvinist attitudes have been defied. There is now no hesitation in separating sex and love, and Vestdijk is typical of many Dutch writers today in his treatment of erotic themes. By combining his understanding of the physiological aspect of man with his insight into depth psychology, Vestdijk is able to infuse his characters with the living reality of modern life.

Without resorting to the naturalistic details beloved by some contemporary novelists, he nevertheless strips bare the relationship between the sexes. That is why he is able to make us understand the real relationship between Nol and Trix. She admits that she loves him, but even on their last night together before her death, she does not sleep with him. Yet we find out later that Trix has been the mistress of some of the most respectable men in town. She enjoys the power over men that sex gives her. Just as the bandmaster cannot be saved from the effects of his destructive craving for alcohol, so his daughter is the victim of her sexual desires. In spite of Nol's idealistic love for her, their very different natures, even more than social distinctions, meant that they could never join their lives in a conventional middle-class marriage.

As a boy Vestdijk enjoyed playing the piano, and his love of music has remained with him all his life. It appears as a recurrent theme in his novels, in a manner reminiscent of Thomas Mann. In *Back to Ina Damman*, Haydn's Minuet in D Major becomes associated in Anton's mind with his love for the cold little heroine. *The Garden Where the Brass Band Played* contains long passages of musical description. Vestdijk unites music with a perceptive treatment of the psyche of a child, when he has young Nol awaken from a terrifying dream about an imaginary crocodile in the brass garden with a new determination to learn to play the piano. Vestdijk combines music with another favorite theme, the lost love of one's youth. This is an element in his work that recalls German romanticism.

In *De dokter en het lichte meisje* (*The Doctor and the Prostitute*, 1951), Vestdijk turns the mirror of memory back on his own early years in the medical profession, and presents another view of the relationship between a young man and woman of very different social origins. This time the setting is Amsterdam, but whether it is in a small town or a huge metropolis, the hypocrisy of society is not much different. The citizen who does not abide by social conventions, however irrelevant they may seem, will be punished by his neighbors.

Both the plot and structure of the novel are simple: the man, a doctor, has a number of love affairs, finds a perfect mistress in Cor, the prostitute, loses her for a time, and then regains her in the end. The physiological and psychological aspects of the male-female relationship are fully illuminated; sex and love are not made identical with each other. Hormones become more important than the traditional concept of romantic love.

The doctor comes to realize that he is defenseless against women. He not only seduces the servant girls, but he is not insensitive to the charms of the wives of his professional colleagues. And yet is it all his fault? Why do they wiggle their hips at him so invitingly as they walk by? This goes beyond the theme of the emancipated woman, a familiar figure in fiction even fifty years ago. Nor is this the much older picture of woman as temptress or seductress. Like some other contemporary Dutch writers, Vestdijk depicts women as equal and willing sexual partners.

As in *The Garden Where the Brass Band Played*, Vestdijk makes use of the first-person narrative form, which has remained popular in contemporary Dutch fiction. This is well adapted to the simple plot and the episodic nature of the narrative. At the same time, it lends immediacy and verisimilitude to the novel. Nature as landscape plays almost no role in this novel of city life, which takes place in rooms and streets in modern Amsterdam. Vestdijk takes us to a dance hall, and introduces us to the *demimonde*.

He is more inventive than most of his contemporaries in the creation of character, and he has peopled this novel with a number of fascinating urban types. There is the retired postal official, who acquires the doctor's mistress for a while, and her uncle, the ex-convict and former assistant in the anatomy laboratory at the medical school. We also meet her former "landlady," who is adept at bamboozling the police. Such characters give a roundness and animation to this novel of urban social life.

Vestdijk, like Mann, is fond of adopting ancient myths and giving them modern content. At the beginning of *The Doctor and the Prostitute,* the hero compares himself with the classical picture of Hercules, who is forced to choose between the broad path to the voluptuous woman and the narrow path to the virtuous one. Hercules, of course, chooses the narrow path of virtue. What else could he do? As if there were really such a thing as free choice! Only men believe in that. "But yet he did what the tradition of the Ancients ascribed to him. He did climb the steep path." After two World Wars it is difficult to want to climb steep paths! The parody and skepticism are those of a modern man, who no longer believes in the old faith and traditions. He cannot take the heroic myth seriously and even pokes fun at it. Thus, Hercules' club "is rounded off at one end like a mythological barstool."

In explaining how it was her uncle who reported the heroine to the police, Vestdijk reinterprets the Biblical story of Cain and Abel, with her Communist father as Abel and her uncle, a convert to Catholicism, as Cain. Vestdijk takes a satirical, rather than a naïve point of view, and adds that Cain was even more concerned with respectability than Abel, since Abel was not sure of exactly which view of sexual morality was current in Russia at that time.

Vestdijk questions not only the mythical and the conventional, but the normal. He is not alone in this among contemporary Dutch novelists, of course, but in his earlier novels he sometimes showed a preference for the physically or psychologically abnormal. The heroes of his later novels are quite "normal," but as an expert analyst of the human psyche, he knows how thin a line separates the normal from the abnormal. In his characterization of Willempje, one of the doctor's passing loves, Vestdijk gives us a penetrating psychological analysis of not only Willempje, but of all women. "As a medical man I cannot call Willempje completely normal. But real women are probably never that."

In continuing his description later, Vestdijk displays his remarkable ability to blend the physical and the psychological. Physiology and psychology become physiognomy.

Some readers will understand me when I say that she was a perfect lover with her eyes, her mouth, her tender embrace. But this did not save her from a tendency to scream and jump, during which her chin receded and her turned-up nose foolishly and conceitedly came forward the moment love began to race toward the limits of love. I am inclined to consider these phenomena among the noblest expressions of the human spirit, although medically they are part of hysteria, which is a completely meaningless statement in itself. Mad romanticism was Willempje's element; the fact that she fell short in other respects only indicated a wise division of powers by Mother Nature.[6]

In *The Doctor and the Prostitute*, Vestdijk attacks rigidity and provincialism in society. The doctor, an outsider, is a rebel against all modern society. With a skeptical view of his profession, he is not sure that his social position differs greatly from the prostitute's. "To be at everyone's service, to take money for questionable arts, to lie. There was no need for me to be proud of myself." Highly critical of the professions and the middle class, Vestdijk by no means idealizes the proletariat. He is fully aware of the shortcomings of human beings in their relationships with one another, even at the lowest levels of society. There is no place in Vestdijk's *Weltanschauung* for dogma. On the whole, Communism has never been a significant force in the Netherlands, and very few Dutch writers adhere to it.

Vestdijk has taken religion seriously, although it is not certain that he accepts God and Christianity. In *De kellner en de levenden* (*The Waiter and the Living*), he takes up the whole question of human existence. The waiter is a Christ figure. This novel, as much as any other, shows his interest in the essay and his talent for incorporating it into the modern novel, as Mann and other European writers have done.

The versatility and range of Vestdijk's genius are extraordinary. He has cultivated the historical novel, a form that has fallen out of fashion in some modern literatures. In this genre he displays a tremendous range and vast erudition, for he is an intellectual writer. He is able to develop complicated figures in psychological depth, and thus gives a picture of the age. In *Het vijfde zegel* (*The Fifth Seal*), for example, he paints a portrait of El Greco in Spain at the end of the sixteenth century.

A naturalist who incorporates romantic and, occasionally, surrealistic elements in his novels, he has used interior monologue, first-person narrative, myth, religious allegory, the historical form, the autobiographical form, and the series form. He has also used the technique of the novel within a novel. At times he has engaged in joint authorship, which is not a unique practice in the Dutch novel.

Like Hermann Hesse, he has sometimes been playful in his use of historical and mythical figures. As a critic of society, he has occasionally antagonized his more puritanical compatriots with the shock effect of his novels. A virtuoso in the application of depth psychology to the technique of the modern novel, he has specialized in the individual portrait, rather than in the portrayal of a class. If he is often subjective, he is honestly occupied with the search for self in this world. Yet his emphasis has always been on man, and he is constantly examining the human condition in this difficult and questionable existence. No wonder that Menno ter Braak, one of the most important writers and critics of the thirties, even then called him *de duivelskunstenaar* or "the wizard."

Jan-Albert Goris (b. 1899), who writes under the pen name of Marnix Gijsen, is one year younger than Vestdijk. He has successfully combined his career as a Belgian diplomat with his literary pursuits as a novelist, essayist, and journalist. Trained as an economist at the University of Louvain, he wrote a doctoral dissertation on the Portuguese, Spanish, and Italian merchant colonies in Antwerp in 1488–1567. In 1925, the same year that his dissertation appeared, Gijsen published a significant collection of poems. Glad to escape the life of commerce that had been planned for him, he joined the group around the magazine *Ruimte* (*Space*). Although he enjoyed a greater reputation as a poet than Vestdijk, after World War II he also turned to the novel, and has become one of the leading contemporary Dutch novelists.

Like Vestdijk, he sees ancient myths from a completely modern point of view; he, too, is a parodist and satirist. He has been acclaimed for his reinterpretation of the Biblical story of Susanna and the Elders, *Het boek van Joachim van Babylon* (*The Book of Joachim of Babylon*, 1946), which provoked replies in the form of books by three different writers.[7] In this novel Gijsen has turned the old myth of Susanna into a portrait of a modern wife, self-righteous in her virtue and insufferable in her hypocrisy. As an agnostic, he does not bother with the myth's religious significance. The myth serves instead as a convenient framework for an essentially modern story, as a disguise for a reinterpretation of Gijsen's experience.

Susanna's husband is very much a skeptical intellectual of today, and in pouring new meanings into old myths, Gijsen assumes that he is writing for an intellectual audience. His readers know the story of Susanna not only from the Apocrypha, but from its various representations in the history of painting and in several periods of literature. In the same way, he alludes to Fénelon's *Télémaque* in

Telemachus in the Village. But having assumed the familiarity of the myth to his readers, Gijsen can no longer take it seriously.

This sophisticated modern writer cannot interpret the Bible literally, with the Biblicist's naïve faith. He reflects on the nature of myth and on the transmutation of truth, or what passes for truth, into legend. The Daniel he offers is not the Biblical Daniel. His Susanna in time becomes a national institution. The two old men who spied on her are transformed into young admirers. But eventually Susanna's fame is eclipsed; she grows old, and her story is forgotten.

Gijsen, like Vestdijk, cannot ignore his knowledge of Freudian psychology. He explains the tensions that build up between Joachim and Susanna entirely in terms of modern psychological theories. Perfect, cold Susanna mothers her husband, so that he complains, "It was as if I were living with beauty itself, not with a woman." Gijsen's use of the sensuous imagery of the Song of Solomon adds irony to the parody, for the beautiful Susanna is sterile.

As Joachim gazes at Susanna's ineffable beauty and desire rises within him, she reassures him of her response by reminding him that she was brought up in Babylon. "Then, dropping into the Babylonian dialect, which we used as a precaution against indiscreet servants, she added: 'Et je sais bien que les enfants ne se font par l'oreille.'"

In this parable for moderns, Israel is the Dutch-speaking cultural entity, and Babylon the French-speaking one. Is Babylon also France or even the United States? In any case, it has a broad significance for the modern world, which has paid so dearly for its smug nationalisms. Gijsen has as little use for chauvinism as Vestdijk does. "They would begin their disquisitions with the words: 'We Babylonians . . .' and in this they were very sincere," writes Gijsen. "They had not been given Babylonia as a fatherland, they had chosen it." They are the words of Gijsen the traveler and diplomat, who has lived in Israel and Babylon, and who knows the ways of each and the tensions between them. They are also the words of Gijsen the scholar and essayist, who has written a book about the national character of the Flemings and another about the Americans, who knows the American experience, and who has called himself "the Euro-American Homunculus." Finally, they are the words of Gijsen the novelist, who chose American backgrounds for several of his novels.

Like Vestdijk, Gijsen is also a social novelist and satirist. He is merciless toward provincialism, including Flemish provincialism, and his *Telemachus in het dorp* (*Telemachus in the Village*, 1948), gives us a picture of Belgian small-town life that is sharply etched in acid. Yet the little town of Blaren also serves as the microcosm of the great world.

That's the way the Blaren of my youth was, a village just like thousands of others, without a history except for the memory of a little skirmish during the Napoleonic wars, without elements to disturb the peace, without much future, without many visible dramas for whoever traveled through it on his way to Holland or to Bergen, the big city. Once Philip van Lierde, in a lyrical outburst, had compared it with a limpid pool, in which the fish swam lazily and peacefully around in regular circles. It took me all of my youth before I understood that there were more sharks and octopuses living in these still waters than I later saw swimming around the coral reefs of the tropical islands. But then it was already too late for me.[8]

The picture is not without its warmth, for Gijsen possesses both irony and humor. He knows well the life and the little villages whereof he writes. These villages are so thoroughly Flemish that very few of the ordinary people know any French. Tradition and the power of the Church are dominating forces. Gijsen himself has been in revolt against both of these forces; he is modern, skeptical, anticlerical. He knows that pious respectability often serves as a mask for ordinary rascality. Gijsen mocks the stubborn attempts to cling to the ways of the past in a closed, provincial society. The plan to build a movie theater arouses great opposition, and brings forth an angry denunciation from the local paper, which asks "whether the presence of so many strangers in the village during the summer was not already enough of a danger to morals. Was it now necessary to bring in this devilish innovation, produced by Jews and Protestants?"

Gijsen is not the only modern Dutch writer in Catholic Belgium to present an anticlerical point of view. Gerard Walschap, who is also a skilled satirist, came into conflict with the ecclesiastical authorities because of his realistic art and attitude. He left the Church, but more than ten years later he published *Zuster Virgilia* (*Sister Virgilia*, 1951), the story of a Flemish country girl who becomes a nun. He juxtaposes the Catholic and the Humanistic points of view in this novel.

In *Klaaglied om Agnes* (*Lament for Agnes*, 1951), Gijsen treats a theme that has been one of Vestdijk's favorite subjects, as he recalls the lost love of his youth. There is a poignancy in this tragic story that adds another dimension to his autobiographical novels. As so often in Gijsen's novels and in contemporary literature, the hero is a lonely and sensitive young man, something of an outsider. The crude, sometimes sordid, atmosphere of his everyday life in army barracks forms a counterpoint to the tenderness of first love. When tuberculosis takes Agnes from him and puts an end to his dreams of their life together, maturity comes to a young man through sorrow and suffering.

Although Gijsen speaks frankly about the relationship between the sexes, he does not fill his pages with explicit detail. This attitude he shares with Vestdijk, and it is representative of most Dutch novelists writing today. Some Dutch writers have separated sex from love. Thus sex does not play much of a role in Joachim's thoughts about Susanna, for, as he explains, "biology was no great passion of mine." Nor could he see why the earth had to be a place of misery. Why did nature put such enormous effort into creation, only to destroy the results with such careless nonchalance?

Like Vestdijk, Gijsen is strongly autobiographical in his novels, which are usually parts of his life recounted in the first person. He has been accused of lacking inventiveness, and it is true that his plots are simple; very little happens in his stories. Ideas, wit, and satire carry the reader's interest along. Gijsen is concerned with the relationship of the individual to society and with what happens to man in the time between birth and death. "Happiness lies in the moment," says Joachim, "unhappiness lies in time."

While Gijsen's skepticism is essentially modern, there is something classical, even stoic, about his attitudes. His writing and his philosophy express restraint and control. Gijsen's heroes are not swept away by passions; they are too intellectual and reflective for that. They observe life, and question whether it is really worth living. Man, not nature, holds the center of the stage in Gijsen's novels. As Joachim expresses it, "the only thing that excited interest in me [was] man, his behavior and the excuses and explanations that he can give for this behavior."

It is part of Gijsen's modern skepticism that he is also a moralist. (Weisgerber credits him with "perpetuating the tradition of the *conte moral*.[9]) In *Goed en kwaad* (*Good and Evil*, 1950), he examines the question of morality and society. Both the style and structure of his novels are derived from his moralist's view of the world. His use of the first-person narrative form gives him a detachment and distance from his own personal experience. In a novel like *Joachim* this can create a certain tension, for there is something exciting about having a character from the Bible speak in the first person. If Gijsen's forte is not the ability to create memorable scenes, he is a supreme stylist who never wastes words. He presents both the European and American scenes through the eyes of a cultivated intellectual observer.

The psychological novel has been an important genre in Belgium too, and some outstanding examples have appeared since the end of World War II. In *De man die zijn haar kort liet knippen* (*The Man Who Had His Hair Cut Short*, 1947), Johan Daisne (b. 1912) has recreated the harrowing experiences of a madman.[10] Written in the first person singular, with no breaks for paragraphs, it is one long outpouring of the troubled, muddled mind of its hero. Daisne, whose deep interest in Russian literature has led him to write a history of it, has admitted that he got the idea for his novel from Gogol's story *The Diary of a Madman*. The Flemish novelist's devotion to the cinema—he is administrator of the Royal Belgian Film Library—is evident in this novel. Like some other contemporary European novelists he has transferred techniques from the film to the novel.

His protagonist is an antihero, who has to screw up his courage before he can bring himself to take a cold shower. And it is through his eyes that the reader sees the critical events of his life. The novel begins in a mental hospital, where he has at last found a kind of tranquillity, sheltered from society which created so many difficulties for him. Such views as the grisly autopsy scene are replete with realistic details. But Daisne, who is a proponent of "magic realism," is skillful in combining the real with the unreal. Did it all really happen as the deranged narrator has recorded it for us? Or are most of the events his wild imaginings? Daisne leads the reader to ponder the nature of life itself. There may be as little logic to its patterns as the view we get through the eyes of the madman.

While Daisne's harrowing tour de force has carried the psychological novel beyond Vestdijk, two young writers in the Netherlands, Willem Frederik Hermans and Harry Mulisch, represent a break with tradition that is an important aspect of life in the Netherlands today. Hermans (b. 1921) is a controversial figure, who makes effective use of polemics. His *Mandarijnen op zwavelzuur* (*Mandarins in Sulphuric Acid*, 1963), has left no literary reputation unscathed. Both its surrealistic illustrations and its style make this volume of literary criticism characteristic of the younger generation.

Hermans mocks the large number of novels supporting the notion that the most important adventures that can befall a Dutchman take place while he is attending high school. He has sought instead to involve his readers in the cataclysmic events of the greater world. In order to accomplish this he is willing to shock and even irritate his reader. He does not shrink from frank sexual detail, obscenity, profanity, or violence, and he is willing to use language as well as situation for shock effect. Nor does he hesitate to question the existence today of such traditional virtues as family love, patriotism, loyalty, and honor. His scorn for the Establishment has given him a reputation as one of Holland's angry young men.

In his novels Hermans deals with the years during and after World War II. *De tranen der acacia's* (*The Tears of the Acacias*, 1949), portrays the horrors of the Nazi occupation in Amsterdam and of the first weeks of the liberation in Brussels. *De donkere kamer van Damocles* (*Damocles' Darkroom*), also has the occupation period as a background. It begins with a shocking murder, and contains a good measure of sex and violence.

The loss of Indonesia was a blow to Dutch pride, and only the glow of wartime friendship for the Americans was able to suppress the resentment that the surrender of this rich colony took place under pressure from the United States. In 1951 Hermans created a sensation with *Ik heb altijd gelijk* (*I Am Always Right*), a novel about a soldier who has returned from the Indonesian campaign. He spares no feelings, and heaps his scorn not only on old traditions and the older generation, but even on old relationships. The hero questions his father's submissive role during the occupation, and at the same time, points cynically to the postwar success of former collaborators. As he returns to his homeland, he reflects that the whole Indonesian campaign has been a humiliating and miserable experience. He despises the pretension of his countrymen that they are a force in the international power structure.

We stand on our historic rights! We are completely independent! If other powers had not found our freedom advantageous, we'd have been on our ass for more than a hundred years already![11]

Protest against the Establishment has led to riots in Amsterdam. *Provos,* as the young rebels of the metropolis are known in the Netherlands, have come to play a role in Dutch life, along with the usual beatniks. This typical phenomenon of the modern European welfare state is all the more remarkable in the Netherlands, for the country has been notably free of labor strife since the war.

For Harry Mulisch the old order is gone. His latest book *Bericht aan de rattenkoning* (*Report to the King of the Rats*) is an account of the groups and events that led to the riots in Amsterdam. It begins with a quotation from Mao, but Mulisch sees East and West as forming one great consumer society.

The frequently surrealistic visions of his fiction may thus be quite appropriate to the apocalyptic events of our age. Since he was born in 1927, he does not see the Second World War in terms of the historical and political developments witnessed by the older generation. In *Het stenen bruidsbed* (1959), which has been published in the United States as *The Stone Bridal Bed*,[12] he concentrates on the death and destruction that were the end results of that war. These are familiar subjects to the people of Holland, who were among the very first victims of Hitler's bombers and who still remember the annihilation of Rotterdam. But Mulisch's views are by no means traditional, and he has outraged many of his readers.

The setting is thoroughly contemporary, an international congress of dentists in bombed-out Dresden. Like so many of his fellow countrymen today, Mulisch feels himself a European. He suffers from no compulsion to prove himself a Dutchman in his writing. The professionally organized congress fosters this international ambiance, but in the East German city of Dresden the tensions between Communism and democracy are evident enough. In spite of the long periods of postwar political stability in the Netherlands and the weight of tradition, the Dutch are sensitive to these tensions themselves.

It is of particular significance, therefore, that Mulisch's antihero is an American and a former bomber pilot, who participated in one of the bombing raids that destroyed Dresden. Forced to bail out, he landed in Russian territory. The workings of the modern bureaucratic state produce an invitation to the congress, where Corinth finds very little that interests him. Haunted by memories of the war, his face scarred by burns, he thinks about the European catastrophe that was World War II. In the surrealistic passages or "songs," which present his bombing flight over Dresden with cinematic effect, he remembers how he fired on helpless civilians who had taken refuge in the Elbe from the burning city. Later the body of his dead buddy, half of whose head had been shot away, is dumped through the bomb bay doors to lighten the burning plane.

Now he feels that the bombing of the city was meaningless, that it was one of those lapses in the history of man that he calls "anti-history." Corinth, who is Jewish, admits that he did not hate the Nazis. It is the "code," society, that demands that we hate the enemy. Communism is the supercode. Like the other angry young men of the new generation, Mulisch rejects the past. He attacks society, but not just middle-class society, which had been the target of Vestdijk and the generation before World War II. In this nihilistic novel, Mulisch denounces society in general. "Society consists of gangsters in makeup acting in a play by Schiller, who say words, but don't understand them, and are savages."

Corinth's antagonist is Schneiderhahn, a West German, who collects pictures of ruins. Corinth suspects him of having been a Nazi, even of having played some role in the concentration camps. He taunts Schneiderhahn by reminding him of the dentists of Auschwitz, who had the job of removing the gold teeth and crowns from the corpses in the death factories. Yet it is typical of Mulisch that he abandons traditional views of good and evil, discarding sharp patterns of white and black. It turns out that Schneiderhahn was a spy. Mulisch places all of mankind in the balance, and it is Schneiderhahn who says, "Then we are the first generation on earth without a future." Corinth himself calls him "a romantic personality," and says of him, "It must be splendid to have a character." At least one critic sees Schneiderhahn as the representative of humanity.

This novel of violence and destruction also offers a contemporary view of love and sex. The Dutch novel usually does not include explicit detail in love scenes, and Mulisch does not offer such descriptions either. It is not until almost the end of the novel that the theme of homosexuality is introduced. There is a directness in the unromantic relationship between the sexes, however, that corresponds to the author's view of the postwar world and produces the intended shock effect. As Corinth, who is married, begins to make love to Hella, a divorcée, he tells her, "Marriage is something like war; vagueness, untidiness." The morning after she goes to bed with him, she sees him making love to one of the young girls at the congress, but she hopes he will continue their relationship.

If Gijsen's characters are shy and find it difficult to approach others, if their own sensitivities lead them to seek revenge on others in their social relationships, Mulisch's characters have adopted the manners of the postwar world in their personal relationships. The dialogue in the novel is no longer polite conversation, but the acid question and the pointed reply, so that it takes on a polemic quality. Where the speakers have guilty consciences, challenge and accusation replace amiable chitchat. There is a sharpness of tone that is completely contemporary. Although Mulisch suggests psychological overtones, communication between the people of the novel is direct and often blunt.

Hate assumes a more important place than love in this novel of postwar Europe. It is not necessary to know a man, says Mulisch, to hate him. The dark forces of life are thus important for the writer, who creates surrealistic passages that remind us of Brueghel. At one point Corinth rides through a street filled with cripples, all carrying fruit.

Mulisch even uses a kind of black imagery. Dresden is a city of stone, prepared like a bride, hence the title of the novel. He takes Vestdijk's view of man as a physiological organism a step further, and portrays him as a thing of secretions and decay. Thus, in one image the destruction of Dresden is fused with Corinth's own disintegration. "His kidneys were two villas that had collapsed in desolate gardens, his back was the charred church at the cross-roads."

It is only necessary to recall Vestdijk's use of the garden in *The Garden Where the Brass Band Played* to see that it is still an important *topos* in the modern Dutch novel. It reappears several times in *The Stone Bridal Bed*. At the beginning of the book Corinth receives his invitation as he comes from the garden. At the end he enters a garden. He himself reveals that his hobby is gardening. The garden is apparently identified with peace and tranquillity, for great bewilderment is expressed over the fact that a gardener could be an arsonist.

It is a long way from Van Schendel, or even Vestdijk and Gijsen, to Hermans and Mulisch, a whole world and a war away. A new generation has brought with it a new attitude toward world events and toward contemporary life. Times have changed in the Netherlands and Belgium, but this change has enriched the range and diversity of Dutch literature.

REFERENCES

1. Maria Dermoût, *The Ten Thousand Things* (New York, 1958); *Only Yesterday* (New York, 1959).

2. Arthur van Schendel, *The Waterman* (London, 1963).

3. Simon Vestdijk, *The Garden Where the Brass Band Played* (New York, 1965).

4. *Ibid.*, pp. 121–22.

5. *Ibid.*, p. 205.

6. Simon Vestdijk, *De dokter en het lichte meisje* (Amsterdam, 1951), p. 49.

7. Marnix Gijsen, *The Book of Joachim of Babylon* (New York, 1951).

8. Marnix Gijsen, *Telemachus in het dorp* ('s-Gravenhage, 1952), p. 20.

9. Jean Weisberger, *Formes et Domaines du Roman Flamand*, 1927–1960 (Brussels, 1963), p. 235.

10. Johan Daisne, *The Man Who Had His Hair Cut Short* (New York, 1965).

11. Willem Frederik Hermans, *Ik heb altijd gelijk* (Amsterdam, 1951), p. 25.

12. Harry Mulisch, *The Stone Bridal Bed* (New York, 1962).

NOTES ON CONTRIBUTORS

NOTES ON CONTRIBUTORS

ROBERT ALTER, born in 1935 in New York City, is Assistant Professor of English at Columbia University. He is the author of *Rogue's Progress: Studies in the Picaresque Novel* (Cambridge, 1964). Mr. Alter, a frequent contributor to *Book Week* and *Midstream*, writes a regular column for *Commentary*. At present, he is a Guggenheim Fellow and is writing a book on Fielding.

SEYMOUR L. FLAXMAN, born in 1918, is Professor of German and Comparative Literature at The City College of The City University of New York. He is also a member of the doctoral faculty in German and in Comparative Literature at the Graduate Center there. Mr. Flaxman is the author of *Herman Heijermans and His Dramas* (The Hague, 1954) and editor of the newsletter *Neerlandica Americana*.

N. V. M. GONZALEZ, born in 1915 in Romblon, the Philippines, is Associate Professor of English and Comparative Literature at the University of the Philippines. The author of *A Season of Grace* (Manila, 1956); *The Bamboo Dancers* (Manila, 1959); *Children of the Ash Covered Loam and Other Stories* (Manila, 1954); and *Look, Stranger, On This Island Now* (Manila, 1963), he was the winner of the 1960 Republic Cultural Heritage Award and the 1961 Rizal Pro-Patria Award.

HOWARD HIBBETT, born in 1920 in Akron, Ohio, is Professor of Japanese Literature and Chairman of the Department of Far-Eastern Languages at Harvard University. The Author of *The Floating World in Japanese Fiction* (New York, 1959), Mr. Hibbett has also translated Tanizaki Junichirō's *The Key* (New York, 1961), *Seven Japanese Tales* (New York, 1963), and *The Diary of a Mad Old Man* (New York, 1965). He has spent approximately four years in residence in Japan, studying at Kyoto and Tokyo Universities.

ERWIN N. HIEBERT, born in 1919 in Saskatchewan, Canada, is Professor of the History of Science at the University of Wisconsin. He is the author of *The Impact of Atomic Energy* (Newton, Kansas, 1961) and *Historical Roots of the Principle of Conservation of Energy* (Madison, 1962). His interest has been the history of physical science and thought since 1800, with special emphasis on the history of thermodynamics.

VALÉRIE KOREK, born in 1906, is a literary critic and frequent contributor to Hungarian literary magazines published in the West. She is the author of *Budai Latogátás*, a novel in Hungarian. In the past years, she has been engaged in work on the Hungarian novelist, Zoltán Ambrus.

CZESLAW MILOSZ, born in 1911 in Lithuania, is Professor of Slavic Languages and Literature at the University of California at Berkeley. He is the author of several volumes of poetry in Polish; *The Captive Mind* (New York, 1953); *La Prise du Pouvoir* (a novel, Paris, 1953); *Tal der Issa* (a novel, Köln, 1961). Mr. Milosz has also translated French, American, and English poetry into Polish.

EMIR RODRIGUEZ MONEGAL, born in 1921 in Melo, Uruguay, is Editor-in-Chief of *Mundo Nuevo*, a magazine concerned with Latin American affairs and published in Paris under the auspices of the Instituto Latino-americano de Relaciones Internacionales. He is the author of *José E. Rodó en el Novecientos* (Montevideo, 1950); *El juicio de los parricidas* (Buenos Aires, 1956); *Las raíces de Horacio Quiroga* (Montevideo, 1960); *Narradores de esta América* (Montevideo), 1961); and *El viajero inmóvil, Introducción a Pablo Neruda* (Buenos Aires, 1966).

HENRI PEYRE was born in Paris, France, in 1901. He is now Sterling Professor of French at Yale University. Mr. Peyre has written some 25 books, the latest being *Literature and Sincerity* (1963), plus some 400 articles in a great variety of reviews and journals.

COSTAS M. PROUSSIS, born in Cyprus in 1911, is Director of Studies and Professor of Classics at the Holy Cross Greek Orthodox Theological School in Brookline, Massachusetts. He is the author of *Grammar of Modern Greek* (Cyprus, 1934); *Latin Grammar* (Cyprus, 1943); *The Poet Costis Palamis* (1943); *Aesthetic Culture* (1946); and *Cyprus Prose Writing* (1949). He has also edited the magazines: *Essay and Criticism* (Athens, 1932); *Cyprus Letters* (Cyprus, 1934–48); and *Cyprus Studies* (Cyprus, 1940–48).

GEORGE N. SFEIR, born in 1922 in Lebanon, is Assistant Manager and Counsel for the Intra Bank S. A. in New York City. Mr. Sfeir has written articles on contemporary Arab writers for *The New York Times Book Review*, and is the author of numerous articles, both in Arabic and English, in the fields of Arab banking, government, and law.

INDEX

INDEX

Index

Index